Hands-On Cloud-Native Applications with Java and Quarkus

Build high performance, Kubernetes-native Java
serverless applications

Francesco Marchioni

BIRMINGHAM - MUMBAI

Hands-On Cloud-Native Applications with Java and Quarkus

Commissioning Editor: Kunal Chaudhari
Acquisition Editor: Alok Dhuri
Content Development Editor: Pathikrit Roy
Technical Editor: Gaurav Gala
Copy Editor: Safis Editing
Senior Editor: Rohit Singh
Project Coordinator: Francy Puthiry
Proofreader: Safis Editing
Indexer: Priyanka Dhadke
Production Designer: Aparna Bhagat

First published: December 2019

Production reference: 1131219

Published by Packt Publishing Ltd.
Livery Place
35 Livery Street
Birmingham
B3 2PB, UK.

ISBN 978-1-83882-147-0

www.packt.com

To my wife Linda, who is happy she married somebody "with no special talent, but who is passionately curious." And I'm so glad to be such.

Packt.com

Subscribe to our online digital library for full access to over 7,000 books and videos, as well as industry leading tools to help you plan your personal development and advance your career. For more information, please visit our website.

Why subscribe?

- Spend less time learning and more time coding with practical eBooks and Videos from over 4,000 industry professionals

- Improve your learning with Skill Plans built especially for you

- Get a free eBook or video every month

- Fully searchable for easy access to vital information

- Copy and paste, print, and bookmark content

Did you know that Packt offers eBook versions of every book published, with PDF and ePub files available? You can upgrade to the eBook version at www.packt.com and as a print book customer, you are entitled to a discount on the eBook copy. Get in touch with us at customercare@packtpub.com for more details.

At www.packt.com, you can also read a collection of free technical articles, sign up for a range of free newsletters, and receive exclusive discounts and offers on Packt books and eBooks.

Foreword

I've been involved with Java and enterprise Java since 1995-96 and over the intervening years, I've been impressed by the passion of the developers within communities who find innovative ways to improve their own productivity and that of others. Various significant changes to our industry have occurred and Java has continued to remain relevant. Whether it's service-oriented architecture, RESTful development, Internet of Things, microservices, or hybrid cloud, Java has found a way to ensure that developers can bring much of what they've learned prior to the advent of these waves with them so they don't have to re-invent the wheel.

However, sometimes that wheel does need a bit of shaking up. Not everything that is applicable to one type of deployment environment is necessarily going to be useful to another. And we've seen that with the cloud, Platform-as-a-Service and, specifically, Kubernetes and Linux containers. The Java Virtual Machine (JVM) represents a huge and impressive amount of work by countless developers from several vendors over two decades.

Despite the fact that Java began life aimed at constrained devices, it rapidly evolved into a world where the assumptions are quite different compared to the cloud today, such as, the ability to consume a lot of memory, the requirements to dynamically update the running application/environment, and other runtime optimizations. Concerns about Java (performance, runtime memory footprint, boot time, and so on) have caused some to re-evaluate their investment with Java and consider some of the newer languages, despite the fact that many of those languages don't yet have the rich ecosystem of tools, utilities, and so on that have been built up over the years by the Java community.

This is where Quarkus comes in! It aims to make Java relevant in the modern Kubernetes world. I've seen frameworks and stacks come and go over the decades, with some of them being massively successful for their time. However, whether it's DCE, CORBA, JBoss, or Spring, I've never seen anything quite like Quarkus in terms of almost instantaneous popularity, the ability to capture the imagination of people, being able to mine a deep-rooted need for Java developers, and to create a new wave: true Kubernetes-native Java middleware.

And I try to say that objectively, given that I've been involved with Quarkus since the very beginning. As you're about to find out when you read this book, it truly feels like "a paradigm shift." It enables developers to bring their Java skills to Kubernetes and feel like they can be as (or more) productive as developers using other languages and even other Java frameworks/stacks.

I'm really pleased to see this book coming out so quickly on the back of the initial Quarkus release and thus filling an important need for existing Quarkus developers and those thinking about trying it out. The fact the author works within Red Hat JBoss Middleware, from where Quarkus originated, and specifically in our QE group, gives a unique view that readers interested in learning about Quarkus and developers interested in using it can both enjoy and benefit from. I hope you find it as interesting to read the book as I did!

Mark Little

Red Hat's Vice President, Middleware Engineering

Contributors

About the author

Francesco Marchioni is a **Red Hat Certified JBoss Administrator (RHCJA)** and **Sun Certified Enterprise Architect (SCEA)** working at Red Hat in Rome, Italy. He started learning Java in 1997, and since then he has followed all the newest application program interfaces released by Sun. In 2000, he joined the JBoss community, when the application server was running the 2.X release.

He has spent years as a software consultant, where he has enabled many successful software migrations from vendor platforms to open source products, such as JBoss AS, fulfilling the tight budget requirements necessitated by the current economy. Over the last 10 years, he has authored many technical articles for O'Reilly Media and has run an IT portal focused on JBoss products.

> *I have a long list of people that I'd like to thank for their contribution in writing this book. I'd like to thank, in strict random order, Clement Escoffier, Guillaume Smet, Georgios Andrianakis for their valuable hints that made my journey through Quarkus Land smooth and safe. Many thanks to Mark Little for writing the incipit of this book.*
>
> *Also, last but not least, a huge thanks to the reviewers and proofreaders of this book, Alessio Soldano, Guillame Smet, Max Andersen, and Nicola Ferraro.*

About the reviewers

Nicola Ferraro is a passionate software developer contributing to many open source projects. He is a committer and a PMC member of Apache Camel as well as a co-creator of the Camel K serverless integration platform, which leverages the power of Quarkus. He works as a collaborator for the Knative project. He is also developing Syndesis, a no-code integration platform, and the Fabric8 development tools for Kubernetes. Nicola currently works as a principal software engineer for Red Hat.

I would have never finished the review of this book without the help of my beloved son, Alessandro, who kept me out of bed for so many nights. Love you!

Alessio Soldano was born in Varese, Italy, in 1979. He started his career working on distributed systems in the financial/credit field and fell in love with JBoss. After years of J2EE practice, he finally got the chance to deal with web services. He contributed to the JBoss Web Services project by finding and fixing some bugs and eventually was hired by JBoss (a division of Red Hat) to continue doing that. Later on, Alessio took on project leadership, represented Red Hat at JCP (JSR 224) and W3C (Web Services Resource Access Working Group), and contributed to multiple JBoss and Apache projects. More recently, he has shifted his attention to the REST world; he's been leading RESTEasy for a few years and because of that he's also involved in Quarkus.

Packt is searching for authors like you

If you're interested in becoming an author for Packt, please visit authors.packtpub.com and apply today. We have worked with thousands of developers and tech professionals, just like you, to help them share their insight with the global tech community. You can make a general application, apply for a specific hot topic that we are recruiting an author for, or submit your own idea.

Table of Contents

Preface

Despite its age, Java still remains one of the most popular choices among developers, having made it through almost 20 years of constant improvements and having developed a full stack of libraries for enterprise systems. As we are living in a fast-paced industry, we cannot deny that many things have changed in the last few years with the introduction of containers, microservices, reactive applications, and cloud platforms. To remain a first-class citizen in this changing world, Java needs a boost. And we, at Red Hat, believe that this boost can be Quarkus!

Quarkus has been designed from the ground up to be a Kubernetes-native Java framework that is a perfect fit for creating microservice applications with a minimal memory footprint and fast execution. At the same time, Quarkus does not dump the rich set of libraries, such as Hibernate, and REST services that most developers are familiar with. On the contrary, they are part of a larger picture that includes the game-changing MicroProfile API, reactive programming models such as Vert.x, and a ton of other features that can be easily plugged into your services.

Quarkus provides an effective solution for running Java in this new world of serverless, microservices, containers, Kubernetes, **Function as a Service** (**FaaS**), and the cloud because it has been designed with these in mind. Its container-first approach to cloud-native Java applications unifies imperative and reactive programming paradigms for microservices development and offers an extensible set of standards-based enterprise Java libraries and frameworks combined with extreme developer productivity that promises to revolutionize the way we develop in Java.

Who this book is for

This book is for Java developers and software architects who are interested in learning about a very promising microservice architecture for building reliable and robust applications. Some knowledge of Java, Spring, and REST APIs is assumed.

What this book covers

Chapter 1, *Introduction to Quarkus Core Concepts*, explains the container-first (minimal-footprint Java applications are optimal for running in containers), cloud-native (Quarkus embraces the 12-factor architecture of environments such as Kubernetes), and microservice-first (Quarkus brings lightning-fast start up times and code turnaround times to Java apps) approaches. We will examine the various tools available for developing Quarkus applications. For this, we will install an IDE and GraalVM, which is required for native applications.

Chapter 2, *Developing Your First Application with Quarkus*, takes you through building your first application with Quarkus. We will see how to use Maven/Gradle plugins to bootstrap your application. You will learn how to import the application in your IDS, and how to run and test the application. Next, we will discuss creating a native application from your Java project.

Chapter 3, *Creating a Container Image of Your Application*, looks at how to build a Docker image of your application, how to run an application on Docker, how to install a single-node cluster of OpenShift, and how to run an application on Minishift.

Chapter 4, *Web Application Development*, looks at the use case of a customer store application that will use REST and the CDI stack and a web frontend. We will see how to deploy the application and see changes without restarting Quarkus.

Chapter 5, *Managing Data Persistence with Quarkus*, discusses data persistence with Quarkus. We will see how to add persistence to the customer store example as well as setting up a database (PostgreSQL) to run the example. We will then take the application to the cloud. Finally, we will show you how Hibernate Panache can simplify application development.

Chapter 6, *Building Applications Using the MicroProfile API*, teaches you how to complement the Enterprise API that we have already discussed with the full stack of Eclipse MicroProfile specifications (https://microprofile.io/).

Chapter 7, *Securing Applications*, will explore how to secure our example application with built-in security APIs such as the Elytron Security stack, the Keycloak extension, and the MicroProfile JWT extension.

Chapter 8, *Advanced Application Development*, gets into advanced application development techniques such as advanced application configuration management, life cycle events, and firing scheduled tasks.

Chapter 9, *Unifying Imperative and Reactive*, takes you through the non-blocking programming model with Quarkus and an example application using the Vert.x programming model with Quarkus. We will also explore how to leverage Vert.x's reactive SQL API to build non-blocking database applications.

Chapter 10, *Reactive Messaging with Quarkus*, explains how to implement reactive data streaming applications using a CDI development model and Kafka and AMQP as a broker. We will also explain how to implement a full streaming architecture in the cloud by deploying our application on OpenShift.

To get the most out of this book

Hands-On Cloud-Native Applications with Java and Quarkus is a complete end-to-end development guide that will give you hands-on experience with building Kubernetes-native applications in serverless environments. To get the most out of this book, we recommend using a development environment that is integrated with Apache Maven (such as IntelliJ IDEA or Eclipse) and import it into our example code files. That will help you to follow our projects step-by-step and, when needed, to debug them.

Download the example code files

You can download the example code files for this book from your account at www.packt.com. If you purchased this book elsewhere, you can visit www.packt.com/support and register to have the files emailed directly to you.

You can download the code files by following these steps:

1. Log in or register at www.packt.com.
2. Select the **Support** tab.
3. Click on **Code Downloads**.
4. Enter the name of the book in the **Search** box and follow the onscreen instructions.

Once the file is downloaded, please make sure that you unzip or extract the folder using the latest version of:

- WinRAR/7-Zip for Windows
- Zipeg/iZip/UnRarX for Mac
- 7-Zip/PeaZip for Linux

The code bundle for the book is also hosted on GitHub at `https://github.com/PacktPublishing/Hands-On-Cloud-Native-Applications-with-Java-and-Quarkus`. In case there's an update to the code, it will be updated on the existing GitHub repository.

We also have other code bundles from our rich catalog of books and videos available at `https://github.com/PacktPublishing/`. Check them out!

Download the color images

We also provide a PDF file that has color images of the screenshots/diagrams used in this book. You can download it here: `https://static.packt-cdn.com/downloads/9781838821470_ColorImages.pdf`.

Code in Action

Please visit the following link to see the Code in Action videos: `http://bit.ly/2LKFbY1`

Conventions used

There are a number of text conventions used throughout this book.

`CodeInText`: Indicates code words in text, database table names, folder names, filenames, file extensions, pathnames, dummy URLs, user input, and Twitter handles. Here is an example: "An `index.html` page is provided as a marker in our project, as shown in the project's hierarchy."

A block of code is set as follows:

```
// Create new JSON for Order #1
   objOrder = Json.createObjectBuilder()
          .add("id", new Long(1))
          .add("item", "mountain bike")
          .add("price", new Long(100))
```

When we wish to draw your attention to a particular part of a code block, the relevant lines or items are set in bold:

```
@POST
@RolesAllowed("admin")
public Response create(Customer customer)
```

Any command-line input or output is written as follows:

```
$ tree src
```

Bold: Indicates a new term, an important word, or words that you see on screen. For example, words in menus or dialog boxes appear in the text like this. Here is an example: "Once you have some data, other actions (such as **Edit** and **Delete**) will be available."

Warnings or important notes appear like this.

Tips and tricks appear like this.

Get in touch

Feedback from our readers is always welcome.

General feedback: If you have questions about any aspect of this book, mention the book title in the subject of your message and email us at customercare@packtpub.com.

Errata: Although we have taken every care to ensure the accuracy of our content, mistakes do happen. If you have found a mistake in this book, we would be grateful if you would report this to us. Please visit www.packt.com/submit-errata, selecting your book, clicking on the Errata Submission Form link, and entering the details.

Piracy: If you come across any illegal copies of our works in any form on the internet, we would be grateful if you would provide us with the location address or website name. Please contact us at copyright@packt.com with a link to the material.

If you are interested in becoming an author: If there is a topic that you have expertise in, and you are interested in either writing or contributing to a book, please visit authors.packtpub.com.

Reviews

Please leave a review. Once you have read and used this book, why not leave a review on the site that you purchased it from? Potential readers can then see and use your unbiased opinion to make purchase decisions, we at Packt can understand what you think about our products, and our authors can see your feedback on their book. Thank you!

For more information about Packt, please visit `packt.com`.

Section 1: Getting Started with Quarkus

In this section, we will learn about the foundations of the Quarkus architecture, install the tools we need to develop applications, and develop our first cloud-native application.

This section includes the following chapters:

- Chapter 1, *Introduction to Quarkus Core Concepts*
- Chapter 2, *Developing Your First Application with Quarkus*
- Chapter 3, *Creating a Container Image of Your Application*

Introduction to Quarkus Core Concepts

Java was introduced to the open source community over 20 years ago. Since then, we cannot think of a single large IT company or organization that doesn't use Java. For this reason, Java is often regarded as a **corporate** language, which is not a bad thing *per se*: Java is the enterprise standard, and it's an extremely mature language with a huge ecosystem of tools and libraries around it and still the most used language by developers in the world.

20 years in the IT industry is, however, a considerable amount of time. Since the beginning, Java has gone through a long list of optimizations with the burden of keeping backward compatibility with earlier releases. Today, however, the IT landscape has significantly changed with the rise of new standards such as the cloud, containers, microservices, and Reactive Programming. Do we still need to use Java to address the latest application architectures and reach a higher level of productivity and efficiency? Yes! This book promises to do this while teaching you about **Quarkus**, a Kubernetes-native framework that will take supersonic, subatomic Java to new heights!

In the first part of this book, we will learn how to create Quarkus applications with simple tools while using a development environment to code, execute, and debug them. After completing all the green bars, we will concentrate on advanced topics to show you how to combine multiple Quarkus extensions to produce a serverless infrastructure.

As far as this chapter is concerned, we will have a quick tour of the Quarkus technology by covering these topics:

- An overview of the IT landscape, showing the benefits of cloud-native applications and microservices
- The basics of the Quarkus architecture
- Installing the required software (GraalVM to compile code natively and a development environment)

Technical requirements

You can find the source code for the project in this chapter on GitHub at `https://github.com/PacktPublishing/Hands-On-Cloud-Native-Applications-with-Java-and-Quarkus/tree/master/Chapter01`.

From the big data hype to Kubernetes

About 10 years ago, the biggest buzz in the IT industry was the term *big data*. Every major enterprise was racing to harness the mystical powers of massive, yet supposedly manageable, silos of data. Equipped with big data, no problem would prove insurmountable, and all forecasts would be met.

But lately, these forecasts appear to have faded, and the worst-kept secret in the IT industry is that big data is dead – at least as we knew it. This doesn't mean that the volume or growth of data has broken down – or the opposite. It's just the underlying technology that has changed, which means that the architectures of applications that use big data have too.

Take Hadoop as an example, which has been the icon of the big data hype. It was designed based on a set of assumptions that dramatically changed in a short time. One of these assumptions was that, in order to process a large batch of data, network latency was the evil and cloud-native storage simply wasn't an option. At that time, most of the IT industry data was on-premise, so the focus was on avoiding moving around big sets of information. This meant that data was to be co-located in order to compute it efficiently.

Today, this scenario has changed quite a bit: most applications still use large amounts of data, but data is now processed on the fly. That is to say, we now stream data instead of processing the whole dataset multiple times.

Besides this, the network latency barrier has become less of an issue for cloud providers and there are even multiple cloud sources to choose from. Also, companies now have the option to deploy their own private cloud on-premise, leading to new scenarios such as **hybrid clouds**.

Therefore, the focus is what really changed: today, big data does not merely mean a **big** quantity of datasets but flexible storage options for a big quantity of data.

This is where containers and, specifically, Kubernetes fits in. In a nutshell, you can think of a container as a packaged application that contains just the libraries that are needed to run it, and Kubernetes is like an orchestrating system that makes sure all the containers have the appropriate resources while managing their life cycle.

Kubernetes runs images and manages containers using **Docker**. However, Kubernetes can use other engines too (for example, `rkt`). Since we will be building our applications on top of Kubernetes, we will provide a short overview of its architecture in the next section.

The Kubernetes architecture in a nutshell

The architecture of Kubernetes is focused around the concept of a loosely coupled, flexible mechanism for service discovery. Like most other distributed middleware platforms, a Kubernetes cluster is composed of one or more master nodes and multiple compute nodes. The following diagram depicts a high-level view of a Kubernetes cluster:

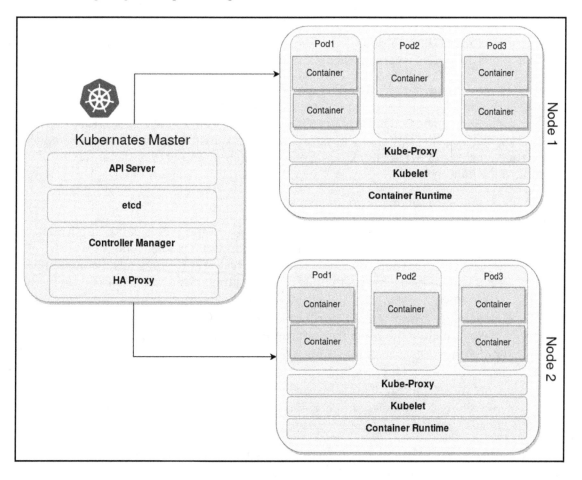

Kubernetes Master nodes essentially make up the brain of the cluster. They are responsible for managing the overall cluster, exposing APIs, and scheduling deployments. **Kubernetes nodes** (right-hand side of the preceding diagram) contain the services that are needed to run applications in components called Pods.

Each **master node** contains the following components:

- **API Server**: This synchronizes and validates the information running in Pods and services.
- **etcd**: This provides consistent and highly available storage for the cluster data. You can think of `etcd` as the brain's shared memory.
- **Controller Manager server**: This checks for changes in the `etcd` service and uses its API to enforce the desired state.
- **HAProxy**: This can be added when we're configuring HA masters to balance loads between several master endpoints.

Kubernetes nodes (simply called **nodes**) can be considered workhorses of a Kubernetes cluster. Each node exposes a set of resources (such as computing, networking, and storage) to your applications. The node also ships with additional components for service discovery, monitoring, logging, and optional add-ons. In terms of infrastructure, you can run a node as a **virtual machine** (**VM**) in your cloud environment or on top of bare-metal servers running in the data center.

Each node contains the following components:

- **Pod**: This allows us to logically group containers and pieces of our application stacks together. A Pod acts as the logical boundary for such containers with shared resources and contexts. Pods can be scaled at runtime by creating Replica sets. This, in turn, ensures that the required number of Pods is always run by the deployment.
- **Kubelet**: This is an agent that runs on each node in the Kubernetes cluster. It makes sure that the containers are running in a Pod.
- **Kube-Proxy**: This maintains network rules on nodes to allow network communication between Pods.
- **Container Runtime**: This is the software that is responsible for running containers. Kubernetes supports multiple container runtimes (such as Docker, `containerd`, `cri-o`, and `rktlet`).

Now that we've covered the basics of the Kubernetes architecture, let's look at the top advantages that it can bring to your organization.

Benefits of using Kubernetes

The advantages that Kubernetes can bring to your organization are as follows:

- Kubernetes greatly simplifies container management. As you have learned, when using Kubernetes, there's no need to manage containers directly. Instead, you just to have manage Pods. In order to have your applications available in your Pods, Kubernetes introduced an abstraction called a **service**. It defines a logical set of Pods with their IP address. This level of abstraction enhances fault tolerance and reduces downtime by launching containers on different machines.

- Kubernetes speeds up the process of building, testing, and releasing software by supporting a wide range of programming languages (Java, Go, Python, and so on) and offering advanced deployment features (automated rollouts and rollbacks, canary deployments, and more). This makes it a lot easier to configure effective **Continuous Integration/Continuous Delivery (CI/CD)** pipelines for your software.

- Kubernetes provides the fastest and least costly horizontal scalability for your pods, so when the number of users for your application increases, you can configure the replication service to fire new Pods and balance the load across them to avoid downtime.

- It's worth mentioning that Kubernetes is able to manage both stateless and stateful applications, because it allows ephemeral storage and persistent volumes. It also supports a number of storage types, such as NFS, GlusterFS, and cloud storage systems. Furthermore, a **persistent volume (PV)** life cycle doesn't depend on any pod using it, so you can keep the data as long as you need it.

The benefits of using Kubernetes as a service orchestrator in your industry are clearly evident, but the next question is, how do we write our services to get the most out of this architecture? Can we still write our applications using the same standards we have learned about in the last few years? The next section will address this dilemma.

From Java EE to MicroProfile

Java Enterprise Edition (EE) has reached an outstanding level of maturity and has a huge adoption in the IT Enterprise. A Java EE application is typically packaged as a monolithic application and deployed in an application server, which can host multiples of them.

A monolithic application can be thought of as a self-contained application that includes both the user interface and the business components that are required to run the applications.

This approach has been widely used for years. The reason is simple: monolithic applications are conceptually simple to develop and package because everything is contained in a bundle and can be edited with a single IDE. Also, scaling monolithic applications is simple: all you need to do is scale a single component.

As a result, the traditional way of coding enterprise applications produced an extremely large set of applications that were supposed to be available as long-running processes and needed an application server to manage their **High Availability** (**HA**). In turn, some other tooling was needed to manage server restarts in the case of failures and to check the overall health of the system.

As server-based monolithic applications continued growing, several disadvantages became evident, as follows:

- **Difficult to maintain**: This is due to the size of the applications, which makes it complex to create a patch for them.
- **Limited scalability**: You can scale the whole application, not the single services.
- **Longer release cycles**: Any changes that are made to the code require that we deploy the whole application, which complicates things when multiple teams are working on the same application.
- **Less isolation**: Deploying multiple applications in an application server can potentially lead to a whole system failure from a single application misbehaving.
- **Slower startup**: The startup time of a full monolithic stack is ill-famed to be slow, especially if multiple applications are deployed at the same time and potentially competing for the same resources.
- **Complex monitoring**: It is harder to monitor and tune the activity of a single monolithic application which delivers a myriad of metrics.
- **More complex CI/CD**: Configuring a CI/CD pipeline for multiple monolithic applications is equally as hard.

In this scenario, a new paradigm called **microservices** emerged around a simple yet not new idea. The main theme behind microservices is that, for certain types of applications, once they are split into smaller and composable pieces, it's easier to build and maintain them. In a service-based architecture, we don't need to measure the uptime of our applications in weeks or months anymore since we can activate our services when they are needed. Therefore, the timing factor can be as little as minutes or seconds.

In such an architecture, each component has its own life cycle spanning from development to testing, and the resulting application is simply the combination of all these single components. This approach marks a sensible departure from **monolithic** applications, where everything is built and tested as a single unit.

Applications that are built as a set of smaller modular components are simpler to understand, easier to test/debug, and easier to maintain over the application life cycle. A microservice architecture leverages the agility of your company by reducing the time it takes to deploy improvements to production. This approach has been tried and tested and is superior for the following reasons:

- **Increased resilience**: The microservice architecture increases the system's overall capability to withstand any kind of unexpected failures or faults of components or networks by spinning up another component, even as the remaining application continues to function.
- **Developer independence**: By working in smaller teams in parallel, you can speed up the work that's being done, especially for large enterprise applications that are composed of teams that are geographically and culturally diverse.
- **Scalability**: Fewer resources are demanded by smaller components. This means we can easily scale them to meet the increasing demand of only that specific component.
- **CI/CD life cycle automation**: Single components fit smoothly into CD pipelines and scenarios that have complex deployment.
- **Simpler mapping with the business**: Microservice architectures are easier to map with the business domain logic since they have increasing independence and transparency across the organization.

To obtain the best results from our **Software as a Service** (**SaaS**), a methodology is required. In the next section, we will discuss the Twelve-Factor App methodology, which is recommended by developers for smoothly working and delivering applications with a focus on microservices.

The Twelve-Factor App methodology

In 2011, the Heroku founder Adam Wiggins published **the Twelve-Factor App** methodology, which soon became a key reference for building **Software as a Service** (SaaS) based on their own experiences. This methodology is not exclusive to any programming language but is compatible with a microservices architecture and is based on containers and CI/CD pipelines. Let's take a look at the 12 factors:

- **Code base**: You should build your application on top of one code base, tracked by a **Version Control System** (**VCS**). You should rely on a base repository for an individual application to ease CI/CD pipelines. It follows that deployments should be automatic so that everything can run in different environments without anything needing to be done.

- **Dependencies**: Don't push any dependencies to your project code base. Instead, use a package manager so that you will have all the dependencies synced across your environments to make sure you reproduce the same behavior.

- **Config**: Store your configuration in environment variables. The configuration should be well parted from the code so that the configuration varies in terms of where the application has been deployed.

- **Backing services**: Services should be easily interchangeable so that you can manage your backing services as attached resources. You must be able to easily exchange the backing services from one provider to another without changing your code. This maximizes portability and helps maintain your system.

- **Build, run, release**: There should be a clear and strict separation between the build, release, and run stages. You can achieve this by assigning a unique release ID and allowing releases to roll back. The automation between these stages should be as easy as possible.

- **Stateless processes**: This factor lies at the core of the microservices architecture. You should not be introducing state into your services. Any data that needs to be persisted must be stored in a backing service, typically a database or another storage.

- **Port binding**: By this factor, your application should be completely self-contained. It should not depend on the runtime startup of a web server into the execution environment to create a frontend service. The web app should make HTTP applications as a service available by binding the service to a port.

- **Concurrency**: You should break down your application into much smaller pieces. Smaller, well-defined apps allow you to scale out as needed to handle varying loads. You should be able to individually scale the single component.

- **Disposability**: You should aim to maximize the robustness of your systems by coding applications with a fast startup and graceful shutdown. This means you should be able to handle unexpected failures. A recommended approach consists of using a robust async backend that returns notifications when failures occur.
- **Dev/prod Parity**: You should aim to keep the development, staging, and production phases similar and homogeneous to limit deviation and errors. This also implicitly encourages a DevOps culture where software development and operations are unified.
- **Logs**: Logging is a key factor for debugging and monitoring your application's general health. The place where logs are stored shouldn't be a concern for developers. Instead, these logs should be treated as a continuous stream that's being separately captured and stored by a service.
- **Admin Processes**: In many cases, developers perform one-off administrative or maintenance tasks, such as database migrations, application patching, or one-time script execution for the app. It is essential to run one-off admin processes in an environment that is similar to the regular long-running processes of the app.

Although some of the preceding patterns may seem trivial at first glance, they become essential building blocks as your services start to grow. Therefore, when designing your microservices applications, keep in mind that most challenges are not related just to coding, but rather to getting the basics wrong. As a matter of fact, even good teams fail at microservices when they don't have a culture that embraces DevOps and key building blocks such as the Twelve-Factor App methodology.

The MicroProfile initiative

Having discussed the methodology of microservices, we will now cover some aspects related to the specific API that can be used to develop microservices.

While, at first glance, it appears that Java and microservices don't really match, it would be a bad idea to discard the entire Java EE ecosystem (rebranded as **Jakarta EE** and transferred to the Eclipse Foundation) that has been created. A lot of effort has already gone into reusing Java EE for coding microservices.

As a matter of fact, many major vendors, including IBM, Red Hat, and Payara, have already provided a lightweight and extensible runtime to power microservices and cloud deployments. Their individual efforts were naturally followed by an open collaboration within the **MicroProfile.io** initiative.

MicroProfile components are built upon the model of Java EE, thereby making the transition to microservices development natural. This means you will be able to reuse the valuable knowledge of Java EE you have accumulated over the years to flexibly use multiple vendor specs to define application requirements.

In its initial release, the MicroProfile initiative included just a small cutdown of the Java EE API (JAX-RS 2.0, CDI 1.2, and JSON-P 1.0).

In a short time, however, new MicroProfile projects have been added. In 2018 alone, we saw the advent of MicroProfile 1.3, 1.4, 2.0, and 2.1, and the projects contained in them. The current release of the MicroProfile initiative extends the standards with functionality that isn't part of Java EE, such as configuration, resiliency, monitoring, health checking, and distributed tracing.

The following diagram depicts the building blocks of MicroProfile projects according to the latest specification (at the time of writing this book):

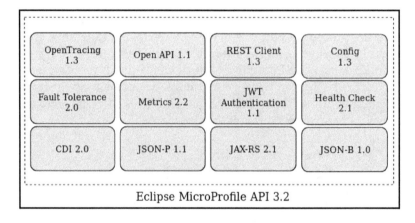

MicroProfile alone, however, is mostly insufficient when it comes to developing a complex enterprise application. For example, it does not include an API for persistence, transaction, or **Security Socket Layer** (**SSL**) management out of the box. For this reason, we need a framework that leverages the MicroProfile API with extensible functionalities and can be orchestrated by Kubernetes, which is going to be the new application server, from the management point of view.

Quarkus – a Kubernetes-native Java framework

One of the main challenges of a microservices architecture is that the proliferation of services can increase the complexity of your systems unless you have a valid framework to orchestrate them from. Also, without a centralized function for authentication, data management, and an API gateway, the advantages of a microservices architecture are invalidated by these challenges.

In this sense, the arrival of Kubernetes is a real revolution in IT patterns. With the help of Kubernetes-based orchestration, you can enhance efficiency and resource utilization by managing and scheduling your microservices in a dynamic manner. This also adds an advanced resiliency level. You can continue to operate as demand varies, without worrying about container failure. To close the circle and unify all the components, we need a framework that has been specifically thought of to work in this kind of architecture. Let's meet **Quarkus**.

Quarkus emerges as a first-class citizen when it comes to managing cloud-native enterprise applications and has lots of amazing features that can enable scenarios that haven't been possible before. As you will see in the upcoming sections, Quarkus is able to build thin native code from Java classes and create container images out of it that you can run on top of Kubernetes or OpenShift. Quarkus also leverages the best of the breed of Java libraries you have been working with for years, such as RESTEasy, Hibernate, Apache Kafka, Vert.x, and much more. Let's look at the highlights of this framework in more detail.

Native code execution

Native code execution has been attempted several times during the long history of Java, but it never got much adoption by developers. First of all, it required some external tooling as this isn't provided out of the box by the platform's vendor. For monolithic applications, the advantage of native execution is minor because, in the long run, due to the advancement in the Hot Spot technology, the speed of Java can become closer to native execution (provided that you are willing to pay for a slower application bootstrap).

Nevertheless, in a microservice scenario, spinning up a bunch of native services plays a crucial role, and even optimizing seconds or a fraction of a second can play a huge difference. In much the same way, if you aim to reach the highest memory density requirements, the maximum requests' throughput, along with a consistent CPU performance, Quarkus' native execution fits neatly in the picture.

On the other hand, you can smoothly transition to Quarkus using plain Java bytecode, still delivering applications with high memory density requirements, excellent CPU raw performance, advanced garbage collections tactics, a large set of libraries or monitoring tools that require the standard JDK, and the ubiquitous *compile once and run everywhere*.

The following table summarizes some typical use cases for choosing between native applications and Java applications when developing with Quarkus:

Quarkus Native applications	Quarkus Java applications
Highest memory density requirements	High memory density requirements
More consistent CPU performance	Best raw performance (CPU)
Fastest startup time	Fast startup time
Simpler garbage collection	Advanced garbage collection
Highest throughput	A large set of libraries and tools that only work with JDK
No JIT spikes	Compile once, run anywhere

As resulting from this picture, Quarkus is a breakthrough as it leverages native code execution while preserving the capability for you to run your services with OpenJDK and use Hot Spot's rich dynamic code execution capabilities when required.

Container first

As anticipated, one of the most promising features of Quarkus is the capability to automatically generate container images out of your applications. The minimal footprint of native applications is optimized to be run inside a container.

Generating container images of your native applications also defeats one common pitfall related to native execution, which is potential conflicts or errors when the build was done with a different OS. Since the container wraps the OS of your choice, you can provide container-safe native builds of your applications without hitting the risk of crash dumps or the infamous blue screen scenario.

Unifying the imperative and Reactive Programming models

Most Java developers are familiar with the imperative programming model, which translates into a sequence of instructions that are used to modify an object's state. On the other hand, asynchronous programming has always been a challenge for Java developers due to its inherent complexity and the lack of a solid pattern for propagating asynchronous changes. In this context, a paradigm called **Reactive Programming** has gained popularity due to its ability to conjugate the asynchronous programming pattern with data streams and the propagation of change.

Quarkus has been designed from the ground up to unify the two models in the same platform so that you can take the benefits of both programming models and use them in your IT organization.

Coding that sparks joy

Even the most powerful framework available wouldn't gain widespread adoption if it were overly complex to use and required lots of coding and configuration to accomplish even minor functions.

As we have learned from Spring Boot's success, developers are more productive with a framework that doesn't require you to spend lots of time on its setup or configuration. Out of the box, Quarkus provides the following:

- A unified configuration that can be easily maintained in a single property file
- A large set of defaults so that you can actually write applications, even with no configuration at all

Besides this, you can have extraordinary features, such as the following:

- Live reload of applications, without any third-party plugins
- Straight to container generation with native executables
- Simplified testing by adding testing extensions built specifically for Quarkus

Best-of-breed Java libraries and standards

The criterion that makes a development stack a successful one is a combination of various things, such as an active number of contributors, a high degree of recognition and use by top industrial actors, compliance to well-known standards, and strong and active criteria validators.

On this matter, Quarkus brings a cohesive, full-stack framework by leveraging the best-of-breed libraries you are already familiar with, which are automatically wired together to produce the final artifact. Quarkus extensions include the full Eclipse MicroProfile Stack, a persistence API (JPA), a transaction manager (Narayana), a reactive framework (Vert.x), an asynchronous event-driven network application framework (Netty), and much more.

Quarkus also includes an extension framework that third-party component authors can leverage to extend the framework. The Quarkus extension framework greatly reduces the complexity of making third-party frameworks run on Quarkus and compile to a native binary.

Quarkus architecture

Now that we know about some of the highlights of Quarkus, let's have a more in-depth look at the architecture of this framework.

At the heart of Quarkus, there is the **core** component that does the hard work of rewriting our application in the build phase so that super-optimized native executable and Java-runnable applications can be generated. To do that, Quarkus **core** requires the cooperation of a set of tools:

- **Jandex**: This is a space-efficient Java annotation indexer and offline reflection library that's able to index all runtime visible Java annotations and class hierarchies for a set of classes into a memory-efficient representation.
- **Gizmo**: This is a bytecode generation library used by Quarkus to produce Java bytecode.
- **GraalVM**: This is a set of components. Every component has a specific function, such as a compiler, an SDK API for the integration of Graal languages and the configuration of native images, and a runtime environment for JVM-based languages.
- **SubstrateVM**: This is a subcomponent of GraalVM that allows for the **ahead-of-time** (**AOT**) compilation of Java applications of Java programs into self-contained executables.

Moving on to the list of available Quarkus extensions, first and foremost, Quarkus fully implements the MicroProfile specifications. Quarkus also includes a set of extensions for Hibernate ORM for handling persistence, a transaction manager (Narayana), a connection pool manager (Agroal), plus several more, such as an API for Apache Kafka, Camel Routes, and the ability to run reactive applications (Vert.X).

The following diagram summarizes the core components of the Quarkus architecture, although the list of available extensions cannot be exhaustive for the sake of brevity:

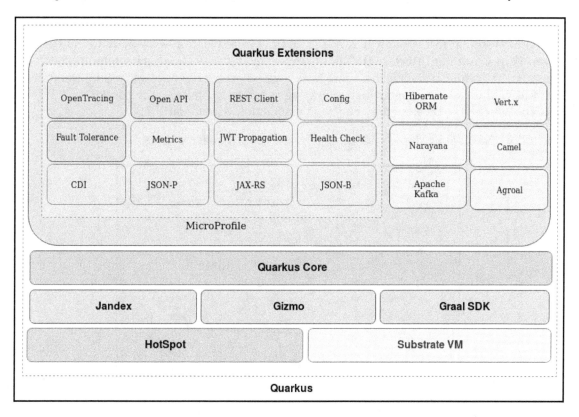

Having covered the basics of the Quarkus architecture, without further ado, we will now shift our attention to the installation of the tools that we'll need in order to build and run Quarkus applications. Our to-do list isn't that long and will be addressed shortly. In the next section, we will be installing GraalVM and a development environment for our applications.

Getting started with GraalVM

To compile Java code into native executables, you will need an extension of the virtual machine called **GraalVM**. To be precise, GraalVM is a universal virtual machine that facilitates the compilation of the bytecode of various languages (such as Python, JavaScript, Ruby, and so on). In addition to this, it allows for the integration of those languages in the same project. It has a few other features as well, among which is one that offers **Substrate VM**, a framework that allows AOT compilation for applications written in various languages. It also allows us to compile JVM bytecode into a native executable.

GraalVM is similar to any other JDK available from other vendors, except that it has **Java-based JVM Compiler Interface (JVMCI)** support, and it uses Graal as its default JIT compiler. Therefore, it can't *just* execute Java code but also languages such as JS, Python, and Ruby. This can be done through a language abstract syntax tree interpreter called **Truffle**, which was developed by Oracle in association with GraalVM.

The following diagram depicts a high-level view of the GraalVM stack:

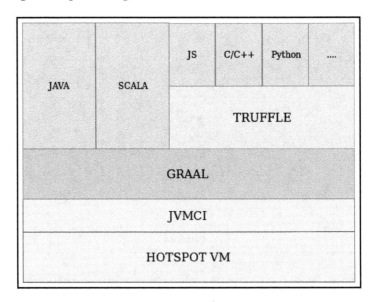

All of this sounds great, but GraalVM comes with a price as well. The dynamic nature of Java is severely constrained; for example, there's the default reflection mechanism, which will not work unless a class/member has been explicitly registered for reflection. Also, class loading at runtime, dynamic proxies, and static initializers require, at best, some changes/workarounds in order to work.

How does Quarkus overcome these limitations? The trick is to move as much framework initialization at build time. During this phase, Quarkus is able to discover which classes need reflection at runtime through metadata discovery (such as annotations). Quarkus uses a set of tools such as Jandex to optimize annotation processing and bytecode generation. Also, to overcome other limitations of GraalVM, Quarkus uses a single-pass, single class loader and programmatically provides compiler hints to enable extensive dead code elimination, thereby substantially cutting down the size of the executable file.

To get started, we will install GraalVM from `https://www.graalvm.org/`. As you will see from the **Downloads** page, the Community and Enterprise GraalVM editions are available. In this book, we will be using the Community Edition, so proceed by downloading the community version that fits with your OS.

Installing GraalVM

There are several ways to get started with GraalVM. You can either download the zipped binary for your operating system or build it from the source. For the purpose of this book, we will choose the former option. The installation steps are as follows:

1. Navigate to the **Downloads** page and choose **Community Edition**. You will be redirected to the GitHub project where the project is hosted. Download the archive that matches with operating system. **Please note that the recommended version of GraalVM to use with Quarkus 1.0.0.final is the version 19.2.1**. As a matter of fact, the newer 19.3.0 version does not meet the requirements of Quarkus 1.0.0.final.
2. Extract the archive to your filesystem.

You should have the following top-level structure in the folder where GraalVM has been extracted:

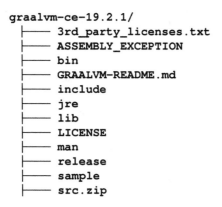

```
graalvm-ce-19.2.1/
├──── 3rd_party_licenses.txt
├──── ASSEMBLY_EXCEPTION
├──── bin
├──── GRAALVM-README.md
├──── include
├──── jre
├──── lib
├──── LICENSE
├──── man
├──── release
├──── sample
├──── src.zip
```

As you can see, the top-level structure of GraalVM is quite similar to the JDK. In the `bin` folder, you will find many utilities and replacements for JDK tools. Notably, when you use the `java` command in GraalVM, it runs the JVM and the default compiler, which is Graal. `javac` can be used to compile your code. Apart from this, the following commands are essentials when it comes to leveraging the native and polyglot functionalities of GraalVM:

- `js`: This command can be executed to run plain JavaScript code if we pass a set of options and the JavaScript filename as an argument.
- `node`: This command can be used to run Node.js-based applications. It relies on the npm command to install Node.js modules.
- `native-image`: This command takes your Java class(es) and builds an AOT compiled executable or a shared library. It is not included by default in most recent GraalVM installations and you need the `gu` tools to install it.
- npm: This is the package manager for Node.js. It puts modules in place so that `node` can find them and manages dependency conflicts intelligently.
- `lli`: This is an LLVM bitcode interpreter that can execute LLVM bitcode in a managed environment.
- `gu`: This tool can be used to install language packs for Python, R, and Ruby, as well as the native-image tool.

The first thing we are going to do is export the path where GraalVM has been installed into our environment:

```
export GRAALVM_HOME=/path/to/graal
```

In addition, it is recommended to complete the installation adding the `bin` folder of GraalVM to your OS's `PATH`. For example, on Linux, we would do the following:

```
export PATH=$PATH:$GRAALVM_HOME
```

Optionally, you can resolve to the GraalVM installation directory by setting the `JAVA_HOME` environment variable like so:

```
export JAVA_HOME=$GRAALVM_HOME
```

> All the preceding environment settings should be added to the script that initializes your shell. For most Linux distributions, this means putting them in the `.bashrc` file.

After you have set the `PATH` environment variable, it's pretty simple to check language versions with GraalVM's launchers:

```
$ java -version
openjdk version "1.8.0_232"
OpenJDK Runtime Environment (build
1.8.0_232-20191008104205.buildslave.jdk8u-src-tar--b07)
OpenJDK 64-Bit GraalVM CE 19.2.1 (build 25.232-b07-jvmci-19.2-b03, mixed
mode)

$ node -v
v10.16.3

$ lli --version
LLVM (GraalVM CE Native 19.2.1)
```

The executables belonging to all the language runtimes in GraalVM emulate the behavior of the languages' default runtimes. It should be enough to include GraalVM at the beginning of your `PATH` environment variable in order to run your applications with GraalVM.

Running a Java application with GraalVM

To test whether your GraalVM environment works correctly, we will be adding a minimal Java class and running it. Open an editor and create the following `Main` class:

```
public class Main {
 public static void main(String[] args) {
 System.out.println("Hello GraalVM!");
 }
}
```

Compile this class into bytecode and then run it on GraalVM using the following commands:

```
$ javac Main.java
$ java Main
```

This will give us the following output:

```
Hello GraalVM!
```

Building native images

Now that we have tested the compilation and execution of Java bytecode, we will convert the bytecode into native executables to achieve faster startup and a smaller footprint for our applications. In order to do that, we need the `native-image` tool, which allows us to AOT compile Java code into a standalone executable. We can install the `native-image` tool as follows:

```
${GRAALVM_HOME}/bin/gu install native-image
```

Upon successful installation, we can use the `native-image` tool against the same `HelloWorld` Java class we have created. Run the following command to build a native image:

```
$ native-image Main
```

You will see the following output:

```
Build on Server(pid: 7874, port: 38225)*
[main:7874]      classlist:   1,156.93 ms
[main:7874]          (cap):     859.74 ms
[main:7874]        setup:   1,940.59 ms
[main:7874]    (typeflow):   2,415.87 ms
[main:7874]     (objects):     680.43 ms
[main:7874]    (features):     124.69 ms
[main:7874]      analysis:   3,517.35 ms
[main:7874]      universe:     179.14 ms
[main:7874]        (parse):     413.36 ms
[main:7874]       (inline):     728.98 ms
[main:7874]     (compile):   3,642.72 ms
[main:7874]       compile:   5,219.51 ms
[main:7874]         image:     304.89 ms
[main:7874]         write:      97.09 ms
[main:7874]       [total]:  12,891.94 ms
```

This builds an executable file, just 2 MB in size, named `main` in the current working directory:

```
$ ls -al main
-rwxrwxr-x. 1 francesco francesco 2481352 Apr 16 10:06 main
```

Invoking it executes the natively compiled code of the `Main` class, as follows:

```
$ ./main
Hello GraalVM!
```

Once that we have verified that our installation of GraalVM works, we can install a development environment, which will be needed to run the examples contained in this book.

Installing a development environment

Choosing a development environment becomes less significant as we move away from monolithic development, where a large set of plugins is often required to build the complex interaction between the application layers. Therefore, we can choose any IDE that is capable of importing/exporting Maven or Gradle projects natively, as well as a decent set of features for speeding up our code or refactoring it. We will be using **IntelliJ IDEA**, which we can download from `https://www.jetbrains.com/idea/`.

As you will see from the download page (`https://www.jetbrains.com/idea/download/`), both the Ultimate and Community versions are available. We will be using the latter, which can be freely downloaded. Choose to download the latest binary for your operating system. Then, unzip it into a folder of your preference (for example, in your `Home` folder):

```
tar xvzf ideaIC-2019.1.tar.gz -C $HOME
```

Next, move into the `bin` folder of the installation and execute it with the following command:

```
./idea.sh
```

Let's have a minimal overview of the development environment's visual elements.

A brief overview of IntelliJ IDEA

Although we won't be focusing on a specific development environment to learn about Quarkus, we will provide a short overview of the visual elements that comprise IntelliJ IDEA to understand what actions you can do in a quicker and easier manner. As shown in the following screenshot, these are the main elements of the IntelliJ IDEA interface:

Let's have a look at the various highlighted sections:

1. **Menu bar**: The menu bar includes options we can use to create or import projects and other key actions related to projects, such as code refactoring, builds, run, debug, version-control options, and so on.
2. **Toolbar**: The toolbar contains some shortcuts for common execution actions, such as compile, debug, and run. You can also customize it according to your requirements.
3. **Navigation bar**: The navigation bar enables navigation between sources within a project. This feature will come in handy as your code base grows.
4. **Tools tab**: The tools tab, which can show up on either side of the main window, lets you access key tools such as Maven/Ant builds, databases, and so on.

5. **Project perspective**: The project perspective window contains all the elements of your project, such as packages, modules, classes, external libraries, and so on.
6. **Editor window**: This is where you edit your code in IntelliJ IDEA using advanced features such as syntax highlighting, smart completion, quick-fix suggestions, and other useful features.

Great! In the next chapter, we will be creating a simple application with Quarkus that we will import into IntelliJ IDEA.

Installing IntelliJ Plugin for Quarkus

Before closing this chapter, it is worth mentioning that IntelliJ IDEA includes in its plugin marketplace a plugin to bootstrap Quarkus applications. You can install it through the **File | Settings | Plugin** top menu option. Once you have selected the **Plugin** option, search for "quarkus" in the marketplace text field.

Once found it, click on the **Install** button as depicted by the following picture:

Restart the IDE for the changes to take effect. Once that the Plugin has been installed, you can add new Quarkus projects directly from the IDE. Here is a snapshot of the updated list of Projects:

The project wizard will guide you through the selection of the Maven coordinates of your project and the extensions you want to have included in it:

Before sailing into unknown waters, we will pause for a while to briefly recap what we have learned in this chapter. Then, grab a cup of tea and get ready for departure!

Summary

In this chapter, we got an overview of the current landscape of the IT industry. As we have learned, Kubernetes adds a completely new dimension to traditional language-based building blocks by offering a new set of distributed services and a runtime environment for creating distributed systems that spread across multiple nodes. Although the core principles of creating containerized applications don't strictly require that you decompose your monolithic applications in single services, there are evident advantages in doing so in terms of isolation, scalability, team independence, monitoring, resilience, and life cycle automation.

Later, we discussed the actual applications that can run natively by introducing Quarkus, an amazing framework where we can create serverless, native applications without losing the skills we learned as Java developers.

Now that we've installed the required tools to get started with Quarkus, in the next chapter, we will code our first example application.

2
Developing Your First Application with Quarkus

In this chapter, we will be creating our first Quarkus application using the tooling that's available to us. As you will soon see, this is a pretty simple process that can be bootstrapped from the command line and doesn't require you to download any external tools. By using this process, we will be able to compile an application into a native executable and have solid evidence of how fast and thin a Java application can be when it's turned into native code by Quarkus.

In this chapter, we will cover the following topics:

- Using the Quarkus Maven plugin to bootstrap our projects
- Alternative methods to kick-start your projects (Quarkus CLI)
- Creating and executing our first Quarkus application
- Debugging the application from our IDE
- Testing the application with an extension of the JUnit test framework
- Turning our application into native code

Technical requirements

You can find the source code for the project in this chapter on GitHub at `https://github.com/PacktPublishing/Hands-On-Cloud-Native-Applications-with-Java-and-Quarkus/tree/master/Chapter02`.

Getting started with the Quarkus Maven plugin

In order to scaffold our first Quarkus application, we will be using Maven, which is the most common software and release management tool available. It is used by a variety of developers, mostly because it offers the following:

- A standard structure for all your projects
- Centralized and automatic management of dependencies

Maven is distributed in several formats for the user's convenience. You can download it from https://maven.apache.org/download.cgi.

Once you've downloaded Maven, do the following:

1. Unzip the distribution archive (for example, apache-maven-3.6.1-bin.zip) to the directory that you want Maven to be installed in (for example, in your $HOME/apache folder):

   ```
   $ mkdir $HOME/apache
   $ unzip $HOME/Downloads/apache-maven-3.6.1-bin.zip -d $HOME/apache
   ```

2. Add the Maven libraries to your system path, as shown in the following code. This will update the PATH environment variable:

   ```
   $ export PATH=$PATH:$HOME/apache/apache-maven-3.6.1/bin
   ```

3. Once you have completed your installation, you need to check whether Maven has been correctly installed or not. Run mvn --version to verify this:

   ```
   $ mvn --version
   Apache Maven 3.6.1
   Maven home: /home/francesco/apache/apache-maven-3.6.1
   Java version: 1.8.0_191, vendor: Oracle Corporation, runtime:
   /usr/lib/jvm/java-1.8.0-openjdk-1.8.0.191.b13-0.fc29.x86_64/jre
   Default locale: en_US, platform encoding: UTF-8
   OS name: "linux", version: "4.18.16-300.fc29.x86_64", arch:
   "amd64", family: "unix"
   ```

If you get the preceding output, then you have just verified that Maven is installed on your system.

Launching the Quarkus Maven plugin

Now that Maven has been set up, we can bootstrap our first Quarkus application by means of its Maven plugin. A Maven plugin provides a set of goals that can be executed to compile and build our artifacts or extend our project with some features. Each plugin, like every Maven component, is based on the following coordinates:

- `groupId`: The ID of the project's group. This often matches the ID of the package root directory.
- `artifactId`: The ID of the artifact. This often matches with the final artifact name.
- `version`: The version of the artifact under the specified group.

You can reference a Maven plugin from the command line by indicating the `<groupId>:<artifactId>` coordinates. For Quarkus, the `<groupId>:<artifactId>` combination is `io.quarkus:quarkus-maven-plugin`. You can check the available goals and the latest version of it with the following command:

```
$ mvn -Dplugin=io.quarkus:quarkus-maven-plugin help:describe
```

You will see the following output:

```
Name: Quarkus - Maven Plugin
Description: Build parent to bring in required dependencies
Group Id: io.quarkus
Artifact Id: quarkus-maven-plugin
Version: 1.0.0.Final
Goal Prefix: quarkus

This plugin has 11 goals:

quarkus:add-extension
  Description: (no description available)

quarkus:add-extensions
  Description: Allow adding an extension to an existing pom.xml file.
  Because you can add one or several extension in one go, there are 2
  mojos:
    add-extensions and add-extension. Both supports the extension and
    extensions parameters.

quarkus:analyze-call-tree
  Description: (no description available)

quarkus:build
```

```
    Description: (no description available)

  quarkus:create
    Description: This goal helps in setting up Quarkus Maven project with
      quarkus-maven-plugin, with sensible defaults

  quarkus:create-example-config
    Description: (no description available)

  quarkus:dev
    Description: The dev mojo, that runs a quarkus app in a forked process

  quarkus:help
    Description: Display help information on quarkus-maven-plugin.
      Call mvn quarkus:help -Ddetail=true -Dgoal=<goal-name> to display
parameter
      details.

  quarkus:list-extensions
    Description: (no description available)

  quarkus:native-image
    Description: (no description available)

  quarkus:remote-dev
    Description: The dev mojo, that connects to a remote host
```

The source code of our first application can be located in the Chapter02/hello-rest folder of this book's GitHub repository. For reference, we have created the application using the Maven plugin and configured the following set of arguments:

```
$ mvn io.quarkus:quarkus-maven-plugin:1.0.0.Final:create \
  -DprojectGroupId=com.packt.quarkus.Chapter02 \
  -DprojectArtifactId=hello-rest \
  -DclassName="com.packt.quarkus.Chapter02.SimpleRest" \
  -Dpath="/helloworld"
```

As a result of the preceding command, the following directory structure has been generated in the hello-rest folder:

```
├── mvnw
├── mvnw.cmd
├── pom.xml
└── src
    └── main
        │   ├── docker
        │   │   ├── Dockerfile.jvm
        │   │   └── Dockerfile.native
```

```
|        ├──── java
|        |     └──── com
|        |           └──── packt
|        |                 └──── quarkus
|        |                       └──── Chapter02
|        |                             └──── SimpleRest.java
|        └──── resources
|              ├──── application.properties
|              └──── META-INF
|                    └──── resources
|                          └──── index.html
└──── test
      └──── java
            └──── com
                  └──── packt
                        └──── quarkus
                              └──── Chapter02
                                    ├──── NativeSimpleRestIT.java
                                    └──── SimpleRestTest.java
```

In the next section of this chapter, we will learn how to import the project into IntelliJ IDEA (the steps are pretty much the same in any IDE, though). Right now, let's stick to the preceding tree view of the project and look at the files that are included in this project:

- A **Project Object Model** (pom.xml) with the project configuration
- A sample REST service named SimpleRest.java and a test class for it named SimpleRestTest.java, as well as a wrapper class named NativeSimpleRestIT.java for executing the test against the native executable application
- A placeholder for the configuration file (application.properties)
- An index.html file to indicate where we can add static web content
- A Dockerfile so that we can create a container out of our applications
- A Maven wrapper file (mvnw/mvnw.cmd) to allow us to execute Maven goals without prior installation of it

The pom.xml file will be added to the root of your project. There, you will find an upper dependencyManagement section, which imports Quarkus' **Bill Of Materials**. This allows us to automatically link the exact version of each Quarkus extension.

 In the 1.0.0.Final version of Quarkus, you will reference the artifactId named quarkus-universe-bom, which belongs to groupId io.quarkus.

Here, `quarkus-maven-plugin` has also been included to allow you to package your application and generate the native executable:

```xml
<dependencyManagement>
  <dependencies>
    <dependency>
      <groupId>${quarkus.platform.group-id}</groupId>
      <artifactId>${quarkus.platform.artifact-id}</artifactId>
      <version>${quarkus.platform.version}</version>
      <type>pom</type>
      <scope>import</scope>
    </dependency>
  </dependencies>
</dependencyManagement>
<build>
  <plugins>
    <plugin>
      <groupId>io.quarkus</groupId>
      <artifactId>quarkus-maven-plugin</artifactId>
      <version>${quarkus-plugin.version}</version>
      <executions>
        <execution>
          <goals>
            <goal>build</goal>
          </goals>
        </execution>
      </executions>
    </plugin>
</build>
```

Moving into the dependencies section, you will see that the only runtime dependency that's been added is the following one, which allows you to execute a basic REST application:

```xml
<dependency>
    <groupId>io.quarkus</groupId>
    <artifactId>quarkus-resteasy</artifactId>
</dependency>
```

RESTEasy is a portable implementation of the JAX-RS specification that is included by default in the WildFly application server (`http://www.wildfly.org`). You can use it to provide a representation of your service through the standard HTTP methods using stateless communication.

Besides `quarkus-resteasy`, some other libraries have been included in your `pom.xml` file for the purpose of testing your applications. This will be discussed more in detail in the *Testing Quarkus applications* section.

 To add additional libraries to your project, besides editing the `pom.xml` file, you can also use `add-extension`, which can be found in Quarkus' Maven plugin. An example of this is `$ mvn quarkus:add-extension -Dextensions="io.quarkus:quarkus-jsonp,io.quarkus:quarkus-smallrye-health"`.

The following `SimpleRest` class has been automatically generated for you in `src/main/java/com/packt/quarkus/Chapter02`:

```
import javax.ws.rs.GET;
import javax.ws.rs.Path;
import javax.ws.rs.Produces;
import javax.ws.rs.core.MediaType;

@Path("/helloworld")
public class SimpleRest {

    @GET
    @Produces(MediaType.TEXT_PLAIN)
    public String hello() {
        return "hello";
    }
}
```

As you can see, it's a very simple REST endpoint that leverages the JAX-RS API to produce a `TEXT_PLAIN` resource when the `/helloworld GET` requests lands on the default port.

 Simpler than JAX-RS!
As we mentioned previously, Quarkus simplifies code development to provide sensible defaults. However, we don't need to declare an `ApplicationScoped` class to bootstrap the REST service anymore since we will get it as the default option.

Running the application

Now, we are ready to run our application. Execute the `compile` and `quarkus:dev` goals to build it and run it:

```
$ mvn compile quarkus:dev
```

After a few seconds, the application will be compiled and executed, as shown in the following log:

```
[INFO] Scanning for projects...
. . . .
[INFO] --- maven-resources-plugin:2.6:resources (default-resources) @
hello-rest ---
[INFO] Using 'UTF-8' encoding to copy filtered resources.
[INFO] Copying 2 resources
[INFO]
[INFO] --- maven-compiler-plugin:3.8.1:compile (default-compile) @ hello-
rest ---
[INFO] Changes detected - recompiling the module!
[INFO] Compiling 1 source file to /home/francesco/git/packt/Hands-On-Cloud-
Native-Applications-with-Java-and-Quarkus/chapter2/hello-
rest/target/classes
[INFO]
[INFO] --- quarkus-maven-plugin:1.0.0.Final:dev (default-cli) @ hello-rest
---
Listening for transport dt_socket at address: 5005
2019-11-11 13:10:34,493 INFO  [io.qua.dep.QuarkusAugmentor] (main)
Beginning quarkus augmentation
2019-11-11 13:10:35,078 INFO  [io.qua.dep.QuarkusAugmentor] (main) Quarkus
augmentation completed in 585ms
2019-11-11 13:10:35,395 INFO  [io.quarkus] (main) Quarkus 1.0.0.CR1 started
in 1.079s. Listening on: http://0.0.0.0:8080
2019-11-11 13:10:35,397 INFO  [io.quarkus] (main) Profile dev activated.
Live Coding activated.
2019-11-11 13:10:35,397 INFO  [io.quarkus] (main) Installed features: [cdi,
resteasy]
```

Now, you can request the provided endpoint with the browser or a tool such as `curl`:

```
$ curl http://localhost:8080/helloworld
hello
```

You can stop the application with *Ctrl + C*, although we recommend keeping it running as we will be testing the **hot reload** feature soon!

Using the Maven plugin to generate a Gradle project

The Quarkus Maven plugin is pretty agnostic in spite of its name. As a matter of fact, you can also use it to generate **Gradle** projects. A comparison between the two tools is out of the scope of this book; however, a large number of developers prefer Gradle as a build tool since it's modeled in a way that is extensible in the most fundamental ways and has outstanding performance.

That being said, you can generate a Gradle project by simply setting the `buildTool` option to `gradle`, which otherwise defaults to `maven`. Here's how you can generate your project with Gradle:

```
mvn io.quarkus:quarkus-maven-plugin:1.0.0.Final:create \
  -DprojectGroupId=com.packt.quarkus.Chapter02 \
  -DprojectArtifactId=hello-rest \
  -DclassName="com.packt.quarkus.Chapter02.SimpleRest" \
  -Dpath="/helloworld" \
  -DbuildTool=gradle
```

The resulting `build.gradle` file defines the set of available repositories and dependencies and sets the core project attributes such as `quarkusPlatformGroupId`, `quarkusPlatformArtifactId`, and `quarkusPlatformVersion` as variables:

```
buildscript {
    repositories {
        mavenLocal()
    }
    dependencies {
        classpath "io.quarkus:quarkus-gradle-
        plugin:${quarkusPluginVersion}"
    }
}

plugins {
    id 'java'
}

apply plugin: 'io.quarkus'

repositories {
    mavenLocal()
    mavenCentral()
}
```

```
dependencies {
    implementation enforcedPlatform("${quarkusPlatformGroupId}:
    ${quarkusPlatformArtifactId}:${quarkusPlatformVersion}")
    implementation 'io.quarkus:quarkus-resteasy'

    testImplementation 'io.quarkus:quarkus-junit5'
    testImplementation 'io.rest-assured:rest-assured'

    nativeTestImplementation 'io.quarkus:quarkus-junit5'
    nativeTestImplementation 'io.rest-assured:rest-assured'
}

group 'org.acme'
version '1.0.0-SNAPSHOT'

compileJava {
    options.compilerArgs << '-parameters'
}

java {
    sourceCompatibility = JavaVersion.VERSION_1_8
    targetCompatibility = JavaVersion.VERSION_1_8
}
```

All the preceding variables are retrieved from the `gradle.properties` file, which is located at the root of your project.

As you can see from the configuration, a plugin is also included in the default project so that you can easily build your application and start it in development mode, as follows:

./gradlew quarkusDev

Finally, it is worth mentioning that the Gradle extension is still under development, so you may see some changes or updates in the next Quarkus releases.

Now, we will learn how to easily bootstrap our project (either Maven or Gradle) using the online Quarkus project generator.

Kick-starting applications using the Quarkus online application

Another option for bootstrapping your Quarkus application is using the online application, which is available at the following address: `https://code.quarkus.io/`.

By landing on that page, you will be able to generate a basic project with an initial endpoint, as well as all the extensions that you checked out in the user interface:

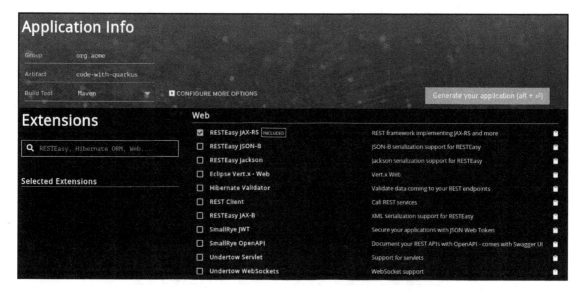

As shown in the preceding screenshot, by default, just the **RESTEasy** extension is selected. From the top-left corner of the interface, you can configure your project coordinates (groupId, artifactId) and the build tool, which can be either Maven or Gradle. More options are available through the **CONFIGURE MORE OPTIONS** panel, which lets you configure the package name and the version for the project.

By scrolling down the list of available extensions, you can also choose to experiment with alternative languages, such as Kotlin or Scala, to develop your Quarkus applications. These options are still work in progress, so consider that their API and/or configuration may change as the extension matures. The Quarkus team, however, does appreciate your feedback if you have tested any preview extension.

When you are done setting your options, just click on **Start a new application** to download the artifact as a compressed folder:

Now, you can just unpack it and import it into your favorite IDE. We will do this in the next section.

Testing live reload from your IDE

In this section, we will use the live reload feature of Quarkus. For this purpose, we will import the project into our IDE so that we can apply some changes.

Navigate to **File** | **Open** and point to the folder where you created the Maven project. It will be automatically imported into your IDE. Here is the **Files** tab view of your Java classes:

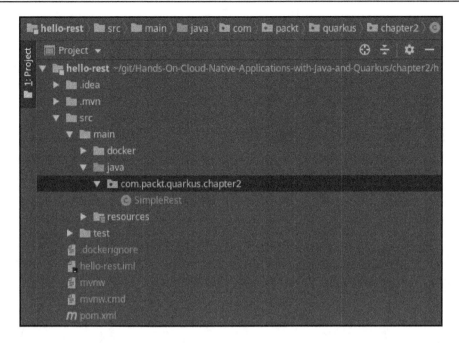

Now, let's look at how live reload works with Quarkus. For this, let's apply a simple change to our code. Here, we have modified the return value for the `hello` method, as follows:

```
public class SimpleRest {

    @GET
    @Produces(MediaType.TEXT_PLAIN)
    public String hello() {
        return "hello changed!";
    }
}
```

Hopefully, you haven't stopped your server. Now, try to call the service once more:

```
$ curl http://localhost:8080/helloworld
hello changed!
```

As you can see, when running in development mode, you can have a live reload of your application. Amazing, isn't it?

Live reload also works for resource files such as web pages or the configuration property file. Requesting the service triggers a scan of the workspace, and if any changes are detected, the Java files are recompiled and the application is redeployed. Your request is then serviced by the redeployed application.

Debugging applications

When running in development mode, Quarkus will automatically listen for a debugger on port 5005. You can check that the debugging is active with a basic shell command, as follows:

```
$ netstat -an | grep 5005
  tcp      0     0 0.0.0.0:5005        0.0.0.0:*              LISTEN
```

Now, let's undo these changes in the hello method and include another hello method, which receives a parameter to be inspected as input:

```
package com.packt.quarkus.chapter2;

import javax.ws.rs.GET;
import javax.ws.rs.Path;
import javax.ws.rs.Produces;
import javax.ws.rs.PathParam;
import javax.ws.rs.core.MediaType;
import org.slf4j.Logger;
import org.slf4j.LoggerFactory;

@Path("/helloworld")
public class SimpleRest {
    protected final Logger log = LoggerFactory.getLogger(this.getClass());
    @GET
    @Produces(MediaType.TEXT_PLAIN)
    @Path("/{name}")
    public String hello(@PathParam("name") String name) {

        log.info("Called with "+name);
        return "hello "+name;
    }

    @GET
    @Produces(MediaType.TEXT_PLAIN)
    public String hello() {
        return "hello";
    }
}
```

By using the `@PathParam` expression in our REST service, we will be able to debug the value of this expression as a method variable from within our IDE. Now, place a breakpoint on the logging statement, as shown in the following screenshot:

```java
package com.packt.quarkus.chapter2;

import javax.ws.rs.GET;
import javax.ws.rs.Path;
import javax.ws.rs.Produces;
import javax.ws.rs.PathParam;
import javax.ws.rs.core.MediaType;
import org.slf4j.Logger;
import org.slf4j.LoggerFactory;

@Path("/helloworld")
public class SimpleRest {
    protected final Logger log = LoggerFactory.getLogger(this.getClass());
    @GET
    @Produces(MediaType.TEXT_PLAIN)
    @Path("/{name}")
    public String hello(@PathParam("name") String name) {
        log.info("Called with "+name);
        return "hello "+name;
    }

    @GET
    @Produces(MediaType.TEXT_PLAIN)
    public String hello() {
        return "hello\n";
    }
}
```

Next, in order to attach the IntelliJ IDEA to the debugger, you have to connect to the debugger's port. In IntelliJ IDEA, you can do this in various ways. The simplest way is to select **Run** | **Attach to Process**. The runnable process of your application will be detected, as shown in the following screenshot:

```
Attach with Java Debugger To
Java
5371 /home/francesco/git/Hands-On-Cloud-Native-Applications-with-Java-and-Quarkus/chapter2/hello-rest/target/hello-rest-dev.jar (5005)
Java Read Only
2846 com.oracle.svm.hosted.server.NativeImageBuildServer
4996 org.jetbrains.idea.maven.server.RemoteMavenServer
5337 org.apache.maven.wrapper.MavenWrapperMain
```

Select it and check that you managed to attach to it successfully. You can do this from the **Debugger Console**:

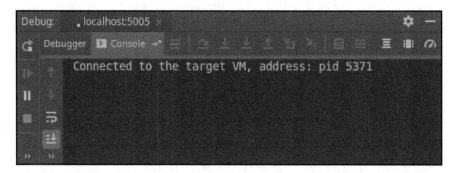

Now, invoke the application by adding an extra parameter at the end of it so that you hit the breakpoint:

```
$ curl http://localhost:8080/helloworld/frank
```

From the debugger prompt, you can inspect the class and method variables from its console. You can also control the execution path (**Step Over**, **Step Into**, **Stop**, and many more) by clicking on the buttons located on the left-hand side of the **Debugger Console**, as follows:

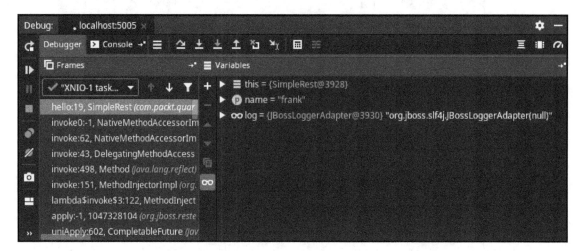

If you want to wait for the debugger to attach before starting your Quarkus application, you can pass –Ddebug on the command line. As soon as your IDE's debugger connects, the Quarkus Augmentor will start and your application will be executed. On the other hand, if you don't want the debugger at all, you can use –Ddebug=false.

Testing Quarkus applications

Along with the sample endpoint, the Maven plugin automatically included a test class for our REST service:

```
package com.packt.quarkus.chapter2;

import io.quarkus.test.junit.QuarkusTest;
import org.junit.jupiter.api.Test;

import static io.restassured.RestAssured.given;
import static org.hamcrest.CoreMatchers.is;

@QuarkusTest
public class SimpleRestTest {

    @Test
    public void testHelloEndpoint() {
        given()
          .when().get("/helloworld")
          .then()
             .statusCode(200)
             .body(is("hello"));
    }

}
```

Under the hood, this test class uses JUnit as the core testing framework and the REST Assured library:

```
<dependency>
    <groupId>io.quarkus</groupId>
    <artifactId>quarkus-junit5</artifactId>
    <scope>test</scope>
 </dependency>
 <dependency>
    <groupId>io.rest-assured</groupId>
    <artifactId>rest-assured</artifactId>
    <scope>test</scope>
 </dependency>
```

REST Assured is a Java library that can be used to write powerful tests for REST APIs using a flexible **Domain Specific Language** (DSL). The Fluent API that's available in REST Assured supports the standard patterns from **Behavior-Driven Development** (BDD) with its Given/When/Then syntax. The resulting test is simple to read and can include all the steps that we need in order to build the test with just one line of code.

Now, we can verify the response body's content and check that the HTTP response status code is 200. We can verify the test's execution by running the following command:

```
$ mvn clean test
```

You should see the following output in your console:

```
[INFO] Running com.packt.quarkus.chapter2.SimpleRestTest
 2019-05-16 11:04:21,166 INFO  [io.qua.dep.QuarkusAugmentor] (main)
Beginning quarkus augmentation
 2019-05-16 11:04:21,832 INFO  [io.qua.dep.QuarkusAugmentor] (main) Quarkus
augmentation completed in 669ms
 2019-05-16 11:04:22,108 INFO  [io.quarkus] (main) Quarkus 1.0.0.Final
started in 0.265s. Listening on: http://[::]:8081
 2019-05-16 11:04:22,109 INFO  [io.quarkus] (main) Installed features:
[cdi, resteasy]
 [INFO] Tests run: 1, Failures: 0, Errors: 0, Skipped: 0, Time elapsed:
2.958 s - in com.packt.quarkus.chapter2.SimpleRestTest

2019-05-16 11:04:23,263 INFO

[io.quarkus] (main) Quarkus stopped in 0.005s
 [INFO]
 [INFO] Results:
 [INFO]
 [INFO] Tests run: 1, Failures: 0, Errors: 0, Skipped: 0
 [INFO]
 [INFO] ------------------------------------------------------------------
----
 [INFO] BUILD SUCCESS
 [INFO] ------------------------------------------------------------------
----
```

As you can see, the test started the Quarkus runtime on the local IP address at port 8081. Therefore, it doesn't interfere with the development/production environment that runs on port 8080 by default.

You can mix and match multiple conditions in your tests by concatenating them using the and() method. This method works as simple syntactic sugar, that is, it helps make the code more readable. Here's an example of how to include a check on the header's Content-Length:

```
@Test
public void testHelloEndpointHeader() {
    given()
      .when().get("/helloworld")
        .then()
```

```
.statusCode(200)
.body(is("hello"))
  .and()
   .header("Content-Length","6");
}
```

By using parameterized tests, you can test multiple scenarios within a single method by providing different sets of records. REST Assured supports two different types of parameters:

- **Query parameters**: These can be appended at the end of a RESTful API endpoint and are identified by the question mark in front of them. Here's an example:

```
@Test
public void testHelloEndpointQueryParam() {
    given()
      .param("name","Frank")
      .when().get("/helloworld")
        .then()
        .statusCode(200)
        .body(is("hello"));

}
```

As you can see, using query parameters only requires that we specify their name and value by concatenating the `param()` method.

- **Path parameters**: These are specified in a similar fashion, that is, by including the `pathParam()` method with the parameter name/value combination:

```
@Test
public void testHelloEndpointPathParam() {

given()
.pathParam("name", "Frank")
.when().get("/helloworld/{name}")
.then()
.statusCode(200)
.body(is("hello Frank"));
}
```

Finally, it's worth mentioning that, since Quarkus aims at top performance, you can also validate your tests based on the response time. This can be done by concatenating `time()` to your condition. Here is an example that sets the time to be less than one second when it comes to returning the response:

```
@Test
public void testTimedHelloEndpointPathParam() {

  given()
  .pathParam("name", "Frank")
  .when().get("/helloworld/{name}")
  .then()
  .time(lessThan(1000L))
  .body(is("hello Frank"));
}
```

In this section, we have covered the most common testing scenarios that we can build with the REST Assured API. If you want to checkout some more advanced patterns, we recommend having a look at its Wiki, which is available at `https://github.com/rest-assured/rest-assured/wiki/usage`.

Choosing a different port for testing

You can change the default port that's used for testing by Quarkus (`8081`) by setting an appropriate value in the `src/main/resources/application.properties` file, which is the general configuration file for Quarkus. For example, in order to shift the test port to `9081`, you would need to add the following information to `application.properties`:

```
quarkus.http.test-port=9081
```

 As an alternative, you can also use the same property at startup by passing the `-Dquarkus.http.test-port=9081` flag.

Turning your application into a native executable

Now, it's time to check what Quarkus can do to turn our bytecode into a native executable. This kind of magic is done under the hood by a Maven profile named native, which is included out of the box when you scaffold your application:

```xml
<profile>
  <id>native</id>
  <activation>
    <property>
      <name>native</name>
    </property>
  </activation>
  <build>
    <plugins>
      <plugin>
        <artifactId>maven-failsafe-plugin</artifactId>
        <version>${surefire-plugin.version}</version>
        <executions>
          <execution>
            <goals>
              <goal>integration-test</goal>
              <goal>verify</goal>
            </goals>
            <configuration>
              <systemProperties>
                <native.image.path>${project.build.directory}
                  /${project.build.finalName}-runner
                </native.image.path>
              </systemProperties>
            </configuration>
          </execution>
        </executions>
      </plugin>
    </plugins>
  </build>
  <properties>
    <quarkus.package.type>native</quarkus.package.type>
  </properties>
</profile>
```

In addition, `maven-failsafe-plugin` has been automatically configured to run `integration-test goal` since we've set the path where the native image has been built as the system property.

 Before building your executable, verify that you have set `GRAALVM_HOME` in your environment, as described in the previous chapter.

Next, create a native executable by executing the following command:

```
$ mvn package -Pnative
```

The plugin will start analyzing the classes and packaging that's used in your application, along with the call tree. The resulting output will be a super lean executable that contains just a thin JVM layer (narrow enough to just execute the application) and the application itself.

You should see something similar to the following at the end of your output:

```
[INFO] [io.quarkus.deployment.QuarkusAugmentor] Quarkus augmentation
completed in 60485ms
```

Along with the JAR file containing the compressed bytecode for your application, the following executable will be generated in the `target` folder:

```
Nov 11 14:49 hello-rest-1.0-SNAPSHOT-runner
```

 The actual name of your application can be varied by setting the `native.image.path` environment variable in your `pom.xml` file, which is `${project.build.directory}/${project.build.finalName}-runner` by default.

As you can see, with approximately 20 MB, we have an executable application runtime that contains all the libraries and just what it needs from the JVM to run our application. You can execute it with the following command:

```
$ target/hello-rest-1.0-SNAPSHOT-runner
```

In as little as 0.006s, we got our service up and running. This can be seen in the console log:

```
2019-11-11 14:53:38,619 INFO  [io.quarkus] (main) hello-rest 1.0-SNAPSHOT
(running on Quarkus 1.0.0.CR1) started in 0.014s. Listening on:
http://0.0.0.0:8080
2019-11-11 14:53:38,619 INFO  [io.quarkus] (main) Profile prod activated.
2019-11-11 14:53:38,619 INFO  [io.quarkus] (main) Installed features: [cdi,
resteasy]
```

Let's check the memory usage of this compact application by executing the ps command:

```
$ ps -o pid,rss,command -p $(pgrep -f hello-rest)
```

Here is the output I have collected from my laptop:

```
PID   RSS   COMMAND
27919 18720 target/hello-rest-1.0-SNAPSHOT-runner
```

Although the output may vary depending on your environment, the **Resident Set Size (RSS)** shows that the process is taking about 18 MB of memory, which is a fraction of the minimum memory size required for a Java application.

Now, let's execute it to check the result:

```
$ curl http://localhost:8080/helloworld
  hello
```

As you can see, the result didn't change when we turned our application into a native application.

Executing integration tests against the native executable

Interestingly, native executable code can be tested. When you generated the sample project, a Native<project>Test class name was included in the test folder. This class differs from Java tests as it's annotated with the @NativeImageTest annotation.

> As a result of the Maven failsafe plugin configuration, all rests ending in *IT* or annotated with @NativeImageTest will be run against the native executable.

In terms of code, there's no need to make any changes as it uses inheritance to execute the native executable tests from our `SimpleRestTest` class:

```
@NativeImageTest
public class NativeSimpleRestIT extends SimpleRestTest {

    // Execute the same tests but in native mode.
}
```

The `verify` goal is required to test native executables. Before that, make sure you have exported the path where GraalVM has been installed into your environment:

```
export GRAALVM_HOME=/path/to/graal
```

Now, you can run the `verify` goal to test the native executable application:

```
$ mvn verify -Pnative
```

Check that the outcome is the same one that we produced in the *Testing Quarkus applications* section, earlier in this chapter:

```
[INFO] Running com.packt.quarkus.chapter2.SimpleRestTest
 2019-05-16 11:35:22,509 INFO  [io.qua.dep.QuarkusAugmentor] (main)
Beginning quarkus augmentation
 2019-05-16 11:35:23,084 INFO  [io.qua.dep.QuarkusAugmentor] (main) Quarkus
augmentation completed in 575ms
 2019-05-16 11:35:23,419 INFO  [io.quarkus] (main) Quarkus 1.0.0.Final
started in 0.319s. Listening on: http://[::]:8081
 2019-05-16 11:35:23,419 INFO  [io.quarkus] (main) Installed features:
[cdi, resteasy]
 2019-05-16 11:35:24,354 INFO  [com.pac.qua.cha.SimpleRest] (XNIO-1 task-1)
Called with Frank
 2019-05-16 11:35:24,598 INFO  [com.pac.qua.cha.SimpleRest] (XNIO-1 task-1)
Called with Frank
 [INFO] Tests run: 5, Failures: 0, Errors: 0, Skipped: 0, Time elapsed:
2.215 s - in com.packt.quarkus.chapter2.SimpleRestTest
```

Great! We have just managed to test our sample application in both scenarios (JVM and native executable).

Summary

In this chapter, we went through our first proof of concept Quarkus project, which was generated through `quarkus-maven-plugin`. The default application is a prototype of the REST service with all the minimal functionalities and a `Test` class that we have progressively enriched. In the second part of this chapter, we saw how to turn the Java application code into a thin native executable using the appropriate native profile of `quarkus-maven-plugin`.

So far, we have only scratched the surface of what we can do with Quarkus. Now, it's time to move on and learn how to create a Container image out of our native application and deploy it in a Kubernetes environment. This is what we are going to discuss in the next chapter.

3
Creating a Container Image of Your Application

In the previous chapter, we had a glimpse of the power of Quarkus applications by running a traditional JVM application and then turning it into a native build. There is much more to Quarkus than lean executables and low resource usage, though, so, in this chapter, we will keep learning how to create container images of our application that can then be deployed into a Kubernetes-native environment. For this purpose, our to-do list includes installing the Docker tool and the Community version of OpenShift, which is called **Origin Community Distribution of Kubernetes**, or simply **OKD**. Then, we will learn how to scale our application so that we can improve its response time even further.

In this chapter, we will cover the following topics:

- Setting up Docker in your environment
- Starting a Quarkus application in a container
- Running a native executable in a container
- Deploying your container image on OpenShift
- Scaling our application to improve its throughput

Technical requirements

You can find the source code for the project in this chapter on GitHub at `https://github.com/PacktPublishing/Hands-On-Cloud-Native-Applications-with-Java-and-Quarkus/tree/master/Chapter03`.

Setting up Docker

Docker is a tool that lets us simplify the creation and execution of containers in our environment. Each container, in turn, wraps up an application and its dependencies into a single standardized unit that includes everything it needs to run, that is, the system tools, code, and other required libraries. This guarantees that your application will always execute in the same way by sharing a simple container image. Docker is available in two versions:

- **Community Edition** (**CE**): The Docker CE, which we will be using in this book, is ideal for developers and small teams looking for a quick start with Docker and container-based applications.
- **Enterprise Edition** (**EE**): The EE features additional capabilities such as a certified infrastructure, image management, and image security scanning.

Although we will be using the Community version of Docker, this isn't going to reduce your application's full potential as we will be able to leverage advanced container capabilities through a native Kubernetes platform, which is an ideal solution for running business-critical applications in production at scale.

The installation of Docker is fully documented at `https://docs.docker.com/install/`. In a nutshell, you can follow several installation tactics, depending on your needs:

- From a midterm perspective, you may want to ease the upgrade of Docker. Most users choose to set up Docker's repositories and install and upgrade from there (`https://docs.docker.com/install/linux/docker-ce/fedora/#install-using-the-repository`).
- Another option, which turns out to be pretty useful if you are installing Docker on a machine that is offline, requires manually installing the RPM package and manually handling upgrades as well (`https://docs.docker.com/install/linux/docker-ce/fedora/#install-from-a-package`).
- Finally, for quick and easy installation, you can use the automated script, which will detect your operating system and install Docker accordingly. For the sake of simplicity, we will choose this option.

Let's proceed with installing Docker by following these steps:

1. The automated script can be downloaded from `https://get.docker.com/`, as follows:

   ```
   $ curl -fsSL https://get.docker.com -o get-docker.sh
   ```

2. Now, execute it with the following command:

   ```
   $ sh get-docker.sh
   ```

 Important! Just like any other shell script, verify its content before executing it! Its content needs to match with the `install.sh` script located at `https://github.com/docker/docker-install`. If the content doesn't match, verify whether the automated script is still being maintained by going to the Docker install page.

3. If you would like to run Docker as a non-privileged user, you should consider adding your user to the `docker` group by executing the following command:

   ```
   $ sudo usermod $(whoami) -G docker -a
   ```

4. For this to take effect, you will need to log out and log in again. We can check that our user is now in the Docker group by checking the output of the following command:

   ```
   $ groups $(whoami)
   ```

5. The output should include `docker` in the list of groups. Now, you can verify that you can run Docker commands without a root user (or `sudo`):

   ```
   $ docker run hello-world
   ```

6. The preceding command will pull the `hello-world` test image from the Docker repository, and run it in a container. When the test image starts, it prints an informative message and exits:

   ```
   Status: Downloaded newer image for hello-world:latest
   Hello from Docker!
   ```

This message shows that your installation appears to be working correctly.

Running Quarkus applications in a container

Once you have installed Docker, you are just ready to build a Docker image out of your Java or native executable application. For this purpose, we will quickly build another simple application that inspects some environment variables to determine the container ID where the application is running.

The source code for this chapter is located in the `Chapter03/hello-okd` folder of this book's GitHub repository. We recommend importing the project into your IDE before you continue.

Let's dive into the code by starting with the REST endpoint class (`HelloOKD`), which returns some information from a **Contexts and Dependency Injection (CDI)** service:

```
package com.packt.quarkus.chapter3;

import javax.ws.rs.GET;
import javax.ws.rs.Path;
import javax.ws.rs.Produces;
import javax.ws.rs.core.MediaType;
import javax.inject.Inject;

@Path("/getContainerId")
public class HelloOKD {
    @Inject
    ContainerService containerService;

    @GET
    @Produces(MediaType.TEXT_PLAIN)
    public String hello() {
        return "You are running on " +
            containerService.getContainerId();
    }
}
```

The following code is for the `ContainerService` class, which is injected into the REST endpoint:

```
package com.packt.quarkus.chapter3;

import javax.enterprise.context.ApplicationScoped;

@ApplicationScoped
public class ContainerService {

    public String getContainerId() {
```

```
            return System.getenv().getOrDefault("HOSTNAME", "unknown");
    }
}
```

This example shows the use of the CDI @ApplicationScoped annotation for injected objects. An object that is defined as @ApplicationScoped is created once for the duration of the lifetime of an application. In our case, it returns the HOSTNAME environment variable, which defaults to the Docker container ID.

In order to test our simple REST service, the following HelloOKDTest has been included in the project under the src/test/java path. Through its testHelloEndpoint method, we verify that the status code of the REST call was a success:

```
package com.packt.quarkus.chapter3;

import io.quarkus.test.junit.QuarkusTest;
import org.junit.jupiter.api.Test;

import static io.restassured.RestAssured.given;
import static org.hamcrest.CoreMatchers.is;

@QuarkusTest
public class HelloOKDTest {

    @Test
    public void testHelloEndpoint() {
        given()
          .when().get("/getContainerId")
          .then()
             .statusCode(200);
    }

}
```

Before we set off on our journey into Docker, let's check that the preceding test passes. The test phase will automatically kick in as we run the install goal of our project:

```
$ mvn install
```

A successful test should produce the following log:

```
[INFO] Tests run: 1, Failures: 0, Errors: 0, Skipped: 0, Time elapsed:
3.174 s - in com.packt.quarkus.chapter3.HelloOKDTest
2019-11-17 19:15:16,227 INFO  [io.quarkus] (main) Quarkus stopped in 0.041s
[INFO]
[INFO] Results:
[INFO]
[INFO] Tests run: 1, Failures: 0, Errors: 0, Skipped: 0
```

Now, let's move on to looking at Docker. If you take a look at the `src/main/docker` folder, you will notice that some of the files have been automatically added to your project:

```
$ tree src/main/docker
 src/main/docker
 ├─────── Dockerfile.jvm
 └─────── Dockerfile.native
```

The first file in the list, `Dockerfile.jvm`, is a Dockerfile that's been specifically written for a JVM environment. Its content is as follows:

```
FROM fabric8/java-alpine-openjdk8-jre
ENV JAVA_OPTIONS="-Dquarkus.http.host=0.0.0.0 -
Djava.util.logging.manager=org.jboss.logmanager.LogManager"
ENV AB_ENABLED=jmx_exporter
COPY target/lib/* /deployments/lib/
COPY target/*-runner.jar /deployments/app.jar
EXPOSE 8080

# run with user 1001 and be prepared for be running in OpenShift too
RUN adduser -G root --no-create-home --disabled-password 1001 \
   && chown -R 1001 /deployments \
   && chmod -R "g+rwX" /deployments \
   && chown -R 1001:root /deployments
USER 1001

ENTRYPOINT [ "/deployments/run-java.sh" ]
```

 A Dockerfile is a plain text file that contains a set of commands that we can use to assemble an image so that it can be executed by Docker. A Dockerfile needs to match with a specific format and set of instructions that have been documented in the Dockerfile reference (`https://docs.docker.com/engine/reference/builder/`).

In our example, the Dockerfile contains instructions for building a Java environment using Fabric8 Java Base Image and enables the JMX exporter (`https://github.com/prometheus/jmx_exporter`) to expose process metrics. Now, we will build the image for our container, as follows:

```
$ docker build -f src/main/docker/Dockerfile.jvm -t quarkus/hello-okd .
```

In your console, you can verify that the Docker pull process will be triggered and that all the commands in the Dockerfile contribute to building the intermediate layers of your quarkus/hello-okd container image:

```
Step 1/9 : FROM fabric8/java-alpine-openjdk8-jre
Trying to pull repository docker.io/fabric8/java-alpine-openjdk8-jre ...
sha256:b27090f384b30f0e3e29180438094011db1fa015bbf2e69decb921bc2486604f:
Pulling from docker.io/fabric8/java-alpine-openjdk8-jre
9d48c3bd43c5: Pull complete
 . . . . . . .
Status: Downloaded newer image for docker.io/fabric8/java-alpine-openjdk8-
jre:latest
 ---> fe776eec30ad
Step 2/9 : ENV JAVA_OPTIONS "-Dquarkus.http.host=0.0.0.0 -
Djava.util.logging.manager=org.jboss.logmanager.LogManager"
 ---> Running in c5d31bae859e
 ---> 01c99aac17db
Removing intermediate container c5d31bae859e
Step 3/9 : ENV AB_ENABLED jmx_exporter
 ---> Running in c867300baaf0
 ---> 52deadd505bc
Removing intermediate container c867300baaf0
Step 4/9 : COPY target/lib/* /deployments/lib/
 ---> aa11b2b30f16
Removing intermediate container dcbd13a3ae0f
Step 5/9 : COPY target/*-runner.jar /deployments/app.jar
 ---> 2f2e1218eff8
Removing intermediate container 4b3861ba33d9
Step 6/9 : EXPOSE 8080
 ---> Running in 93eebaee5495
 ---> 4008a4fdbb9c
Removing intermediate container 93eebaee5495
Step 7/9 : RUN adduser -G root --no-create-home --disabled-password 1001
&& chown -R 1001 /deployments  && chmod -R "g+rwX" /deployments  && chown
-R 1001:root /deployments
 ---> Running in 2a86b3aeaeae
 ---> b21be209f09e
Removing intermediate container 2a86b3aeaeae
Step 8/9 : USER 1001
 ---> Running in fac8d64b8793
```

```
 ---> 94077bb5396a
Removing intermediate container fac8d64b8793
Step 9/9 : ENTRYPOINT /deployments/run-java.sh
 ---> Running in 7bacd02dd631
 ---> 9f269b2041d3
Removing intermediate container 7bacd02dd631
Successfully built 9f269b2041d3
```

Now, let's check that the image is available in your local Docker repository by executing the `docker images` command:

```
$ docker images | grep hello-okd
```

You should see the following output:

```
quarkus/hello-okd                                         latest
9f269b2041d3          2 minutes ago        98.9 MB
```

As you can see, the locally cached image is now available in your local Docker repository. You can run it using the following command:

```
$ docker run -i --rm -p 8080:8080 quarkus/hello-okd
```

In the `run` command, we have included some additional flags, such as `--rm`, which removes the container automatically after it exits. The `-i` flag will connect the container to the Terminal. Finally, the `-p` flag exposes port `8080` externally, thus mapping to port `8080` on the host machine.

Since we will be exporting the service on the host port, that is, `8080`, check that no other service is engaging that port! You should be able to collect this output on the console, which is a log of the agent startup and, at the bottom, a log of our `hello-okd` service:

```
exec java -Dquarkus.http.host=0.0.0.0 -
Djava.util.logging.manager=org.jboss.logmanager.LogManager -
javaagent:/opt/agent-bond/agent-bond.jar=jmx_exporter{{9779:/opt/agent-
bond/jmx_exporter_config.yml}} -XX:+UseParallelGC -XX:GCTimeRatio=4 -
XX:AdaptiveSizePolicyWeight=90 -XX:MinHeapFreeRatio=20 -
XX:MaxHeapFreeRatio=40 -XX:+ExitOnOutOfMemoryError -cp . -jar
/deployments/app.jar
2019-11-11 10:29:12,505 INFO  [io.quarkus] (main) hello-okd 1.0-SNAPSHOT
(running on Quarkus 1.0.0.Final) started in 0.666s. Listening on:
http://0.0.0.0:8080
2019-11-11 10:29:12,525 INFO  [io.quarkus] (main) Profile prod activated.
2019-11-11 10:29:12,525 INFO  [io.quarkus] (main) Installed features: [cdi,
resteasy]
```

The Docker process is now running, which can be confirmed by the following command. This command will display the `Image` name for running containers:

```
$ docker ps --format '{{.Image}}'
```

The following is the output of running the preceding command:

```
quarkus/hello-okd
```

You can test that the application is running in the container with the following command:

```
$ curl http://localhost:8080/getContainerId
```

You should be able to see the same container ID that was printed by the `docker ps` command in the output:

```
You are running on a333f52881a1
```

Now, let's rebuild our container image so that we can use the native executable.

Running the native executable process in a container

As we have seen, the Quarkus Maven plugin has also produced `src/main/docker/Dockerfile.native`, which can be used as a template so that we can run our native executable in a container. Here's the content of this file:

```
FROM registry.access.redhat.com/ubi8/ubi-minimal
WORKDIR /work/
COPY target/*-runner /work/application
RUN chmod 775 /work
EXPOSE 8080
CMD ["./application", "-Dquarkus.http.host=0.0.0.0"]
```

Since there's no need to use a JDK layer to start our application, the base layer for our container will be a stripped-down RHEL image known as `ubi-minimal`.

 Red Hat **Universal Base Images** (**UBI**) are OCI-compliant container OS images that include complimentary runtime languages and other packages that are freely redistributable.

Before building the Docker image, package your application by including the `-Dnative-image.docker-build` option:

```
$ mvn package -Pnative -Dnative-image.docker-build=true
```

Check that the build was successful and then build the image with the following command:

```
$ docker build -f src/main/docker/Dockerfile.native -t quarkus/hello-okd-native .
```

From the console, you will see that the container will be created in much the same way that the Java application was, but using a different initial image (`ubi-minimal`):

```
Sending build context to Docker daemon 32.57 MB
Step 1/6 : FROM registry.access.redhat.com/ubi8/ubi-minimal
 ---> 8c980b20fbaa
Step 2/6 : WORKDIR /work/
 ---> Using cache
 ---> 0886c0b19e07
Step 3/6 : COPY target/*-runner /work/application
 ---> 7e66ae6447ce
Removing intermediate container 2ddc91992af5
Step 4/6 : RUN chmod 775 /work
 ---> Running in e8d6ffbbc14e
 ---> 780f6562417d
Removing intermediate container e8d6ffbbc14e
Step 5/6 : EXPOSE 8080
 ---> Running in d0d48475565f
 ---> 554f79b4cbb2
Removing intermediate container d0d48475565f
Step 6/6 : CMD ./application -Dquarkus.http.host=0.0.0.0
 ---> Running in e0206ff3971f
 ---> 33021bdaf4a4
Removing intermediate container e0206ff3971f
Successfully built 33021bdaf4a4
```

Let's check that the image is available in the Docker repository:

```
$ docker images | grep hello-okd-native
```

You should see the following output:

```
quarkus/hello-okd-native                            latest
33021bdaf4a4        59 seconds ago        113 MB
```

The `quarkus/hello-okd-native` image is now available. Now, run the container image using the following command:

```
$ docker run -i --rm -p 8080:8080 quarkus/hello-okd-native
```

No additional JVM layers will be displayed on the console. Here, we can see that our service was started up in just a few milliseconds:

```
2019-11-11 11:59:46,817 INFO  [io.quarkus] (main) hello-okd 1.0-SNAPSHOT
(running on Quarkus 1.0.0.CR1) started in 0.005s. Listening on:
http://0.0.0.0:8080
2019-11-11 11:59:46,817 INFO  [io.quarkus] (main) Profile prod activated.
2019-11-11 11:59:46,817 INFO  [io.quarkus] (main) Installed features: [cdi,
resteasy]y]
```

Verify that the application returns the container ID when requesting the `getContainerId` URI:

```
curl http://localhost:8080/getContainerId
```

In our case, the output is as follows:

```
You are running on ff6574695d68
```

Great! We just managed to run a native application as a Docker image. Our next task will be deploying our image into a Kubernetes-native environment.

Deploying Quarkus applications on a Kubernetes-native platform

Now that we have verified how simple it is to run Quarkus applications in a container, we will deploy our application into a Kubernetes-native environment. Even if Kubernetes itself is sufficient to orchestrate your services, you can greatly extend its capabilities by installing OpenShift. Besides leveraging Kubernetes features, OpenShift also provides the following:

- Better management of container images through the use of **image streams**, which decouple the actual image from your application
- Advanced CI/CD capabilities to make the whole CI/CD workflow a lot easier, also including a Jenkins certified image

- A simpler build process as it's easier to build a docker image inside OpenShift through the `BuildConfig` component, which can perform automated image builds and push them to its internal registry
- A wealth of certified plugins, such as storage/networking/monitoring plugins
- Support for multitenancy through the **Resource Scheduler** component, which will determine where to run Pods
- A large set of certified databases and middleware products
- A simpler UI web application from where you can easily manage your cluster of services and create new applications

OpenShift is available in several flavors:

- **Red Hat OpenShift Container Platform** (requires a subscription): The supported Kubernetes platform that lets you build, deploy, and manage your container-based applications consistently across cloud and on-premises infrastructures.
- **Red Hat OpenShift Dedicated** (requires a subscription): This provides a supported, private, high-availability Red Hat OpenShift cluster hosted on Amazon Web Services or Google Cloud Platform.
- **Red Hat OpenShift Online** (several plans are available): It provides on-demand access to Red Hat OpenShift so that you can manage containerized applications.
- **Origin Community Distribution of Kubernetes** (**OKD**): This is the Community version of the Red Hat OpenShift Container Platform that you can freely use in any environment.

For the purpose of this book, we will be installing **Minishift**, a simplified version of **OKD**, to launch a single-node cluster inside a virtual machine. This is the simplest approach to get started and try OpenShift on your local machine.

 The current version of Minishift is based on the release 3.x of Openshift. It is highly recommended to move to an Openshift 4.x platform for most advanced examples, such as developing Cloud based reactive applications, which is discussed in the last chapter of this book.

The installation of Minishift is quite simple: all you'll need to do is download and unzip the latest distribution of it. Some prerequisites, however, do exist as you need to prepare your system by installing a hypervisor, which is required to start the virtual environment that OKD is provisioned on.

Installing Minishift

In this section, we will learn how to install Minishift on a machine running Fedora. If you don't run Fedora on your machine, you can check out the prerequisites for your OS at https://docs.okd.io/latest/minishift/getting-started/preparing-to-install. html.

First, you will need to install two kernel modules (libvirt and qemu-kvm), which are needed to manage the various virtualization platforms. These are compliant with the **Kernel-based Virtual Machine (KVM)** technology. Follow these steps to do so:

1. From the shell, execute the following command:

   ```
   $ sudo dnf install libvirt qemu-kvm
   ```

2. Then, to run the virtualization platform with your user, add it to the libvirt group:

   ```
   $ sudo usermod -a -G libvirt $(whoami)
   ```

3. Next, configure the group membership with the user you are currently logged in as:

   ```
   $ newgrp libvirt
   ```

4. Finally, you will need to download and make the KVM driver for your Docker machine executable. As the root user, execute the following commands:

   ```
   $ sudo curl -L
   https://github.com/dhiltgen/docker-machine-kvm/releases/download/v0
   .10.0/docker-machine-driver-kvm-centos7 -o /usr/local/bin/docker-
   machine-driver-kvm
   ```

   ```
   $ sudo chmod +x /usr/local/bin/docker-machine-driver-kvm
   ```

5. Once your user has been set up, download and unpack the latest Minishift release package from the official GitHub repository: https://github.com/ minishift/minishift/releases. At the time of writing, this is the latest version of Minishift that can be downloaded:

   ```
   $ wget
   https://github.com/minishift/minishift/releases/download/v1.33.0/mi
   nishift-1.33.0-linux-amd64.tgz
   ```

6. Once the download has completed, unpack the `.tar` file into a destination folder. For example, to unpack it into your home (~) directory, execute the following command:

```
$ tar xvf minishift-1.33.0-linux-amd64.tgz -C ~
```

Within this package, you will find the `minishift` executable, which can be used to start your Minishift environment.

7. Next, we will run the `minishift` command to start the installation process:

```
$ ./minishift start
```

8. Once complete, you should see a message similar to the following in your Terminal:

```
-- Starting profile 'minishift'
-- Check if deprecated options are used ... OK
-- Checking if https://github.com is reachable ... OK
-- Checking if requested OpenShift version 'v3.11.0' is valid ...
OK
-- Checking if requested OpenShift version 'v3.11.0' is supported
... OK
-- Checking if requested hypervisor 'kvm' is supported on this
platform ... OK
-- Checking if KVM driver is installed ...
. . . .
OpenShift server started.

The server is accessible via web console at:
https://192.168.42.103:8443/console
The server is accessible at:
https://192.168.42.190:8443
You are logged in as: User: developer Password:
To log in as administrator:
oc login -u system:admin
```

And that's it! Minishift has been installed in your environment!

It's recommended that you include the following folders in the `$PATH` environment variable:

- The folder where you have unpacked the `minishift` tool.
- The folder where the `oc` client tool is located. This tool is a command-line utility that you can use to manage your Minishift cluster. Once you start up the cluster, this tool is copied to `~/.minishift/cache/oc/<oc-version>/linux`.

So, for example, if you unpacked Minishift in your home directory, replace `oc-version` with your tool version and execute the following command:

```
export PATH=$PATH:~/minishift-1.33.0-linux-amd64:~/.minishift/cache/oc/<oc-version>/linux
```

You can verify this by opening the OpenShift web console in your default browser (in our case, `https://192.168.42.190:8443`) or by passing the `console` argument to the `minishift` tool:

```
$ minishift console
```

Since the console runs on a secured connection, you will be warned that no signed certificates have been found in your browser. Add a security exception to your browser so that you land on the login page:

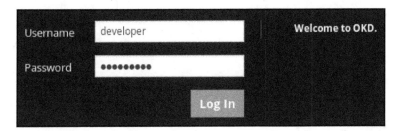

Log in with `developer/developer` to enter the dashboard:

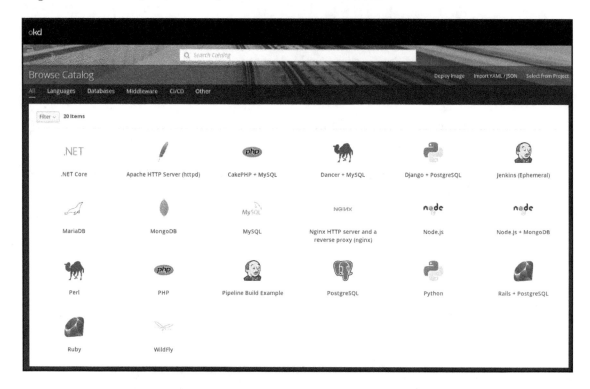

Congratulations! You have installed Minishift and verified it. The next step will be deploying our sample application on it.

Building and deploying a Quarkus application on OKD

Minishift's dashboard contains a set of templates that can be used to build our applications quickly. At the time of writing, there's no Quarkus template; however, we can easily build and deploy our image as a **binary build** that conveys the Dockerfile that we have already tested.

 A **binary build** is a feature that allows developers to upload artifacts from a binary source instead of pulling the source from a Git repository URL.

For this purpose, we will be using the `oc` client tool, which is the Swiss Army knife that's used to configure OpenShift and its objects.

The following set of commands is contained in the `deploy-openshift.sh` file, which is located in the `Chapter03` directory of this book's GitHub repository. If you are impatient to see your application in the cloud, simply execute the script and check that the output matches what we've written in this paragraph.

The first thing we will need to do is create a namespace for our project, which will be created in our current OpenShift namespace. You can create the `quarkus-hello-okd` namespace with the following command:

```
$ oc new-project quarkus-hello-okd
```

The first thing we will need to do is define a binary build object using the `oc new-build` command:

```
$ oc new-build --binary --name=quarkus-hello-okd -l app=quarkus-hello-okd
```

The previous command will produce an image binary build that will be pushed into Minishift's internal registry. The following output describes the resources that were created for this purpose:

```
* A Docker build using binary input will be created
* The resulting image will be pushed to image stream tag "quarkus-hello-
okd:latest"
* A binary build was created, use 'start-build --from-dir' to trigger a new
build

--> Creating resources with label app=quarkus-hello-okd ...
    imagestream.image.openshift.io "quarkus-hello-okd" created
    buildconfig.build.openshift.io "quarkus-hello-okd" created
--> Success
```

Now that the build configuration has been created, we can check its availability by querying the `bc` alias (which stands for build config):

```
$   oc get bc
```

You should see the following output:

```
NAME                 TYPE      FROM      LATEST
quarkus-hello-okd    Docker    Binary    0
```

As it is, the binary build doesn't contain any reference to our Dockerfile. We can add this information using the `oc patch` command, which is a useful shortcut that we can use to edit resources. In our case, we need to set the `dockerfilePath` attribute that refers to the `dockerStrategy` element to the location where our Dockerfile is. From the root of your Quarkus project, execute the following command:

```
$ oc patch bc/quarkus-hello-okd -p
'{"spec":{"strategy":{"dockerStrategy":{"dockerfilePath":"src/main/docker/D
ockerfile.native"}}}}'
```

The following output will be returned:

```
buildconfig.build.openshift.io/quarkus-hello-okd patched
```

If you check the binary build description, you will see that the Dockerfile path has been included:

```
$ oc describe bc/quarkus-hello-okd
```

The output is a bit verbose; however, it should contain the following information:

```
Strategy:          Docker
Dockerfile Path:   src/main/docker/Dockerfile.native
```

Now, we are ready to start the build process, which will take the project's root folder (`.`) as input and will result in uploading `ImageStream` onto your Minishift environment. Execute the following command:

```
$ oc start-build quarkus-hello-okd --from-dir=. --follow
```

The output will notify you that the image has been built and pushed to the Minishift registry:

```
Uploading finished
build.build.openshift.io/quarkus-hello-okd-1 started
Receiving source from STDIN as archive ...
Caching blobs under "/var/cache/blobs".
Pulling image registry.access.redhat.com/ubi8/ubi-minimal ...
. . . .
Writing manifest to image destination
Storing signatures
STEP 1: FROM registry.access.redhat.com/ubi8/ubi-minimal
```

```
STEP 2: WORKDIR /work/
2d94c8983e7ec259aa0e0207c66b0e48fdd9544f66e3c17724a10f838aaa50ab
STEP 3: COPY target/*-runner /work/application
a6d9d0a228023d29203c20de7bcfd9019de00f62b4a4c3fdc544648f8f61988a
STEP 4: RUN chmod 775 /work
e7bf7467d2191478f0cdccd9b480d10ebd19eeae254a7fa0608646cba28c5a97
STEP 5: EXPOSE 8080
29e6198d99e27508aa75cd073290f66fbca605b8ff95cbb6287b4ecbfc1807e5
STEP 6: CMD ["./application","-Dquarkus.http.host=0.0.0.0"]
6c44a4a542ea96450ed578afd4c1859564926405036f61fbbf2e3660660e5f5e
STEP 7: ENV "OPENSHIFT_BUILD_NAME"="quarkus-hello-okd-1"
"OPENSHIFT_BUILD_NAMESPACE"="myproject"
9aa01e4bc2585a05b37e09a10940e326eec6cc998010736318bbe5ed1962503b
STEP 8: LABEL "io.openshift.build.name"="quarkus-hello-okd-1"
"io.openshift.build.namespace"="myproject"
STEP 9: COMMIT temp.builder.openshift.io/myproject/quarkus-hello-
okd-1:d5dafe08
5dafe14a20fffb50b151efbfc4871218a9b1a8516b618d5f4b3874a501d80bcd

Pushing image image-registry.openshift-image-
registry.svc:5000/myproject/quarkus-hello-okd:latest ...
. . .
Successfully pushed image-registry.openshift-image-
registry.svc:5000/myproject/quarkus-hello-
okd@sha256:9fc48bb4b92081c415342407e8df41f38363a4bf82ad3a4319dddced19eff1b3
Push successful
```

As a proof of concept, let's check the list of image streams that are available in the default project using its alias, `is`:

```
$ oc get is
```

You should see the following output:

```
NAME                    IMAGE
quarkus-hello-okd       image-registry.openshift-image-
registry.svc:5000/myproject/quarkus-hello-okd
```

Your `ImageStream` is now available. All we have to do is create an application that uses `ImageStream` `quarkus-hello-okd` as input. This can be done using the following command:

```
$ oc new-app --image-stream=quarkus-hello-okd:latest
```

Now, the resources will be created. This will be confirmed by the resulting output:

```
--> Found image 5dafe14 (2 minutes old) in image stream "myproject/quarkus-
hello-okd" under tag "latest" for "quarkus-hello-okd:latest"

    Red Hat Universal Base Image 8 Minimal
    ---------------------------------------
    The Universal Base Image Minimal is a stripped down image that uses
microdnf as a package manager. This base image is freely redistributable,
but Red Hat only supports Red Hat technologies through subscriptions for
Red Hat products. This image is maintained by Red Hat and updated
regularly.

    Tags: minimal rhel8

    * This image will be deployed in deployment config "quarkus
    -hello-okd"
    * Port 8080/tcp will be load balanced by service "quarkus
    -hello-okd"
      * Other containers can access this service through the hostname
        "quarkus-hello-okd"
    * WARNING: Image "myproject/quarkus-hello-okd:latest" runs as
     the 'root' user which may not be permitted by your cluster
    administrator

--> Creating resources ...
    deploymentconfig.apps.openshift.io "quarkus-hello-okd" created
    service "quarkus-hello-okd" created
--> Success
    Application is not exposed. You can expose services to the
    outside world by executing one or more of the commands below:
     'oc expose svc/quarkus-hello-okd'
    Run 'oc status' to view your app.
```

Now, our application is ready to be consumed. To allow external clients to access it, we need to expose it through a route object, as follows:

```
$ oc expose svc/quarkus-hello-okd
```

The route will be exposed and the following log will be displayed:

```
route.route.openshift.io/quarkus-hello-okd exposed
```

We can verify the route address with the following command, which uses a JSON template to display the virtual host address of our quarkus-hello-okd route:

```
$ oc get route quarkus-hello-okd -o jsonpath --template="{.spec.host}"
```

In our case, the route is accessible at the following address:

```
quarkus-hello-okd-myproject.192.168.42.5.nip.io
```

 Please note that the actual IP address of the route is determined by the hypervisor according to your network configuration, so don't be surprised if it differs from the address that was exposed in this example.

You should be able to acknowledge this information from the web console, which shows that the application is up and running and that a single Pod has been started:

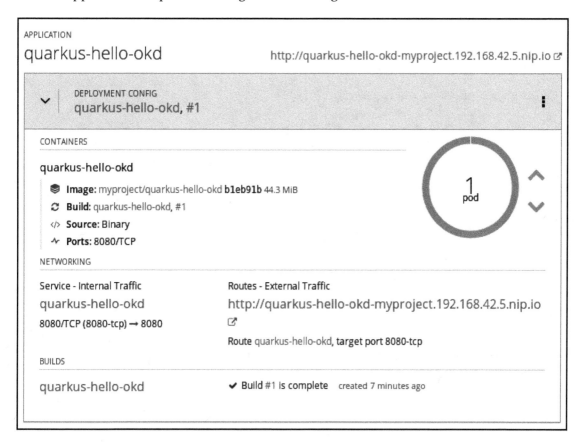

If you go to the route host/port you have been assigned (in our case, `http://quarkus-hello-okd-myproject.192.168.42.5.nip.io`), you will see the following welcome screen:

Your new Cloud-Native application is ready!

Congratulations, you have created a new Quarkus application.

Why do you see this?

This page is served by Quarkus. The source is in `src/main/resources/META-INF/resources/index.html`.

What can I do from here?

If not already done, run the application in *dev mode* using: `mvn compile quarkus:dev`.

- Add REST resources, Servlets, functions and other services in `src/main/java`.
- Your static assets are located in `src/main/resources/META-INF/resources`.
- Configure your application in `src/main/resources/application.properties`.

How do I get rid of this page?

Application

GroupId:
com.packt.quarkus.chapter3

ArtifactId: hello-okd

Version: 1.0-SNAPSHOT

Quarkus Version: 0.13.1

Next steps

Setup your IDE

Getting started

Quarkus Web Site

This is a simple static page that has been included in `src/main/resources/META-INF/resources/index.html` to show you that your application is available and contains some useful information about where you can place static assets and configuration. Your REST service, on the other hand, is still available through the REST URI:

```
$ curl quarkus-hello-okd-myproject.192.168.42.5.nip.io/getContainerId
```

Since the application is running on the `quarkus-hello-okd-1-84xwq` Pod, the expected output is as follows:

```
You are running on quarkus-hello-okd-1-7k2t8
```

Now, let's learn how to scale our Quarkus service by adding some replicas of our application.

Scaling our Quarkus service

So far, you've learned how to deploy a Quarkus application on Minishift. The application is running in a Pod, which is allocated in its own internal IP address and is the equivalent of a machine running a container. In our case, the application is running on one Pod in an OpenShift node. This is sufficient to guarantee the availability of our applications since some liveness and readiness probes are periodically executed. If your Pods stop responding, the OpenShift platform will automatically restart them.

On the other hand, your application probably needs to satisfy a minimum throughput. This requirement usually can't be met with just one Pod unless the number of requests is pretty low. In this case, the simplest strategy is horizontal Pod scaling, which will improve the number of available resources that will be automatically balanced when a request for your application arrives on the router.

Before scaling up our application, we will need to define an upper memory limit for it, in order to reduce the impact it will have on the cluster in terms of system resources. Since our Quarkus application doesn't require a large amount of memory, we will set a limit of 50 MB as the upper limit, which is quite reasonable, and definitely thinner than an average Java application.

Execute the following command to set the memory limit to 50 MB. This will update the **deployment configuration** of your application:

```
$ oc set resources dc/quarkus-hello-okd --limits=memory=50M
```

A deployment configuration (whose alias in the command line is simply dc) describes the state of a particular component of the application as a Pod template. When you update the deployment configuration, a deployment process occurs to scale down the application and scale it up with a new deployment configuration and a new replication controller for the application.

The following output should be returned:

```
deploymentconfig.apps.openshift.io/quarkus-hello-okd resource requirements
updated
```

As a proof of concept, you can verify the deployment configuration through the describe command:

```
$ oc describe dc/quarkus-hello-okd
```

The output of the `describe` command is a bit verbose; however, you should be able to see the following setting in the `Limits` section:

```
Limits:
memory:          50M
```

Now, let's scale our application to 10 instances. This will be pretty fast since we have set a memory limit on the resources that are consumed by each Pod:

```
$ oc scale --replicas=10 dc/quarkus-hello-okd
```

The following is the expected output:

```
deploymentconfig.apps.openshift.io/quarkus-hello-okd scaled
```

Moving to the web console, in the **Overview** panel, we will see that our application has scaled to 10 Pods:

Now that we have a large number of available Pods, let's try to run a load test against our application:

```
for i in {1..100}; do curl quarkus-hello-okd-
myproject.192.168.42.5.nip.io/getContainerId ; echo ""; done;
```

Now, you should be able to see the response that was produced by the REST application in your console. This displays the ID of the Pod that executed the request (the output has been truncated for brevity):

```
You are running on quarkus-hello-okd-2-jzvp2\n
You are running on quarkus-hello-okd-2-fc7h9\n
You are running on quarkus-hello-okd-2-lj67f\n
You are running on quarkus-hello-okd-2-qwm9j\n
You are running on quarkus-hello-okd-2-n6kn6\n
You are running on quarkus-hello-okd-2-bbk84\n
You are running on quarkus-hello-okd-2-d5bj6\n
You are running on quarkus-hello-okd-2-skc2h\n
You are running on quarkus-hello-okd-2-bw5f9\n
You are running on quarkus-hello-okd-2-p24jl\n
You are running on quarkus-hello-okd-2-jzvp2\n
...
```

Although measuring the performance of our applications is beyond the scope of this book, you can go ahead and measure the time that's needed to run the equivalent Java application in the same cluster. You will notice a different response in terms of time and memory consumption!

That was our last task for this chapter. When you are done with this example, and you want to clean up the resources we created in our project, simply execute the following command, which will perform a bulk cleanup of resources:

```
oc delete all --all
```

The output may vary, depending on the number of Pods available. However, it should look similar to the following:

```
pod "quarkus-hello-okd-1-7k2t8" deleted
pod "quarkus-hello-okd-1-build" deleted
pod "quarkus-hello-okd-1-deploy" deleted
replicationcontroller "quarkus-hello-okd-1" deleted
service "quarkus-hello-okd" deleted
deploymentconfig.apps.openshift.io "quarkus-hello-okd" deleted
buildconfig.build.openshift.io "quarkus-hello-okd" deleted
imagestream.image.openshift.io "quarkus-hello-okd" deleted
route.route.openshift.io "quarkus-hello-okd" deleted
```

The preceding log confirms that all the deleted resources have been successfully evicted.

Summary

In this chapter, we ran a simple REST application in a Docker container and then ran it in a Kubernetes-native environment, that is, Minishift. We saw how simple it is to make our applications highly available with a sound throughput by leveraging the features of a bundled distribution of OKD.

Now, it's time to add some more features to our application. In the next chapter, we will learn how to configure the Undertow extension, which can be added to provide web server capabilities to our application. It also includes some UI assets, which we will look at in brief.

Section 2: Building Applications with Quarkus

2

In this section, we will learn how to use all of Quarkus' core extensions, learn how to utilize Hibernate ORM/Panache, and look at the MicroProfile API and security concerns.

This section includes the following chapters:

- Chapter 4, Adding Web Interfaces to Quarkus Services
- Chapter 5, Managing Data Persistence with Quarkus
- Chapter 6, Building Applications Using the MicroProfile API
- Chapter 7, Securing Applications

4
Adding Web Interfaces to Quarkus Services

So far, we have learned how to build a simple REST application with Quarkus and covered the actions that should be put in place to build, test, and deploy our application on a Kubernetes environment.

We could stop at this point and be happy with what we have achieved; however, there are still lots of milestones to reach. For example, we haven't used any web interfaces to access Quarkus services. As you will see in this chapter, Quarkus features some extensions that allow us to reuse standard enterprise APIs such as Servlets and web sockets. At the same time, you can use lighter JavaScript/HTML 5 frameworks as user interfaces for your services. We will explore both approaches in this chapter.

In this chapter, we will cover the following topics:

- Adding web content to Quarkus applications
- Running our application on Minishift
- Adding enterprise web components to our application such as Servlet and WebSockets

Technical requirements

You can find the source code for the project in this chapter on GitHub at `https://github.com/PacktPublishing/Hands-On-Cloud-Native-Applications-with-Java-and-Quarkus/tree/master/Chapter04`.

Adding web content to Quarkus applications

In the examples we've discussed so far, we've tested the web server capabilities of Quarkus by adding RESTful services. Under the hood, Quarkus uses the following core components to handle web requests:

- **Vert.x Web server**: It is the core web component in Quarkus delivering RESTful services as long as **real-time** (server push) web applications. We will discuss more in detail about Vert.x in `Chapter 9`, *Unifying Imperative and Reactive with Vert.x* of this book.
- **Undertow Web server**: It is a flexible product, built by combining different small single-purpose handlers, that comes into play in Quarkus when delivering `WebSocket` applications.

As already discussed, we can add static web content (HTML, JavaScript, images) to our applications by including them under the `resources/META-INF/resources` folder of your project. What is the purpose of having static web content in a microservice-styled application? As a matter of fact, static content can be used in several contexts, including microservices. For example, we could provide helper pages for the service itself. We could also mix and match Quarkus with existing frameworks such as Swagger UI to test our REST endpoints without even writing complex user interfaces.

With this premise, we are going to demonstrate how to build a **Create, Read, Update, Delete** (**CRUD**) application that uses JSON to consume and produce data. Then, we will enrich our application with a thin web interface made from a JavaScript-based web framework.

Building a CRUD application

Within the GitHub source folder for this chapter, you will find two examples. The first one is located in the `Chapter04/customer-service/basic` folder and will be discussed in this section. We recommend importing the project into your IDE before you move on.

If you take a look at the project's structure, you will see that it is made up of three main components:

1. First of all, there is a model class that records customer entries:

```
package com.packt.quarkus.chapter4;

public class Customer {
    private Integer id;
```

```
    private String name;
    private String surname;

    public Integer getId() {
        return id;
    }

    public void setId(Integer id) {
        this.id = id;
    }

    public String getName() {
        return name;
    }

    public void setName(String name) {
        this.name = name;
    }

    public String getSurname() {
        return surname;
    }

    public void setSurname(String surname) {
        this.surname = surname;
    }
}
```

The Customer class is the minimal definition of a Customer record. It is defined as a Plain Old Java Object that should be stored in memory.

2. Next, take a look at the CustomerRepository class, which contains the core functionalities that we'll use to manage our model:

```
package com.packt.quarkus.chapter4;

import javax.enterprise.context.ApplicationScoped;
import java.util.ArrayList;
import java.util.List;


@ApplicationScoped
public class CustomerRepository {

    List<Customer> customerList = new ArrayList();
    int counter;

    public int getNextCustomerId() {
```

```
                    return counter++;
                }

        public List<Customer> findAll() {
            return customerList;
        }

        public Customer findCustomerById(Integer id) {
            for (Customer c:customerList) {
                if (c.getId().equals(id))   {
                    return c;
                }
            }
            throw new CustomerException("Customer not found!");
        }

        public void updateCustomer(Customer customer) {
            Customer customerToUpdate =
             findCustomerById(customer.getId());
            customerToUpdate.setName(customer.getName());
            customerToUpdate.setSurname(customer.getSurname());
        }

        public void createCustomer(Customer customer) {
            customer.setId(getNextCustomerId());
            findAll().add(customer);
        }

        public void deleteCustomer(Integer customerId) {
            Customer c = findCustomerById(customerId);
            findAll().remove(c);
        }
    }
```

As you can see, it's just a vanilla implementation of a repository that serves as a pattern that stores and retrieves our data. In upcoming chapters, we will be adding other features, such as persistent storage and asynchronous behavior. Due to this, it's good to start with a service-agnostic example.

3. The customer service is completed by the `CustomerEndpoint` class, which has the following implementation:

```
package com.packt.quarkus.chapter4;

import javax.enterprise.context.ApplicationScoped;
import javax.inject.Inject;
import javax.ws.rs.*;
```

```java
import javax.ws.rs.core.Response;
import java.util.List;


@Path("customers")
@ApplicationScoped
@Produces("application/json")
@Consumes("application/json")
public class CustomerEndpoint {

    @Inject CustomerRepository customerRepository;

    @GET
    public List<Customer> getAll() {
        return customerRepository.findAll();
    }

    @POST
    public Response create(Customer customer) {
        customerRepository.createCustomer(customer);
        return Response.status(201).build();

    }

    @PUT
    public Response update(Customer customer) {
        customerRepository.updateCustomer(customer);
        return Response.status(204).build();
    }
    @DELETE
    public Response delete(@QueryParam("id") Integer customerId) {
        customerRepository.deleteCustomer(customerId);
        return Response.status(204).build();
    }

}
```

As you can see, `CustomerEndpoint` is a thin REST layer over the `CustomerRepository` class and contains a method for each CRUD action, where it maps each one to the appropriate HTTP method. When using this approach, it would suffice to have a single REST path for the whole application (`/customers`) since the REST engine will call the appropriate method based on the HTTP request method.

Adding a UI to our customer service

As we mentioned in Chapter 1, *Introduction to Quarkus Core Concepts*, you can include static resources such as HTML pages, JavaScript, CSS, or images in the src/main/resources/META-INF/resources folder. An index.html page is provided as a marker in our project, as shown in the project's hierarchy:

```
$ tree src
src
├── main
│   ├── docker
│   ├── java
│   │   └── com
│   │       └── packt
│   │           └── quarkus
│   │               └── chapter4
│   │                   ├── CustomerEndpoint.java
│   │                   ├── Customer.java
│   │                   ├── CustomerRepository.java
│   └── resources
│       ├── application.properties
│       └── META-INF
│           └── resources
│               ├── index.html
```

In order to connect to our REST endpoint, we will include a JavaScript framework called AngularJS and some CSS styling in the head section of our index.html page:

```html
<link rel="stylesheet" type="text/css" href="stylesheet.css" media="screen"
/>
<script
src="//ajax.googleapis.com/ajax/libs/angularjs/1.4.8/angular.min.js"></scri
pt>
```

Also, within the head section of the index.html page, we will include the **AngularJS Controller**, which contains a function that we can use to access REST endpoint methods. We will pass the HTML form data as an argument, which we will discuss next:

```javascript
<script type="text/javascript">
    var app = angular.module("customerManagement", []);
    angular.module('customerManagement').constant('SERVER_URL',
     '/customers');
    //Controller Part
    app.controller("customerManagementController", function
     ($scope, $http, SERVER_URL) {
      //Initialize page with default data which is blank in this
      //example
```

```
$scope.customers = [];
$scope.form = {
  id: -1,
  name: "",
  surname: ""
};
//Now load the data from server
_refreshPageData();
//HTTP POST/PUT methods for add/edit customers
$scope.update = function () {
  var method = "";
  var url = "";
  var data = {};
  if ($scope.form.id == -1) {
    //Id is absent so add customers - POST operation
    method = "POST";
    url = SERVER_URL;
    data.name = $scope.form.name;
    data.surname = $scope.form.surname;
  } else {
    //If Id is present, it's edit operation - PUT operation
    method = "PUT";
    url = SERVER_URL;
    data.id = $scope.form.id;
    data.name = $scope.form.name;
    data.surname = $scope.form.surname;
  }
  $http({
    method: method,
    url: url,
    data: angular.toJson(data),
    headers: {
      'Content-Type': 'application/json'
    }
  }).then(_success, _error);
};
//HTTP DELETE- delete customer by id
$scope.remove = function (customer) {

  $http({
    method: 'DELETE',
    url: SERVER_URL+'?id='+customer.id
  }).then(_success, _error);
};
//In case of edit customers, populate form with customer
// data
$scope.edit = function (customer) {
  $scope.form.name = customer.name;
```

```
          $scope.form.surname = customer.surname;
          $scope.form.id = customer.id;
      };
         /* Private Methods */
      //HTTP GET- get all customers collection
      function _refreshPageData() {
        $http({
          method: 'GET',
          url: SERVER_URL
        }).then(function successCallback(response) {
          $scope.customers = response.data;
        }, function errorCallback(response) {
          console.log(response.statusText);
        });
      }
      function _success(response) {
        _refreshPageData();
        _clearForm()
      }
      function _error(response) {
        alert(response.data.message || response.statusText);
      }
      //Clear the form
      function _clearForm() {
        $scope.form.name = "";
        $scope.form.surname = "";
        $scope.form.id = -1;
      }
    });
  </script>
</head>
```

An in-depth discussion of AngularJS is beyond the scope of this book; however, in a nutshell, Angular applications rely on controllers to manage their flow of data. Each controller accepts $scope as a parameter. This parameter refers to the module or application that the controller needs to handle.

The purpose of our controller will be to reach out to our REST application using different HTTP methods (GET, POST, PUT, and DELETE).

The final part of the index.html page contains the form data, which can be used to insert new customers and edit existing ones:

```html
<body ng-app="customerManagement" ng-
controller="customerManagementController">
 <div class="divTable blueTable">
     <h1>Quarkus CRUD Example</h1>
     <h2>Enter Customer:</h2>
     <form ng-submit="update()">
         <div class="divTableRow">
             <div class="divTableCell">Name:</div>
             <div class="divTableCell"><input type="text"
              placeholder="Name" ng-model=
              "form.name" size="60"/></div>
         </div>
         <div class="divTableRow">
             <div class="divTableCell">Surname:</div>
             <div class="divTableCell"><input type="text"
              placeholder="Surname" ng-model="form.surname"
             size="60"/>
         </div>
         </div>
         <input type="submit" value="Save"/>
     </form>
     <div class="divTable blueTable">
         <div class="divTableHeading">
             <div  class="divTableHead">Customer Name</div>
             <div  class="divTableHead">Customer Address</div>
             <div  class="divTableHead">Action</div>
         </div>
         <div class="divTableRow" ng-repeat="customer in customers">
             <div class="divTableCell">{{ customer.name }}</div>
             <div class="divTableCell">{{ customer.surname }}</div>
             <div class="divTableCell"><a ng-click="edit( customer )"
             class="myButton">Edit</a>
             <a ng-click="remove( customer )"
             class="myButton">Remove</a></div>
         </div>
     </div>
 </body>
</html>
```

Now that we're done with the index.html page, we can write a test class for our application.

Testing our application

Before testing our application, it is worth mentioning that the `quarkus-jsonb` dependency has been included in this project in order to produce JSON content through the REST endpoint and to create JSON objects programmatically in the test class. The following is the dependency we have included in the `pom.xml` file:

```
<dependency>
    <groupId>io.quarkus</groupId>
    <artifactId>quarkus-jsonb</artifactId>
</dependency>
```

The following is our `CustomerEndpointTest` class, which can be used to validate the `Customer` application:

```
@QuarkusTest
public class CustomerEndpointTest {

    @Test
    public void testCustomerService() {

        JsonObject obj = Json.createObjectBuilder()
                .add("name", "John")
                .add("surname", "Smith").build();

        // Test POST
        given()
                .contentType("application/json")
                .body(obj.toString())
                .when()
                .post("/customers")
                .then()
                .statusCode(201);

        // Test GET
        given()
                .when().get("/customers")
                .then()
                .statusCode(200)
                .body(containsString("John"),
                    containsString("Smith"));

        obj = Json.createObjectBuilder()
                .add("id", "0")
                .add("name", "Donald")
                .add("surname", "Duck").build();
```

```
            // Test PUT
            given()
                    .contentType("application/json")
                    .body(obj.toString())
                    .when()
                    .put("/customers")
                    .then()
                    .statusCode(204);

            // Test DELETE
            given()
                    .contentType("application/json")
                    .when()
                    .delete("/customers?id=0")
                    .then()
                    .statusCode(204);


        }
    }
```

Let's switch gears and look a little more closely at the test class. Most of the content here should look familiar to you, except for the `Json.createObjectBuilder` API, which is a convenient factory method that we can use to fluently create JSON objects. In our code, we have used it to produce two instances of `javax.json.JsonObject`. The first one has been serialized as a string and sent to our `CustomerEndpoint` via an HTTP POST call. The second one has been adopted to update the customer via the HTTP PUT call.

You can package and test the application with the following command:

```
$ mvn package
```

The output will show the test result, which should be successful:

```
[INFO] Results:
[INFO] Tests run: 1, Failures: 0, Errors: 0, Skipped: 0
```

The `testCustomerService` method completed successfully. Now that we have a tested REST application, we'll learn how to get our application running in a browser.

Running the example

Now that the full project is at our fingertips, let's see it in action! You can start the application with the following command:

```
$ mvn quarkus:dev
```

Then, go to the home page at `http://localhost:8080`. You should be able to see the following UI, where you can add new customers:

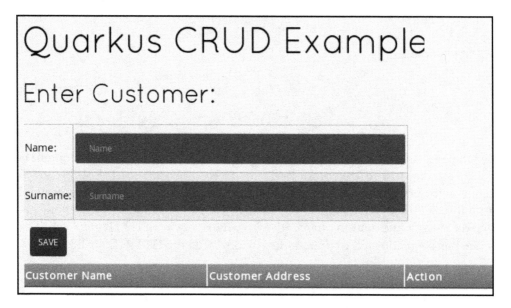

 As you already know, the embedded Vert.x server will serve content from under the root context. If you want to vary this, you can configure the `quarkus.http.root-path` key in `application.properties` to set the context path.

Once you have some data, other actions (such as **Edit** and **Delete**) will be available:

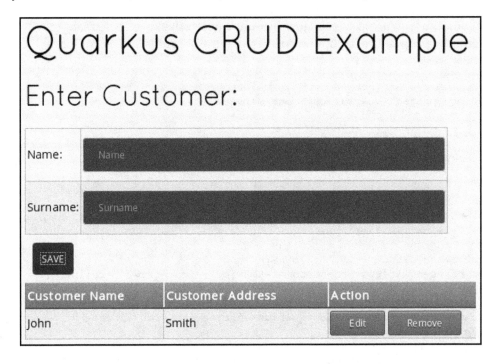

Cool! You can try editing and deleting data to verify that all the REST methods work properly. Now, we will learn how to deploy our application on Minishift.

Running our application on Minishift

Start your Minishift environment as usual and execute the following command to build the native executable Docker image of your application and deploy it in a Pod:

```
$ mvn package -Pnative -Dnative-image.docker-build=true
```

Building the native image of your application will take a minute or so. Next, we will upload the application as a binary build into a Minishift namespace. You should already be familiar with these steps, so we will just include the script to be executed, along with some inline comments. Execute each line and verify that the output is successful for all the commands:

```
#Create a new Project named quarkus-customer-service
$ oc new-project quarkus-customer-service

# Binary Build definition
$ oc new-build --binary --name=quarkus-customer-service -l app=quarkus-
customer-service

# Add the dockerfilePath location to our Binary Build
$ oc patch bc/quarkus-customer-service -p
'{"spec":{"strategy":{"dockerStrategy":{"dockerfilePath":"src/main/docker/D
ockerfile.native"}}}}'

# Uploading directory "." as binary input for the build
$ oc start-build quarkus-customer-service --from-dir=. --follow

# Create a new application using as source the Binary Build
$ oc new-app --image-stream=quarkus-customer-service:latest

# Create a Route for external clients
$ oc expose svc/quarkus-customer-service
```

Now, you should be able to see the Pod where your application is running in the **Overview** panel, which can be reached through the **Route - External Traffic** link: **http://quarkus-customer-service-quarkus-customer-service.192.168.42.53.nip.io** (the actual route address depends on the IP address that's been assigned to your environment):

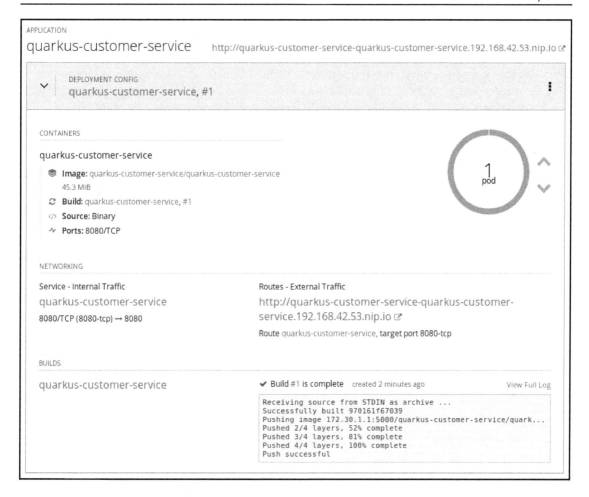

By clicking on the **Route - External Traffic** link, you will be able to verify that your application works in a Kubernetes environment, just like your local copy does.

Configuring Cross-Origin Resource Sharing in Quarkus

In this chapter, we have used JavaScript to drive a request into Quarkus' service. In a more complex scenario where your JavaScript code is deployed in its own service on a distinct host or context, you will have to implement **Cross-Origin Resource Sharing** (**CORS**) to make it work. In a nutshell, CORS allows web clients to make HTTP requests to servers hosted on different origins. By **origin**, we mean a combination of the URI scheme, hostname, and port number.

This is especially challenging for client-side languages such as JavaScript because all modern browsers require a same-origin policy for scripting languages.

To make this work, we need to put our server applications in charge of deciding who can make requests and what type of requests are allowed in using HTTP headers. In practice, when the server receives a request from a different origin, it can reply and state which clients are allowed to access the API, which HTTP methods or headers are allowed, and finally whether cookies are allowed in the request.

How does that translate into Quarkus configurations? As you may have guessed, the configuration has to be applied to the application.properties file, under the quarkus.http.cors namespace. The following is a sample configuration that allows CORS for all domains, all HTTP methods, and all common headers:

```
quarkus.http.cors=true
quarkus.http.cors.origins=*
quarkus.http.cors.methods=GET,PUT,POST,DELETE, OPTIONS
quarkus.http.cors.headers=X-Custom,accept, authorization, content-type, x-
requested-with
quarkus.http.cors.exposed-headers=Content-Disposition
```

In real-world scenarios, you would probably set the list of allowed origins to the domain asking to connect remotely, as follows:

```
quarkus.http.cors.origins=http://custom.origin.com
```

Now that we've clarified this, we can look at another example where we'll use a Java Enterprise component, such as WebSocket, to reach our Quarkus service.

Adding Enterprise web components

In our customer service example, the frontend application used a JavaScript structural framework (AngularJS) to test our application. Now, we will consider a different use case: a new external service is going to connect to our application using a different protocol stack. Besides JAX-RS endpoints, Quarkus has native support for the WebSocket technology that runs in the embedded Undertow web server. Therefore, in this example, we will add a WebSocket endpoint to our existing application. This will be paired with another WebSocket running in a different application.

Introducing WebSockets

First off, let's briefly introduce new components for our application. WebSocket, as defined by its enterprise specification, is an API that establishes **socket** connections between a browser and a server endpoint. This is pretty much similar to standard TCP sockets due to its persistent connection between the client and the server, where both parties can start sending data at any time.

Typically, you would open a WebSocket connection simply by calling the WebSocket constructor in your JavaScript code:

```
var connection = new WebSocket('ws://localhost:8080/hello');
```

 Notice the URL schema for WebSocket connections (ws:). We also have wss: for secure WebSocket connections, which is used in the same way as https: is for secure HTTP connections.

We can attach some event handlers to the connection to help us determine when the connection status is open, receiving messages, or when errors occur.

We can declare a Java class WebSocket server endpoint on the server-side by annotating it with @ServerEndpoint. The URI where the endpoint is deployed needs to be specified as well, as shown in the following example:

```
@ServerEndpoint(value = "/hello")
public class WebSocketEndpoint {
    @OnOpen
    public void onOpen(Session session) throws IOException {
        // Establish connection
    }
    @OnMessage
    public void onMessage(Session session, Message message) throws
    IOException {
        // Handle Websocket messages
    }
    @OnClose
    public void onClose(Session session) throws IOException {
    }
    @OnError
    public void onError(Session session, Throwable throwable) {
    }
}
```

In the next section, we will be adding a WebSocket layer to our existing project and then creating another thin project to remotely access WebSocket and add new customers.

Building a project that uses Websockets

You will find two distinct projects within the `Chapter04/customer-service/websockets` folder in this book's GitHub repository:

- An updated `customer-service` project that ships with a `WebSocket` endpoint
- A project called `customer-service-fe` that features a minimal JavaScript frontend for our `WebSocket` application

You should import both projects into your IDE before moving on.

First, let's discuss the `customer-service` project. The main enhancement we have added is a `WebSocket` endpoint, which is in charge of inserting a new customer (using the `CustomerRepository` bean) and returning a tabular view of our customers. The following is the content of the `WebsocketEndpoint` class:

```
@ServerEndpoint(value="/customers", encoders = {MessageEncoder.class})

public class WebsocketEndpoint {
    @Inject
    CustomerRepository customerRepository;

    public List<Customer>  addCustomer(String message, Session
    session) {
        Jsonb jsonb = JsonbBuilder.create();

        Customer customer = jsonb.fromJson(message, Customer.class);
        customerRepository.createCustomer(customer);
        return customerRepository.findAll();
    }
    @OnOpen
    public void myOnOpen(Session session) {
        System.out.println("WebSocket opened: " + session.getId());
    }
    @OnClose
    public void myOnClose(CloseReason reason) {
        System.out.println("Closing a due to " +
         reason.getReasonPhrase());
    }
    @OnError
    public void error(Throwable t) {

    }

}
```

There are two things to notice here, as follows:

- The method tagged with @OnMessage receives the customer to be added in JSON format as input and returns an updated list of customers.
- This class uses an **encoder** in order to customize the message that's returned to the client. An encoder takes a Java object and produces its serialized representation, which can then be transmitted to the client. For example, an encoder is typically in charge of producing JSON, XML, and binary representations. In our case, it encodes the customer list in JSON format.

Now, let's take a look at the MessageEncoder class:

```
public class MessageEncoder implements
Encoder.Text<java.util.List<Customer>>  {

    @Override
    public String encode(List<Customer> list) throws EncodeException {
        JsonArrayBuilder jsonArray = Json.createArrayBuilder();
        for(Customer c : list) {
            jsonArray.add(Json.createObjectBuilder()
                    .add("Name", c.getName())
                    .add("Surname", c.getSurname()));
        }
        JsonArray array = jsonArray.build();
        StringWriter buffer = new StringWriter();
        Json.createWriter(buffer).writeArray(array);
        return buffer.toString();
    }

    @Override
    public void init(EndpointConfig config) {
        System.out.println("Init");
    }

    @Override
    public void destroy() {
        System.out.println("destroy");
    }

}
```

As you can see, an Encoder must implement either of the following interfaces:

- Encoder.Text<T> for text messages
- Encoder.Binary<T> for binary messages

In our case, `List<Customer>` is received as a generic type in the `encode` method and transformed into a JSON string array.

To be compiled, our project needs the `quarkus-undertow-websockets` extension, which can be added manually into the `pom.xml` file. Alternatively, you can let the Maven plugin do it for you with the following command:

```
$ mvn quarkus:add-extension -Dextensions="quarkus-undertow-websockets"
```

You will see the following output on your console, which confirms that the extension has been added to our configuration:

```
Adding extension io.quarkus:quarkus-undertow-websockets
```

The server project is now complete. You can compile it and run it with the following command:

```
$ mvn compile quarkus:dev
```

Now, let's create a new frontend project with a thin `WebSocket` JavaScript client.

Creating a WebSocket client project

`WebSocket` clients, just like their server counterparts, can be written in many different languages. Since modern browsers have native support for `WebSocket`, we will write a simple JavaScript client so that we don't have to install any additional tools or SDKs to run our example.

Within the `customer-service-fe` folder, you will find the frontend project that can be used to reach our `WebSocket` example.

Our project contains a landing page named `index.html`, which is served when we request the root web context of our application. Within this page, we have included an HTML form and a table to display a list of customers:

```
<html>
 <head>
    <meta http-equiv="content-type" content="text/html; charset=ISO-
    8859-1">
    <link rel="stylesheet" type="text/css" href="stylesheet.css"
    media="screen" />
    <script src="https://ajax.googleapis.com/ajax/libs/jquery/2.1.1
      /jquery.min.js"></script>
    <script src="functions.js"></script>
```

```
</head>

<meta charset="utf-8">
<body>
<h1 style="text-align: center;">Connect to Quarkus Websocket Endpoint</h1>
<br>

<div>
    <form id="form1" action="">
        <div><h3>Enter Customer</h3></div>
        <div class="divTableRow">
            <div class="divTableCell">Name:</div>
            <div class="divTableCell"><input type="text"
             placeholder="Name" name="name" size="60"/></div>
        </div>
        <div class="divTableRow">
            <div class="divTableCell">Surname:</div>
            <div class="divTableCell"><input type="text"
             placeholder="Surname" name="surname"
             size="60"/></div>
        </div>

        <br/>
        <input onclick="send_message()" value="Insert" type="button"
         class="myButton">
    </form>
    <br/>

</div>

<table id="customerDataTable" class="blueTable" />
<div id="output"></div>
</body>
</html>
```

The connection to the `WebSocket` endpoint takes place in an external JavaScript file named `function.js` (you can find this in the `customer-service-fe/src/main/resources/META-INF/resources` folder in this book's GitHub repository). Then following is the content of this file:

```
var wsUri = "ws://localhost:8080/customers";

function init() {
    output = document.getElementById("output");
}

function send_message() {
    websocket = new WebSocket(wsUri);
```

```
        websocket.onopen = function(evt) {
            onOpen(evt)
        };
        websocket.onmessage = function(evt) {
            onMessage(evt)
        };
        websocket.onerror = function(evt) {
            onError(evt)
        };
    }

    function onOpen(evt) {
        doSend(name.value);
    }

    function onMessage(evt) {
        buildHtmlTable('#customerDataTable', evt.data);
    }

    function onError(evt) {
        writeToScreen('<span style="color: red;">ERROR:</span>
          ' + evt.data);
    }

    function doSend(message) {
        var json = toJSONString(document.getElementById("form1"));
        websocket.send(json);

    }
```

As you can see, there are several callback methods (onOpen, onMessage, onError) that are coupled with server events once the connection is established. Here, we will be adding a new customer, serialized as a JSON string, in the doSend method, while the onMessage callback method will receive the list of customers that was produced by our WebSocket encoder. This data will eventually be included in an HTML table.

You can run the project with the following command:

```
$ mvn compile quarkus:dev -Dquarkus.http.port=9080 -Ddebug=6005
```

As you can see, we have shifted the HTTP and debug port with an offset of 1000 so that it doesn't conflict with the customer-service project.

Browsing to `http://localhost:9080` will let you into the `WebSocket` client application. Add some sample data to verify that customers can be included in the table:

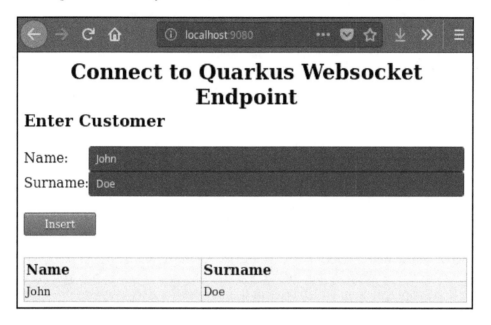

Verify that the same data is also displayed in the AngularJS frontend, which is available at `http://localhost:8080`.

Adding an AJAX handler

Our JavaScript client is primarily required when it comes to testing our `WebSocket` example. However, one more enhancement you will find in this project is a Java Servlet that will let you remove any hardcoded links to your backend so that both services can still communicate as we move our example to a different machine or port.

The following Servlet determines server endpoint information from an environment variable named `CUSTOMER_SERVICE` by using the `ws://localhost:8080/customers` string:

```
@WebServlet("/AjaxHandler")
public class AjaxHandler extends HttpServlet {

    public AjaxHandler() {
        super();
    }
```

```
    protected void doGet(HttpServletRequest request,
    HttpServletResponse response)
    throws ServletException, IOException {
        String endpoint = System.getenv("CUSTOMER_SERVICE")
        != null ? System.getenv("CUSTOMER_SERVICE") :
        "ws://localhost:8080/customers";

        PrintWriter out = response.getWriter();
        out.println(endpoint);
        out.flush();

    }

    protected void doPost(HttpServletRequest request,
        HttpServletResponse response) throws
        ServletException, IOException {
        doGet(request, response);
    }
}
```

This change needs to be reflected in our JavaScript client so that it doesn't use a hardcoded endpoint for our web socket. In the final version of the `function.js` file, you will find the following JavaScript function, which queries our Servlet via AJAX:

```
var wsUri = "";
function callAjax() {

    httpRequest = new XMLHttpRequest();

    if (!httpRequest) {
        console.log('Unable to create XMLHTTP instance');
        return false;
    }
    httpRequest.open('GET', 'AjaxHandler');
    httpRequest.responseType = 'text';
    httpRequest.send();
    httpRequest.onreadystatechange = function() {
        if (httpRequest.readyState === XMLHttpRequest.DONE) {
            if (httpRequest.status === 200) {
                wsUri = httpRequest.response;
            } else {
                console.log('Something went wrong..!!');
            }
        }
    }
}
```

This function is called when the HTML page is loaded:

```
<body onload="callAjax()">
```

Now, start the server from the same shell so that it reads the environment variable:

```
$ mvn quarkus:dev
```

Now, go to `http://localhost:9080` and verify that the output produced by the `WebSocket` request is the same as when the server endpoint address was statically defined.

You can take this example one step further by varying `quarkus.http.port` in your `customer-service` application. For example, you could set it to `8888`:

```
$ mvn quarkus:dev -Dquarkus.http.port=8888
```

`customer-service-fe` will be able to connect to the `WebSocket` endpoint once you have set the `CUSTOMER_SERVICE` environment variable accordingly:

```
$ export CUSTOMER_SERVICE=ws://localhost:8888/customers
```

Great! In this section, we removed any static hardcoded information from our client application, which now uses an environment variable to reach out to the customer service.

Summary

In this chapter, we looked at the different paths we can take to add web content to our Quarkus applications. First, we learned how to create a CRUD in-memory application to manage a set of Java objects. The example application was then accessed by a JavaScript layer (AngularJS) with some peculiar APIs to handle REST calls. We also looked at some configuration parameters that are needed when we want to enable CORS in Quarkus projects. Next, we added a `WebSocket` layer to introduce full-duplex communication between the initial project and the client frontend.

By completing this chapter, you now know how to use the embedded Vert.x and Undertow server to leverage REST APIs (`quarkus-resteasy`) and `WebSocket`/Servlet APIs (`quarkus-undertow-websockets`).

In the next chapter, we will add database storage for our application using the Hibernate ORM and Hibernate Panache extensions.

5
Managing Data Persistence with Quarkus

So far, we have developed some basic applications using in-memory structures that can be accessed through REST channels. But this is just the beginning. In real-world examples, you don't just rely on in-memory data; instead, you persist your data structure either on a relational database or somewhere else, such as in NoSQL storage. Therefore, in this chapter, we will leverage the essential skills we need in order to build applications in Quarkus that persist data into a relational database. We will also learn how to use an **Object Relational Mapping** (**ORM**) tool such as Hibernate ORM to map a database as storage and how to simplify its usage with the **Hibernate ORM with Panache** extension.

In this chapter, we will cover the following topics:

- Adding an ORM layer to the customer service
- Configuring and running an application to reach an RDBMS
- Taking both services (application and database) into the cloud
- Adding Hibernate ORM with Panache on top of your application to simplify the ORM

Technical requirements

You can find the source code for the project in this chapter on GitHub at https://github.com/PacktPublishing/Hands-On-Cloud-Native-Applications-with-Java-and-Quarkus/tree/master/Chapter05.

Adding an ORM layer to our applications

If you've ever worked on an Enterprise project before, you will know that almost every Java application uses an ORM tool to map an external database. The advantages of mapping a database structure with Java objects are as follows:

- **Database neutrality**: Your code will not be database-specific, so you don't need to adapt your code to a specific database SQL syntax, which may vary between vendors.
- **Developer friendly workflow**: You don't need to write complex SQL structures to access your data – you simply need to refer to Java fields.

On the other hand, it's also true that, by writing native SQL statements, you can be truly aware of what your code is actually doing. Also, in most cases, you can achieve maximum performance benefits by writing direct SQL statements. For this reason, most ORM tools include an option to execute native SQL statements to bypass the standard ORM logic.

In the Quarkus toolkit, you can use the `quarkus-hibernate-orm` extension to map your Java classes as entity objects. Hibernate ORM sits between the Java application data access layer and the relational database. You can use Hibernate ORM APIs to perform operations such as query, delete, store, and on domain data.

First of all, let's define the domain model for our application. We will start with the simple **Customer** object since we already know what it is. To make our example a bit more interesting, we will add another object, called **Orders**, that is related to our **Customer** object. To be precise, we will declare a **one-to-many** relationship between a **Customer** and its **Orders**:

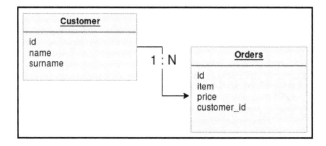

To get started, let's check the first example for this chapter, which is located in the `Chapter05/hibernate` folder in this book's GitHub repository. We recommend importing the project into your IDE before moving on.

If you inspect the `pom.xml` file of this project, you will find several new extensions included in it:

- `quarkus-hibernate-orm`: This extension is the core dependency that we need in order to use Hibernate's ORM tool in our application.
- `quarkus-agroal`: This extension buys us the Agroal connection pool, which will handle JDBC connection management for us.
- `quarkus-jdbc-postgresql`: This extension contains the JDBC modules that we need in order to connect to the PostgreSQL database.
- `quarkus-resteasy-jsonb`: This extension is needed so that we can create JSON items at runtime and produce a JSON response.

The following code shows the additional dependencies as XML elements:

```xml
<dependency>
        <groupId>io.quarkus</groupId>
        <artifactId>quarkus-hibernate-orm</artifactId>
</dependency>
<dependency>
        <groupId>io.quarkus</groupId>
        <artifactId>quarkus-agroal</artifactId>
</dependency>
<dependency>
        <groupId>io.quarkus</groupId>
        <artifactId>quarkus-jdbc-postgresql</artifactId>
</dependency>
<dependency>
        <groupId>io.quarkus</groupId>
        <artifactId>quarkus-resteasy-jsonb</artifactId>
</dependency>
```

Now that we've looked at the project's configuration, let's inspect the single components that make up our application.

Defining the entity layer

The first thing we need to check is the list of entity objects that will map the database tables. The first one is the `Customer` `@Entity` class, as follows:

```java
@Entity
@NamedQuery(name = "Customers.findAll",
        query = "SELECT c FROM Customer c ORDER BY c.id",
        hints = @QueryHint(name = "org.hibernate.cacheable", value =
        "true") )
```

```
public class Customer {
    @Id
    @SequenceGenerator(
            name = "customerSequence",
            sequenceName = "customerId_seq",
            allocationSize = 1,
            initialValue = 1)
    @GeneratedValue(strategy = GenerationType.SEQUENCE, generator =
      "customerSequence")
    private Long id;

    @Column(length = 40)
    private String name;

    @Column(length = 40)
    private String surname;

    @OneToMany(mappedBy = "customer")
    @JsonbTransient
    public List<Orders> orders;

  // Getters / Setters omitted for brevity
  }
```

Let's go through the single annotations we have included in the entity class:

- The @Entity annotation makes this class eligible for persistence. It can be coupled with the @Table annotation to define the corresponding database table to a map. If it's not included, like in our case, it will map a database table with the same name.
- The @NamedQuery annotation (placed at the class level) is a statically defined SQL statement featuring a query string. Using named queries in your code improves how your code is organized since it separates the JPA query language from the Java code. It also avoids the bad practice of embedding string literals directly in your SQL, thus enforcing the use of parameters instead.
- The @Id annotation specifies the primary key of an entity, which will be unique for every record.
- The @SequenceGenerator annotation is used to delegate the creation of a sequence as a unique identifier for primary keys. You will need to check that your database is capable of handling sequences. On the other hand, although this isn't the default option, this is considered a safer alternative since the identifier can be generated prior to executing the INSERT statement.

- The `@Column` annotation is used to tell Hibernate ORM that the Java field maps a database column. Note that we have also specified a constraint in terms of the size of the column. Since we will let Hibernate ORM create our database structures from Java code, all the constraints that are declared in the Java class will effectively turn into database constraints.
- Finally, we had to apply two annotations on top of the `orders` field:
  - The `@OneToMany` annotation defines a one-to-many relationship with the `Orders` table (that is, one customer is associated with many orders).
  - The `@JsonbTransient` annotation prevents mapping the field to the JSON representation (since the reverse mapping for this relationship is included in the `Orders` class, mapping this field to JSON would cause a `StackOverflow` error).

In our code example, we have omitted the getter/setter methods for the sake of brevity. These are, however, needed by Hibernate ORM to perform entity reads and writes against the database. In the *Making data persistence easier with Hibernate Panache* section later in this chapter, we will learn how to make our code leaner and cleaner by extending the `PanacheEntity` API.

The `Customer` entity, in turn, references the following `Orders` class, which provides the other side of the one-to-many annotation:

```
@Entity
@NamedQuery(name = "Orders.findAll",
        query = "SELECT o FROM Orders o WHERE o.customer.id = :customerId
ORDER BY o.item")
public class Orders {
    @Id
    @SequenceGenerator(
            name = "orderSequence",
            sequenceName = "orderId_seq",
            allocationSize = 1,
            initialValue = 1)
    @GeneratedValue(strategy = GenerationType.SEQUENCE, generator =
      "orderSequence")
    public Long id;

    @Column(length = 40)
    public String item;

    @Column
    public Long price;
```

```
      @ManyToOne
      @JoinColumn(name = "customer_id")
      @JsonbTransient
      public Customer customer;

  // Getters / Setters omitted for brevity
  }
```

It's worth noting that the named query for this class is slightly more elaborated since `Orders.findAll NamedQuery` uses a parameter in order to filter the orders by a specific customer.

Since the `Customer` structure and the `Orders` structure make up a bidirectional association, we need to map the corresponding `Customer` field to the `@javax.persistence.ManyToOne` annotation.

We also have included the `@javax.persistence.JoinColumn` annotation to indicate that this entity is the owner of the relationship. In database terms, this means that the corresponding table has a column with a foreign key for the referenced table. Now that we have a class where data will be stored, let's inspect the `Repository` class, which is used to access data from the RDBMS.

Coding the repository classes

In order to access our `Customer` data, we are still relying on the `CustomerRepository` class, which needs to be adjusted. First and foremost, we have injected an instance of the `EntityManager` interface in order to manage the persistence of entity instances:

```
@ApplicationScoped
public class CustomerRepository {

    @Inject
    EntityManager entityManager;

}
```

Once we have a reference to `EntityManager`, we can use it to perform CRUD operations on the rest of the class:

```
public List<Customer> findAll() {
        return entityManager.createNamedQuery("Customers.findAll",
          Customer.class)
                .getResultList();
}
```

```
public Customer findCustomerById(Long id) {
        Customer customer = entityManager.find(Customer.class, id);

        if (customer == null) {
            throw new WebApplicationException("Customer with id of " +
            id + " does not exist.", 404);
        }
        return customer;
}

@Transactional
public void updateCustomer(Customer customer) {
        Customer customerToUpdate = findCustomerById(customer.
         getId());
        customerToUpdate.setName(customer.getName());
        customerToUpdate.setSurname(customer.getSurname());
}

@Transactional
public void createCustomer(Customer customer) {
        entityManager.persist(customer);
}

@Transactional
public void deleteCustomer(Long customerId) {
        Customer c = findCustomerById(customerId);
        entityManager.remove(c);
}
```

It's important to note that we have marked all methods that are performing write operations with the `@javax.transaction.Transactional` annotation. This is the simplest way to demarcate transaction boundaries in a Quarkus application, just like we used to do in Java Enterprise applications. In practice, a `@Transactional` method will run in the context of the caller's transaction, if any. Otherwise, it will start a new transaction before running the method.

Next, we created a `Repository` class, which is also used to manage orders. The `OrderRepository` class is pretty much equivalent to the `CustomerRepository` class, except for the fact that the `findAll` method will filter through the orders of a specific customer:

```
@ApplicationScoped
public class OrderRepository {

    @Inject
    EntityManager entityManager;
```

```
    public List<Orders> findAll(Long customerId) {

      return   (List<Orders>)
        entityManager.createNamedQuery("Orders.findAll")
              .setParameter("customerId", customerId)
              .getResultList();
    }

    public Orders findOrderById(Long id) {

        Orders order = entityManager.find(Orders.class, id);
        if (order == null) {
            throw new WebApplicationException("Order with id of " + id
            + " does not exist.", 404);
        }
        return order;
    }
    @Transactional
    public void updateOrder(Orders order) {
        Orders orderToUpdate = findOrderById(order.getId());
        orderToUpdate.setItem(order.getItem());
        orderToUpdate.setPrice(order.getPrice());
    }
    @Transactional
    public void createOrder(Orders order, Customer c) {
        order.setCustomer(c);
        entityManager.persist(order);

    }
    @Transactional
    public void deleteOrder(Long orderId) {
        Orders o = findOrderById(orderId);
        entityManager.remove(o);
    }
  }
}
```

Now that we've discussed `Repository` and entity classes, let's check out the REST endpoint, which makes the application responsive.

Defining REST endpoints

Our application defines one REST endpoint for each `Repository` class. We already coded `CustomerEndpoint` in the previous chapter, which was blissfully unaware of whether it was using storage or not. Therefore, half of the work has already been done. We've only added `OrderEndpoint` here, which maps CRUD HTTP operations accordingly:

```
@Path("orders")
@ApplicationScoped
@Produces("application/json")
@Consumes("application/json")
public class OrderEndpoint {

    @Inject OrderRepository orderRepository;
    @Inject CustomerRepository customerRepository;

    @GET
    public List<Orders> getAll(@QueryParam("customerId") Long
     customerId) {
        return orderRepository.findAll(customerId);
    }

    @POST
    @Path("/{customer}")
    public Response create(Orders order, @PathParam("customer") Long
     customerId) {
        Customer c = customerRepository.findCustomerById(customerId);
        orderRepository.createOrder(order,c);
        return Response.status(201).build();
    }

    @PUT
    public Response update(Orders order) {
        orderRepository.updateOrder(order);
        return Response.status(204).build();
    }
    @DELETE
    @Path("/{order}")
    public Response delete(@PathParam("order") Long orderId) {
        orderRepository.deleteOrder(orderId);
        return Response.status(204).build();
    }

}
```

Our `OrderEndpoint` is slightly more elaborate since it needs to filter through each order operation by `Customer` ID in the `getAll` method. We also used the `@PathParam` annotation across the code to move the `Customer` and `Orders` data from the client to the REST endpoint.

Connecting to the database

Database connections are made through Quarkus' main configuration file (`application.properties`), which needs, at the very least, the JDBC settings for the database. We will be using PostgreSQL as storage so that the JDBC URL and driver comply with PostgreSQL JDBC's specifications. The following configuration will be used to access the `quarkusdb` database, which uses the `quarkus/quarkus` credentials:

```
quarkus.datasource.url=jdbc:postgresql://${POSTGRESQL_SERVICE_HOST:localhos
t}:${POSTGRESQL_SERVICE_PORT:5432}/quarkusdb
quarkus.datasource.driver=org.postgresql.Driver
quarkus.datasource.username=quarkus
quarkus.datasource.password=quarkus
```

Note that we are using two environment variables (`POSTGRESQL_SERVICE_HOST` and `POSTGRESQL_SERVICE_PORT`) to define the database host and port. If they're left undefined, they will be set to `localhost` and `5432`. This configuration will come in handy when we switch our application from the local filesystem to the cloud.

Next, we configured Hibernate ORM to use the **drop and create** strategy at boot. This is ideal for developing or testing applications as it will drop and regenerate the schema and database objects from the Java Entity each time we start the application:

```
quarkus.hibernate-orm.database.generation=drop-and-create
```

Additionally, we have included the Agroal connection pool settings to define the pool's initial size, the minimum number of connections to be kept available in memory, and the maximum number of simultaneous connections which can be opened:

```
quarkus.datasource.initial-size=1
quarkus.datasource.min-size=2
quarkus.datasource.max-size=8
```

Finally, it can be useful to have some pre-inserted rows in our schema for testing purposes. Hence, we have set the location where the script (`import.sql`) is located using the following property:

```
quarkus.hibernate-orm.sql-load-script=import.sql
```

The following content in the `import.sql` script adds two rows to the `Customer` table:

```
INSERT INTO customer (id, name, surname) VALUES (
nextval('customerId_seq'), 'John','Doe');
INSERT INTO customer (id, name, surname) VALUES (
nextval('customerId_seq'), 'Fred','Smith');
```

The preceding SQL script can be found in the `src/main/resources` folder.

Now that we've inspected our service, we will check the test class, which verifies CRUD operations automatically. Then, we will take a look at the web interface so that we can test the code through a browser.

Coding a test class

Our basic `Test` class assumes that we already have a couple of `Customer` objects available. Therefore, once we verify their count with a `GET` request, we will test all CRUD operations on the `Orders` subordinate entity, as illustrated in the following code:

```
// Test GET
given()
        .when().get("/customers")
        .then()
        .statusCode(200)
        .body("$.size()", is(2));

// Create a JSON Object for the Order
JsonObject objOrder = Json.createObjectBuilder()
        .add("item", "bike")
        .add("price", new Long(100))
        .build();


// Test POST Order for Customer #1
given()
        .contentType("application/json")
        .body(objOrder.toString())
        .when()
        .post("/orders/1")
```

```
        .then()
        .statusCode(201);

// Create new JSON for Order #1
objOrder = Json.createObjectBuilder()
        .add("id", new Long(1))
        .add("item", "mountain bike")
        .add("price", new Long(100))
        .build();

// Test UPDATE Order #1
given()
        .contentType("application/json")
        .body(objOrder.toString())
        .when()
        .put("/orders")
        .then()
        .statusCode(204);

// Test GET for Order #1
given()
        .when().get("/orders?customerId=1")
        .then()
        .statusCode(200)
        .body(containsString("mountain bike"));

// Test DELETE Order #1
given()
        .when().delete("/orders/1")
        .then()
        .statusCode(204);
```

This test class shouldn't be too complex at this point. We are basically testing that the two customers are available in the database using the `org.hamcrest.CoreMatchers.is` construct. Then, we are performing a complete round of operations on the `Orders` entity by creating one item, updating it, querying it, and finally deleting it.

Before running the test, we need an available database where data is going to be persisted. The recommended approach, if you haven't got an active PostgreSQL instance, is to start a `docker` image using the following shell:

```
$ docker run --ulimit memlock=-1:-1 -it --rm=true --memory-swappiness=0 --
name quarkus_test -e POSTGRES_USER=quarkus -e POSTGRES_PASSWORD=quarkus -e
POSTGRES_DB=quarkusdb -p 5432:5432 postgres:10.5
```

Please note that, in addition to the database user, password, and DB settings, we are also enforcing our container via the `--ulimit memlock=-1:-1` setting in order to do unlimited memlocking to prevent swapping. We are also forwarding the database's address and port to all IPv4/IPv6 addresses that are available on the local machine.

The following output will be emitted when the `docker` process is started:

```
2019-07-09 14:05:56.235 UTC [1] LOG:  listening on IPv4 address "0.0.0.0",
port 5432
2019-07-09 14:05:56.235 UTC [1] LOG:  listening on IPv6 address "::", port
5432
2019-07-09 14:05:56.333 UTC [1] LOG:  listening on Unix socket
"/var/run/postgresql/.s.PGSQL.5432"
2019-07-09 14:05:56.434 UTC [60] LOG:  database system was shut down at
2019-07-09 14:05:56 UTC
2019-07-09 14:05:56.516 UTC [1] LOG:  database system is ready to accept
connections
```

Now, you can launch the test class with the following command:

```
$ mvn compile test
```

The expected output should confirm that the test ran successfully:

```
[INFO] Running com.packt.quarkus.chapter5.CustomerEndpointTest
. . . .
[INFO] Tests run: 1, Failures: 0, Errors: 0, Skipped: 0, Time elapsed:
11.846 s - in com.packt.quarkus.chapter5.CustomerEndpointTest
```

Now, we will check the static web pages of the project that we have added so that we can access and manage our service.

Adding a web interface to our application

Our service includes two static web pages to manage the customer service and the orders for each customer. As you know from our previous chapter, static pages are found in the `src/main/resources/META-INF/resources` file of your project by default. We can reuse the same `index.html` page from the previous chapter, which will be our landing page for our application. One enhancement you will find, though, is an action named **Add Order**, which redirects our users to the `order.html` page, which passes a query parameter of the `Customer` information:

```
<div class="divTable blueTable">
    <div class="divTableHeading">
```

```
            <div  class="divTableHead">Customer Name</div>
            <div  class="divTableHead">Customer Address</div>
            <div  class="divTableHead">Action</div>
        </div>
        <div class="divTableRow" ng-repeat="customer in customers">
            <div class="divTableCell">{{ customer.name }}</div>
            <div class="divTableCell">{{ customer.surname }}</div>
            <div class="divTableCell">
                <a ng-href="/order.html?customerId={{ customer.id
                }}&customerName={{ customer.name }}&
                  customerSurname={{ customer.surname }}"
                  class="myButton">Orders</a>
                <a ng-click="edit( customer )" class="myButton">Edit</a>
                <a ng-click="remove( customer )"
            class="myButton">Remove</a>
            </div>
        </div>
    </div>
</div>
```

The order.html page has its own AngularJS Controller that is in charge of displaying the set of Orders for the Customer selected, allowing us to read, create, modify, or delete existing orders. The following is the first part of the Angular Controller, which defines the module and Controller names, and collects the form parameters:

```
var app = angular.module("orderManagement", []);
angular.module('orderManagement').constant('SERVER_URL', '/orders');

//Controller Part
app.controller("orderManagementController", function($scope, $http,
SERVER_URL) {

 var customerId = getParameterByName('customerId');
 var customerName = getParameterByName('customerName');
 var customerSurname = getParameterByName('customerSurname');

 document.getElementById("info").innerHTML = customerName + " " +
customerSurname;

 $scope.orders = [];

 $scope.form = {
 customerId: customerId,
 isNew: true,
 item: "",
 price: 0
 };
 //Now load the data from server
 reloadData();
```

In the second part of our JavaScript code, we have included a `$scope.update` function to insert/edit new `Orders`, a `$scope.remove` function to delete existing orders, and a `reloadData` function to retrieve the list of `Orders` for that `Customer`, as shown in the following code:

```
//HTTP POST/PUT methods for add/edit orders
$scope.update = function() {

var method = "";
var url = "";
var data = {};
if ($scope.form.isNew == true) {
// add orders - POST operation
method = "POST";
url = SERVER_URL + "/" + customerId;
data.item = $scope.form.item;
data.price = $scope.form.price;

} else {
// it's edit operation - PUT operation
method = "PUT";
url = SERVER_URL;

data.item = $scope.form.item;
data.price = $scope.form.price;

}

if (isNaN(data.price)) {
alert('Price must be a Number!');
return false;
}

$http({
method: method,
url: url,
data: angular.toJson(data),
headers: {
'Content-Type': 'application/json'
}
}).then(_success, _error);
};


//HTTP DELETE- delete order by id
$scope.remove = function(order) {
$http({
```

```
method: 'DELETE',
url: SERVER_URL + "/" + order.id
}).then(_success, _error);
};

//In case of edit orders, populate form with order data
$scope.edit = function(order) {
$scope.form.item = order.item;
$scope.form.price = order.price;
$scope.form.isNew = false;
};
/* Private Methods */
//HTTP GET- get all orders collection
function reloadData() {
$http({
method: 'GET',
url: SERVER_URL,
params: {
customerId: customerId
}
}).then(function successCallback(response) {
$scope.orders = response.data;
}, function errorCallback(response) {
console.log(response.statusText);
});
}

function _success(response) {
reloadData();
clearForm()
}

function _error(response) {
alert(response.data.message || response.statusText);
}
//Clear the form
function clearForm() {
$scope.form.item = "";
$scope.form.price = "";
$scope.form.isNew = true;
}
});
```

For the sake of brevity, we haven't included the full HTML page but you can find it in this book's GitHub repository (as we mentioned in the *Technical requirements* section at the beginning of this chapter).

Running the application

The application can be executed from the same shell where we ran our test (so that we still retain the DB_HOST environment variable):

```
mvn quarkus:dev
```

You should expect the following output in the console:

```
Listening for transport dt_socket at address: 5005
2019-07-14 18:41:32,974 INFO  [io.qua.dep.QuarkusAugmentor] (main)
Beginning quarkus augmentation
2019-07-14 18:41:33,789 INFO  [io.qua.dep.QuarkusAugmentor] (main) Quarkus
augmentation completed in 815ms
2019-07-14 18:41:35,153 INFO  [io.quarkus] (main) Quarkus 0.19.0 started in
2.369s. Listening on: http://[::]:8080
2019-07-14 18:41:35,154 INFO  [io.quarkus] (main) Installed features:
[agroal, cdi, hibernate-orm, jdbc-postgresql, narayana-jta, resteasy,
resteasy-jsonb]
```

Now, go to the landing page using the following URL: http://localhost:8080. Here, you will see a prefilled list of customers:

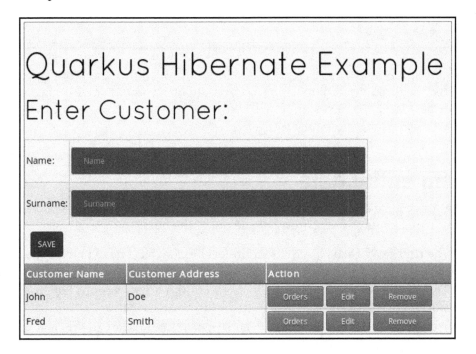

Try adding some orders for customers by clicking on the **Orders** button. You will be taken to the following UI, where you can read, modify, delete, and store new orders for each customer:

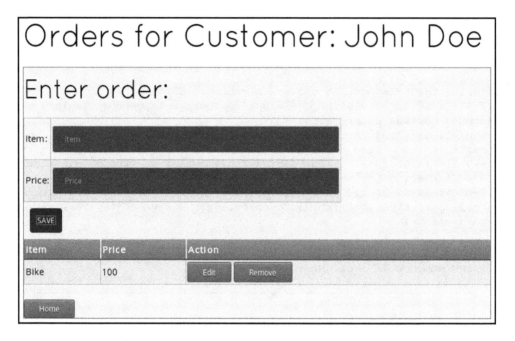

Great! The application works as expected. Can it be improved further? From a performance point of view, the throughput of the application could be improved if we cached data that is frequently accessed. The next section will show you how you can accomplish this using Hibernate ORM's caching mechanisms.

Caching entity data

Caching entities can be easily configured in Hibernate ORM through its advanced caching mechanism. Three kinds of cache are available out of the box:

- The **first-level cache** is a transaction-level cache that's used to track the state of the entities during the current session. It's enabled by default.
- The **second-level cache** is used to cache entities across various Hibernate ORM sessions. This makes it a `SessionFactory`-level cache.
- The **query cache** is used to cache Hibernate ORM queries and their results.

The second-level cache and query cache are not enabled by default due to the large amount of memory they could potentially consume. To make an entity eligible to cache its data, you can annotate it with the `@javax.persistence.Cacheable` annotation, as shown in the following code:

```
@Cacheable
@Entity
public class Customer {

}
```

In this scenario, the customer's field values are cached, except for collections and relationships with other entities. This means that the entity, once cached, can be searched by its primary key without querying the database.

The results of HQL queries can also be cached. This can be quite useful when you want to execute queries for read-mostly entity objects. The simplest way to make an HQL query cacheable is to add a `@javax.persistence.QueryHint` annotation to `@NamedQuery`, with the `org.hibernate.cacheable` attribute set to `true`, as follows:

```
@Cacheable
@Entity
@NamedQuery(name = "Customers.findAll",
        query = "SELECT c FROM Customer c ORDER BY c.id",
        hints = @QueryHint(name = "org.hibernate.cacheable", value =
        "true") )
public class Customer {
}
```

You can easily verify the preceding assertion by turning on SQL logging in your `application.properties` file, as shown here:

```
quarkus.hibernate-orm.log.sql=true
```

Then, if you run the application, you should be able to see a **single** SQL statement you can use to query the `Customer` list in the console, no matter how many times you have requested the page:

```
Hibernate:
    select
        customer0_.id as id1_0_,
        customer0_.name as name2_0_,
        customer0_.surname as surname3_0_
    from
```

```
        Customer customer0_
    order by
        customer0_.id
```

Great! You have reached the first milestone, that is, running the application on your local filesystem and caching frequently used SQL statements in Hibernate ORM's **second-level cache** (**2LC**). Now, it's time to take our application to the cloud!

Taking an application to the cloud

Having tested the application through the local JVM, it's time to bring it natively into the cloud. The interesting part of this process will be connecting the Quarkus application with the PostgreSQL application on OpenShift without touching even one line of code! Let's look at how we can achieve this:

1. Start your Minishift instance and create a new project named `quarkus-hibernate`:

   `oc new-project quarkus-hibernate`

2. Next, we will be adding a PostgreSQL application to our project. A PostgreSQL image stream is included in the `openshift` namespace by default, which you can check with the following command:

   `oc get is -n openshift | grep postgresql`

You should see the following output in your console:

```
postgresql    172.30.1.1:5000/openshift/postgresql    latest,10,9.2 +
3 more...    6 hours ago
```

To create the PostgreSQL application, the following configuration variables need to be set:

- `POSTGRESQL_USER`: Username for the PostgreSQL account to be created
- `POSTGRESQL_PASSWORD`: Password for the user account
- `POSTGRESQL_DATABASE`: Database name

We will be using the same parameters we defined in the `application.properties` file so that we can bootstrap our application with the following command:

```
oc new-app -e POSTGRESQL_USER=quarkus -e POSTGRESQL_PASSWORD=quarkus -e
POSTGRESQL_DATABASE=quarkusdb postgresql
```

In your console logs, check that the following output has been produced:

```
--> Creating resources ...
    imagestreamtag.image.openshift.io "postgresql:10" created
    deploymentconfig.apps.openshift.io "postgresql" created
    service "postgresql" created
--> Success
    Application is not exposed. You can expose services to the
    outside world by executing one or more of the commands below:
     'oc expose svc/postgresql'
    Run 'oc status' to view your app.
```

Let's take a look at the list of available services (`oc get services`) to verify whether `postgresql` is available:

```
NAME                    TYPE        CLUSTER-IP       EXTERNAL-IP    PORT(S)
AGE
postgresql              ClusterIP   172.30.154.130   <none>         5432/TCP
14m
```

As you can see, the service is now active at the cluster IP address `172.30.154.130`. Luckily, we don't need to hardcode this address in our application code since we will be using the service name, `postgresql`, which works like an alias of the cluster address.

Now, we will create a binary build of our project so that it can be deployed into Minishift. Impatient users can just execute the `deploy-openshift.sh` script, which is available on GitHub in the root folder of this chapter. Within it, you will find the following commented list of commands:

```
# Build native application
mvn package -Pnative -Dnative-image.docker-build=true -DskipTests=true

# Create a new Binary Build named "quarkus-hibernate"
oc new-build --binary --name=quarkus-hibernate -l app=quarkus-hibernate

# Set the dockerfilePath attribute into the Build Configuration
oc patch bc/quarkus-hibernate -p
'{"spec":{"strategy":{"dockerStrategy":{"dockerfilePath":"src/main/docker/D
ockerfile.native"}}}}'

# Start the build, uploading content from the local folder:
```

```
oc start-build quarkus-hibernate --from-dir=. --follow

# Create a new Application, using as Input the "quarkus-hibernate" image
stream:
oc new-app --image-stream=quarkus-hibernate:latest

# Expose the Service through a Route:
oc expose svc/quarkus-hibernate
```

At the end of this process, you should be able to see the following route available through the oc get routes command:

```
NAME                    HOST/PORT
PATH        SERVICES                PORT        TERMINATION    WILDCARD
quarkus-hibernate    quarkus-hibernate-quarkus-
hibernate.192.168.42.30.nip.io                quarkus-hibernate    8080-tcp
None
```

The overall status of the applications can be also checked from the web console of your project:

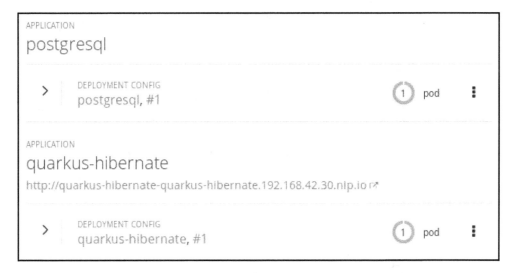

You can now navigate to the external route of the application (the actual route address will vary, depending on your network configuration. In our example, it's **http://quarkus-hibernate-quarkus-hibernate.192.168.42.30.nip.io**) and check that the application works smoothly on the cloud.

Making data persistence easier using Panache API

Hibernate ORM is the standard way to map database structures into Java objects. The main downside of using an ORM tool is that even a simple database structure requires lots of boilerplate code (such as getter and setters methods). Also, you have to include basic query methods in your repository classes, which makes the work quite repetitive. In this section, we will learn how to use Hibernate Panache to simplify and accelerate the development of our applications.

To get started with Hibernate ORM with Panache, let's check the second example for this chapter, which is located in the `Chapter05/hibernate-panache` folder in this book's GitHub repository. We recommend importing the project into your IDE before you move on.

If you take a look at the project's configuration, you will see that we have included `quarkus-hibernate-orm-panache` in the `pom.xml` file:

```xml
<dependency>
        <groupId>io.quarkus</groupId>
        <artifactId>quarkus-hibernate-orm-panache</artifactId>
</dependency>
```

This is the only configuration that we need to use Hibernate Panache. Now comes the funny part. There are two strategies for plugging Panache into your entity:

- Extending the `io.quarkus.hibernate.orm.panache.PanacheEntity` class: This is the simplest option as you will get an ID field that is auto-generated.
- Extending `io.quarkus.hibernate.orm.panache.PanacheEntityBase`: This option can be used if you require a custom ID strategy.

Since we are using a `SequenceGenerator` strategy for our ID field, we will use the latter option. Following is the `Customer` class, which has been rewritten so that it extends `PanacheEntityBase`:

```java
@Entity
@NamedQuery(name = "Customers.findAll",
        query = "SELECT c FROM Customer c ORDER BY c.id" )
public class Customer extends PanacheEntityBase {
    @Id
    @SequenceGenerator(
            name = "customerSequence",
            sequenceName = "customerId_seq",
```

```
            allocationSize = 1,
            initialValue = 1)
    @GeneratedValue(strategy = GenerationType.SEQUENCE, generator =
      "customerSequence")
    public Long id;

    @Column(length = 40)
    public String name;

    @Column(length = 40)
    public String surname;

    @OneToMany(mappedBy = "customer")
    @JsonbTransient
    public List<Orders> orders;
}
```

As you can see, the code has been reduced quite a lot as we haven't used a getter/setter field. Instead, some fields have been exposed as `public` so that they can be accessed directly by the classes. The `Orders` entity has been rewritten using the same pattern:

```
@Entity
@NamedQuery(name = "Orders.findAll",
        query = "SELECT o FROM Orders o WHERE o.customer.id = :id ORDER BY
o.item")
public class Orders extends PanacheEntityBase {
    @Id
    @SequenceGenerator(
            name = "orderSequence",
            sequenceName = "orderId_seq",
            allocationSize = 1,
            initialValue = 1)
    @GeneratedValue(strategy = GenerationType.SEQUENCE, generator =
      "orderSequence")
    public Long id;

    @Column(length = 40)
    public String item;

    @Column
    public Long price;

    @ManyToOne
    @JoinColumn(name = "customer_id")
    @JsonbTransient
    public Customer customer;

}
```

So far, we have seen some of the benefits that are provided by Hibernate Panache. Another aspect worth mentioning is that by extending `PanacheEntityBase` (or `PanacheEntity`), you will be able to use a set of static methods directly on your entity. Following is a table containing the most common methods you can trigger on your entity:

Method	Description
count	Counts this entity from the database (with an optional query and parameters)
delete	Delete this entity from the database if it has already been persisted.
flush	Flushes all pending changes to the database
findById	Finds an entity of this type by ID
find	Finds entities using a query with optional parameters and a sort strategy
findAll	Finds all the entities of this type
list	Shortcut for find().list()
listAll	Shortcut for findAll().list()
deleteAll	Deletes all the entities of this type
delete	Deletes entities using a query with optional parameters
persist	Persists all given entities

The following shows the `CustomerRepository` class, which leverages the new field and methods that are available in the `Customer` entity:

```
public class CustomerRepository {

    public List<Customer> findAll() {
        return Customer.listAll(Sort.by("id"));
    }

    public Customer findCustomerById(Long id) {
        Customer customer = Customer.findById(id);

        if (customer == null) {
            throw new WebApplicationException("Customer with id
            of " +  id + " does not exist.", 404);
        }
        return customer;
    }
    @Transactional
    public void updateCustomer(Customer customer) {
        Customer customerToUpdate = findCustomerById(customer.id);
        customerToUpdate.name = customer.name;
        customerToUpdate.surname = customer.surname;
    }
    @Transactional
```

```
        public void createCustomer(Customer customer) {
            customer.persist();
        }
        @Transactional
        public void deleteCustomer(Long customerId) {
            Customer customer = findCustomerById(customerId);
            customer.delete();
        }
    }
```

The most obvious advantage is that you don't need `EntityManager` as a proxy to manage your entity class anymore. Instead, you can directly invoke static methods that are available in your entity, thus dramatically reducing the verbosity of your `Repository` class.

For the sake of completeness, let's have a look at the `OrderRepository` class, which has been adapted to use Panache objects as well:

```
    public class OrderRepository {

        public List<Orders> findAll(Long customerId) {
            return Orders.list("id", customerId);
        }

        public Orders findOrderById(Long id) {
            Orders order = Orders.findById(id);
            if (order == null) {
                throw new WebApplicationException("Order with id of
                " + id  + " does not exist.", 404);
            }
            return order;
        }
        @Transactional
        public void updateOrder(Orders order) {
            Orders orderToUpdate = findOrderById(order.id);
            orderToUpdate.item = order.item;
            orderToUpdate.price = order.price;
        }
        @Transactional
        public void createOrder(Orders order, Customer c) {
            order.customer = c;
            order.persist();
        }
        @Transactional
        public void deleteOrder(Long orderId) {
            Orders order = findOrderById(orderId);
            order.delete();
        }
    }
```

Nothing else has been changed in your application since switching to Hibernate Panache is completely transparent for our REST endpoint and the web interfaces. Build and run the application as usual with the following command:

```
mvn compile quarkus:dev
```

On the console, you should see that the application has started and the two initial customers have been added:

```
Hibernate:
    INSERT INTO customer (id, name, surname) VALUES (
nextval('customerId_seq'), 'John','Doe')
Hibernate:
    INSERT INTO customer (id, name, surname) VALUES (
nextval('customerId_seq'), 'Fred','Smith')
2019-11-28 10:44:02,887 INFO  [io.quarkus] (main) Quarkus 1.0.0.Final
started in 2.278s. Listening on: http://[::]:8080
2019-11-28 10:44:02,888 INFO  [io.quarkus] (main) Installed features:
[agroal, cdi, hibernate-orm, jdbc-postgresql, narayana-jta, resteasy,
resteasy-jsonb]
```

Now, enjoy your simplified CRUD application powered by Hibernate ORM with Panache!

Summary

In this chapter, we looked at data persistence and covered the well-known Hibernate ORM framework. If you have some years' Enterprise programming under your belt, you shouldn't have found it challenging to apply the same concepts to Quarkus. Now, your overall skills include configuring an RDBMS-based application using Hibernate and its simplified paradigm called Panache. We have also learned how to deploy and connect both RDBMS and our application on the cloud on an OpenShift cluster.

To summarize, we have mastered the major pillars of Enterprise programming (moving from REST services to servlets, CDI, and data persistence).

In the next chapter, we'll learn how we can complement the standard Enterprise API with the MicroProfile API in Quarkus.

6
Building Applications Using the MicroProfile API

At this point, you should have a good understanding of how to use the most common Java APIs (CDI, REST, JSON, JPA) in a Quarkus application. In this chapter, we will be adding a whole bunch of APIs called the MicroProfile specification. By mastering the topics in this chapter, you will be able to shape up components that have built upon the core features of the Java EE, which allows for a straightforward development experience when implementing microservices, increasing the robustness of your applications, and reducing the risk of over-designing and reinventing the same patterns. Topics you will learn to include how to add fault tolerance and health checks to your services, how to check your service's metrics, how to trace and document them, and how to create lean REST clients for your endpoints. Other features, such as configuration, security, and Reactive Messaging, will be covered in upcoming chapters.

In this chapter, we will cover the following topics:

- An overview of the MicroProfile API and how it can complement the Enterprise API
- How the MicroProfile API can fit into your Quarkus projects
- Some exposure on how to run the MicroProfile API in the cloud

Technical requirements

You can find the source code for the project in this chapter on GitHub at `https://github. com/PacktPublishing/Hands-On-Cloud-Native-Applications-with-Java-and-Quarkus/ tree/master/Chapter06`.

Getting started with the MicroProfile API

The Java Enterprise API is a great set of technologies for building applications, but it has historically lacked some features that are needed if you want to move your application to the cloud. For instance, there is no specific API to handle configuration properties that can be injected into your services, nor is there a formal way to describe how clients can interact with REST endpoints. Also, it would definitely help to include some features so that we can monitor an application's health or load-balance requests; these are currently managed by vendors with custom technologies.

The Eclipse MicroProfile project is a collaboration initiative that's driven by top application vendors and aims to optimize the Enterprise API for Java applications, including all the features we have mentioned here.

A bird's-eye view of the Eclipse MicroProfile specification shows how rich this environment is in the 3.2 release:

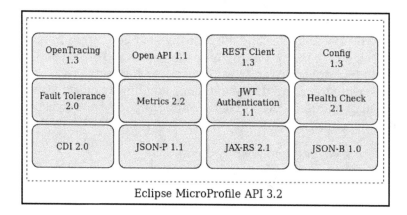

In this chapter, we will delve into the following areas of the MicroProfile specification:

- **The Eclipse MicroProfile Configuration**: Provides a unified way to configure your services by injecting the configuration data from a static file or from environment variables.
- **The Eclipse MicroProfile Health Check**: Provides the ability to probe the state of a service; for example, whether it's running or not, whether it lacks disk space, or whether there is an issue with the database connection.
- **The Eclipse MicroProfile Fault Tolerance**: Allows you to define a strategy in the event of your services failing, for example, configuring timeouts, retry policies, fallback methods, and Circuit Breaker processing.

- **The Eclipse MicroProfile Metrics**: Provides a standard way for MicroProfile services to export monitoring data to external agents. Metrics also provide a common Java API that exposes their telemetry data.
- **The Eclipse MicroProfile OpenAPI**: Provides a set of Java interfaces to document your services in a standard way.
- **The Eclipse MicroProfile OpenTracing**: Provides a set of instrumentation libraries for tracing components such as JAX-RS and CDI.
- **The Eclipse MicroProfile Rest Client**: This builds upon the JAX-RS API and provides a type safe, unified approach for invoking RESTful services over HTTP.

Although not discussed in this chapter, Quarkus also supports MicroProfile **JWT RBAC**, which outlines a proposal for using **OpenID Connect (OIDC)**-based **JSON Web Tokens (JWTs)** for **role-based access control (RBAC)** in your service endpoints. In the next chapter, which is about security, we will cover this topic in more detail.

Getting started with MicroProfile projects

To learn about the single MicroProfile API, you will need the following projects, which can be found under the Chapter06 folder in this book's GitHub repository:

- `fault-tolerance`: A project that shows us how to use the MicroProfile Fault Tolerance API
- `health`: A project that focuses on the MicroProfile Health Check API
- `openapi-swagger`: A project that implements OpenAPI interfaces
- `opentracing`: A project that implements the OpenTracing API
- `rest-client`: A project that focuses on the MicroProfile REST Client API

Most of the preceding projects are derived from the **customer service** Hibernate application that we discussed in Chapter 5, *Managing Data Persistence with Quarkus*. Therefore, a basic requirement is to have a PostgreSQL database up and running so that we can run our projects. We remind you that this can be done with just a one-line script:

```
docker run --ulimit memlock=-1:-1 -it --rm=true --memory-swappiness=0 --
name quarkus_test -e POSTGRES_USER=quarkus -e POSTGRES_PASSWORD=quarkus -e
POSTGRES_DB=quarkusdb -p 5432:5432 postgres:10.5
```

Next, we recommend importing the whole Chapter06 folder into your IDE so that you can have the full set of projects at your fingertips as you continue with this chapter. That being said, we will start by discussing the MicroProfile Health Check API.

The Eclipse MicroProfile Health Check

In the cloud environment, it is essential to allow services to report, and eventually publish, the overall health status to a defined endpoint. This can be achieved through MicroProfile Health Check, which allows a service to report the overall status as "UP" if it is available and "DOWN" if it is unavailable. This information can be collected by a service orchestrator, which can then use the health reports to make decisions.

Let's put these concepts into practice with the Chapter06/health example. First off, in order to use the health extension, we have included the following dependency in the pom.xml file:

```
<dependency>
  <groupId>io.quarkus</groupId>
  <artifactId>quarkus-smallrye-health</artifactId>
</dependency>
```

Once the preceding library is available, we can add an implementation of the org.eclipse.microprofile.health.HealthCheck interface, which allows us to check the service status. The following is the DBHealthCheck class, which verifies the status of the PostgreSQL database connection:

```
@Health
@ApplicationScoped
public class DBHealthCheck implements HealthCheck {

    @ConfigProperty(name = "db.host")
    String host;

    @ConfigProperty(name = "db.port")
    Integer port;

    @Override
    public HealthCheckResponse call() {

        HealthCheckResponseBuilder responseBuilder =
        HealthCheckResponse.named("Database connection
         health check");

        try {
            serverListening(host,port);
            responseBuilder.up();
        } catch (Exception e) {
            // cannot access the database
            responseBuilder.down()
                    .withData("error", e.getMessage());
```

```
    }
    return responseBuilder.build();
  }

  private void serverListening(String host, int port) throws
   IOException
  {
    Socket s = new Socket(host, port);
    s.close();
  }
}
```

This class contains two core implementations of the MicroProfile specifications:

1. First of all, we have the @Health annotation, which works in combination with the @ApplicationScoped CDI context to return the health status check each time a request to http://localhost:9080/health is received.

2. This class also uses the **MicroProfile Configuration API** to inject the PostgreSQL database host and port it into the bean. The following is an excerpt from the application.properties file:

   ```
   db.host=${POSTGRESQL_SERVICE_HOST:localhost}
   db.port=${POSTGRESQL_SERVICE_PORT:5432}
   quarkus.datasource.url=jdbc:postgresql://${db.host}:${db.port}/post
   gres
   ```

 As you can see, if the POSTGRESQL_SERVICE_HOST and POSTGRESQL_SERVICE_PORT environment variables aren't set, the default values (localhost and 5432) are used and stored in the db.host and db.port variables.

The target host and port are reached via a TCP socket and, on a successful attempt, a responseBuilder.up() will be returned. Otherwise, responseBuilder.down() will indicate a failure.

You can start the Quarkus project with the following command:

```
$ mvn compile quarkus:dev
```

Then, assuming that the database is up and running, let's try to access the `http://localhost:9080/health` endpoint:

```
curl http://localhost:8080/health
{
    "status": "UP",
    "checks": [
        {
            "name": "Database connection health check",
            "status": "UP"
        },
        {
            "name": "File system Readiness check",
            "status": "UP"
        }
    ]
}
```

The response acknowledges the status of the database connection. Let's also verify the condition where the database is unavailable. A simple *Ctrl + C* from the PostgreSQL shell will send the appropriate signal to stop the process. You should see the following output on the console:

```
2019-07-27 09:47:25.564 UTC [54] LOG:   shutting down
2019-07-27 09:47:25.601 UTC [1] LOG:   database system is shut down
```

Now, check the status of the database connection through the `/health` endpoint once more:

```
{
    "status": "DOWN",
    "checks": [
        {
            "name": "Database connection health check",
            "status": "DOWN",
            "data": {
                "error": "Connection refused (Connection refused)"
            }
        }
    ]
}
```

As you can see from the preceding output, the JSON that was returned changed the status to `"DOWN"` and set the error message in the error field. This example sets our first milestone: checking the application's health. We can further refine our health check policies by using liveness and readiness checks, which we will discuss in the next section.

Using liveness and readiness checks

According to the newest MicroProfile specifications, health checks are now to be used with a more specific model to help us determine the cause of potential issues. Therefore, it's recommended you migrate the legacy `@HealthCheck` to one of the following checks:

- **Readiness checks**: This check can indicate that a service is *temporarily* unable to serve traffic. This can be due to, for example, the fact that an application may be loading some configuration or data. In such cases, you don't want to shut down the application but, at the same time, you don't want to send it requests either. Readiness checks are supposed to cover this scenario.
- **Liveness checks**: Services running 24/7 can sometimes undergo a transition to broken states, for example, because they have hit `OutOfMemoryError`. Therefore, they cannot recover except by being restarted. You can, however, be notified of this scenario by defining a liveness check that probes the liveness of the service.

In order to implement both checks, you can simply replace the `@org.eclipse.microprofile.health.HealthCheck` annotation with more specific ones, such as `@org.eclipse.microprofile.health.Liveness` and `@org.eclipse.microprofile.health.Readiness`.

In the following example, we have implemented a `@Readiness` check to verify whether a lock file exists (for example, due to a pending task) and emit a `"DOWN"` status when this file is detected:

```
@Readiness
@ApplicationScoped
public class ReadinessHealthCheck implements HealthCheck {

    @Override
    public HealthCheckResponse call() {
        HealthCheckResponseBuilder responseBuilder =
          HealthCheckResponse.named("File system Readiness check");

        boolean tempFileExists =
          Files.exists(Paths.get("/tmp/tmp.lck"));
        if (!tempFileExists) {
            responseBuilder.up();
```

```
        }
        else {
            responseBuilder.down().withData("error", "Lock file
              detected!");
        }
        return responseBuilder.build();
    }
}
```

Readiness checks are verified through the "/health/ready" URI. You can check this by requesting the following URL: http://localhost:8080/health/ready:

```
$ curl http://localhost:8080/health/ready
```

If no file has been detected, you will see something similar to the following output:

```
{
    "status": "UP",
    "checks": [
        {
            "name": "File system Readiness check",
            "status": "UP"
        }
    ]
}
```

Now, let's learn how to add a **liveness check** to our services. We will check the amount of free memory that's needed to run the service and return a liveness check based on a certain memory threshold, which we have set to one gigabyte:

```
@Liveness
@ApplicationScoped
public class MemoryHealthCheck implements HealthCheck {
    long threshold = 1024000000;
    @Override
    public HealthCheckResponse call() {
        HealthCheckResponseBuilder responseBuilder =
          HealthCheckResponse.named("MemoryHealthCheck
        Liveness check");
        long freeMemory = Runtime.getRuntime().freeMemory();

        if (freeMemory >= threshold) {
            responseBuilder.up();
        }
        else {
            responseBuilder.down()
                    .withData("error", "Not enough free memory!
                    Please restart application");
```

```
        }
        return responseBuilder.build();
    }

}
```

You can now verify the service's liveness with cURL, as follows:

```
curl http://localhost:8080/health/live
```

Since the default Quarkus JVM settings don't permit the amount of memory we have set in the threshold, the status of the service will indicate `"DOWN"`, as follows:

```
{
    "status": "DOWN",
    "checks": [
        {
            "name": "MemoryHealthCheck Liveness check",
            "status": "DOWN",
            "data": {
                "error": "Not enough free memory! Please restart
                application"
            }
        }
    ]
}
```

Before we move on to the next API in our checklist, it is worth checking how health checks can be triggered in a cloud environment using Kubernetes probe checks. We'll learn how to do this in the next section.

Letting OpenShift manage unhealthy services

In the examples so far, we have seen how to detect different health checks scenarios. One of the greatest advantages of running a Kubernetes native environment is that you can react automatically to changes in an application's status. More specifically, it is possible to probe the following checks through the application's deployment descriptors:

- **Liveness probe**: Kubernetes provides a liveness probe to determine whether the container that it's been configured in is still running. Should the liveness probe fail, the `kubelet` agent kills and restarts the container.

- **Readiness probe**: Kubernetes provides the readiness probe to signal that an application is temporarily unable to serve traffic, for example, because a configuration is being loaded. In such cases, you don't want to stop the application, but you don't want to allow any requests in either.

As you can see, the preceding probes match the MicroProfile Health Checks that were defined in the latest specifications. As a proof of concept, we will be deploying our example application into MiniShift as a binary build. As usual, we will start by creating a new project from the shell (or the web console, if you prefer doing things this way):

```
oc new-project quarkus-microprofile
```

As you may remember, we need to add a PostgreSQL application to our project that will be found by our checks:

```
oc new-app -e POSTGRESQL_USER=quarkus -e POSTGRESQL_PASSWORD=quarkus -e
POSTGRESQL_DATABASE=quarkusdb postgresql
```

Then, you can finally push the Quarkus MicroProfile Health application we have just built onto the cloud. The following script will be used for this purpose:

```
# Build native application
mvn package -Pnative -Dnative-image.docker-build=true -DskipTests=true

# Create a new Binary Build named "quarkus-microprofile"
oc new-build --binary --name=quarkus-microprofile -l app=quarkus-
microprofile

# Set the dockerfilePath attribute into the Build Configuration
oc patch bc/quarkus-microprofile -p
'{"spec":{"strategy":{"dockerStrategy":{"dockerfilePath":"src/main/docker/D
ockerfile.native"}}}}'

# Start the build, uploading content from the local folder:
oc start-build quarkus-microprofile --from-dir=. --follow

# Create a new Application, using as Input the "quarkus-microprofile"
Image Stream:
oc new-app --image-stream=quarkus-microprofile:latest

# Expose the Service through a Route:
oc expose svc/quarkus-microprofile
```

The preceding script should be nothing new for you, so let's move on to the OpenShift console, where we can check the status of our project:

Now, check the **Deployments** configuration of your project and select **Edit Health Checks**:

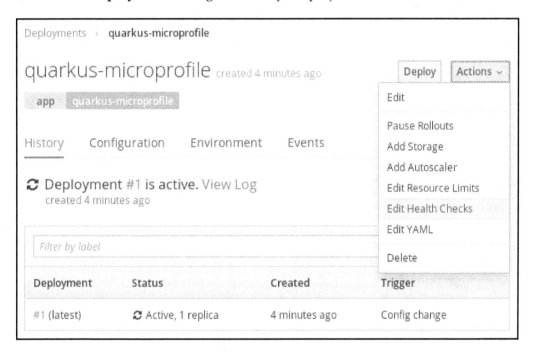

Within the **Health Checks** UI, you can choose which health check you want to add:

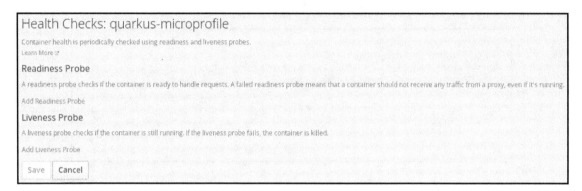

Let's start with the **Readiness Probe**. By selecting it, you will be taken to the following UI:

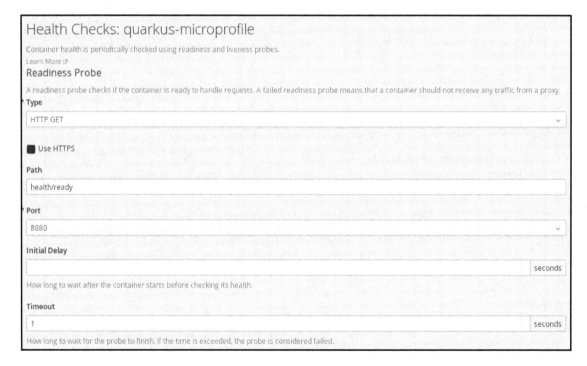

The key parameter to select is **Path**, which should match our MicroProfile readiness URI (`health/ready`). Apart from that, you can also configure the following properties:

- `initialDelaySeconds`: The number of seconds after the container has started before liveness or readiness probes are initiated.

- `timeoutSeconds`: The number of seconds after which the probe times out. Defaults to 1 second. The minimum value is `1`.

Now, let's configure the **Liveness Probe**:

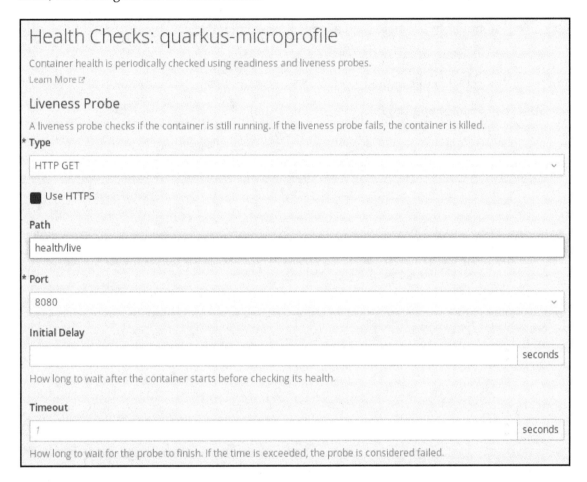

Except for **Path**, which will be `health/live`, we can leave the other default values. Save your changes as-is. Now, let's try to break a few things. For example, we will create a lock file in the Pod where the application is running. This will immediately trigger a failure in the readiness probe. Let's check a list of Pods from the shell with the following command:

```
$ oc get pods
```

The output that's returned is as follows:

```
NAME                              READY    STATUS       RESTARTS    AGE
quarkus-microprofile-1-build      0/1      Completed    0           20m
quarkus-microprofile-1-rxp4r      1/1      Running      0           20m
```

Okay, we will now run a remote shell against this running Pod:

```
$ oc rsh quarkus-microprofile-1-rxp4r
```

We're in. Now, create a file named /tmp/tmp.lck

```
sh-4.4$ touch /tmp/tmp.lck
```

In a couple of seconds (depending on the initial delay setting), your Pod won't be available anymore. You can see this from the **Overview** panel:

This change will also be reflected in system events, which can be captured through the `oc get events` command, as follows:

```
$ oc get events
quarkus-microprofile-3-mzl6f.15b54cfc42ddb728      Pod
spec.containers{quarkus-microprofile}      Warning      Unhealthy kubelet,
localhost
Readiness probe failed: HTTP probe failed with statuscode: 503
```

Finally, it's worth mentioning that our application also includes a liveness check, which verifies that the amount of available memory is greater than a certain threshold. Whether you have hit the threshold or not, the liveness probe depends on the amount of memory allowed at startup for MiniShift. A digression into OpenShift's application memory sizing would take us beyond the scope of this book, but it's worth reading more about it by looking at the official docs: `https://docs.openshift.com/container-platform/3.9/dev_guide/application_memory_sizing.html`.

Maintaining your application's status so that it's healthy is a key element to consider when designing your applications. On the other hand, enabling your services to react to failures or performance degradation is no less important. Don't worry, though – the next section will teach you how to handle failures using the MicroProfile Fault Tolerance API.

The Eclipse MicroProfile Fault Tolerance API

The **Fault Tolerance** specification is a fundamental API that can be used to handle the unavailability of your microservices by endorsing a set of policies that can improve the resiliency of your applications. The following fault tolerance policies are available:

- **Timeout**: Defines a timeout for the execution of a service call
- **Fallback**: Provides a contingency solution when a failure occurs
- **Retry**: Allows you to retry execution based on criteria
- **Bulkhead**: Isolates partial service failures while the rest of the system can still work
- **Circuit Breaker**: Defines criteria for automatic fast-fails to prevent system degradation caused by overloading
- **Asynchronous**: Allows us to invoke an operation asynchronously

Let's look at these concepts in practice by using the `Chapter06/fault-tolerance` example. First off, in order to use the fault-tolerance extension, we have included the following dependency in the `pom.xml` file:

```xml
<dependency>
  <groupId>io.quarkus</groupId>
  <artifactId>io.quarkus:quarkus-smallrye-fault-tolerance</artifactId>
</dependency>
```

Let's start with the Timeout, Fallback, and Retry policies, which are commonly used together since they complement each other.

Using Timeout, Fallback, and Retry to create resilient services

In simple terms, the `@org.eclipse.microprofile.faulttolerance.Timeout` annotation can be used to specify the maximum time (in ms) allowed for returning a response in a method. Here is an example `findAll` method that times out after 250 ms:

```java
@Timeout(250)
public List<Customer> findAll() {

    randomSleep();
    return entityManager.createNamedQuery("Customers.findAll",
Customer.class)
            .getResultList();
}

private void randomSleep() {
    try {
        Thread.sleep(new Random().nextInt(400));
    } catch (java.lang.InterruptedException e) {
        e.printStackTrace();
    }

}
```

The random sleep that's triggered by the finder method can be used to allow some occasional execution failures.

In order to mitigate time-outs or other failures, you can decorate your methods with the `@Fallback` policy so that you can specify an alternate execution path in the case of failure:

```
@Timeout(250)
@Fallback(fallbackMethod = "findAllStatic")
public List<Customer> findAll() {

    randomSleep();
    return entityManager.createNamedQuery("Customers.findAll",
    Customer.class)
            .getResultList();

}
private List<Customer> findAllStatic() {
    LOGGER.info("Building Static List of Customers");
    return buildStaticList();

}
```

In this example, we are redirecting the execution to the `findAllStatic` method if any failure arises in the `findAll` method. The `findAllStatic` method will return a static list of `Customer` objects (please check the source code example for this chapter to see the implementation of this).

Applying a retry policy to your failures

Sometimes, failures in the execution of your methods are caused by temporary issues such as network congestion. If we are confident that the issue can be resolved in accordance with our business SLA, we can include a `@Retry` annotation to allow us to reiterate the execution of failed methods a certain number of times.

For example, by adding the `@Retry(maxRetries = 3)` annotation, we will attempt to load data from the database three more times before using a static list of customers:

```
@Timeout(250)
@Fallback(fallbackMethod = "findAllStatic")
@Retry(maxRetries = 3)
public List<Customer> findAll() {

    randomSleep();
    return entityManager.createNamedQuery("Customers.findAll",
     Customer.class)
            .getResultList();

}
```

It is worth mentioning that the `@Retry` annotation can be configured to retry only a subset of specific exceptions. This can be seen in the following example, where we're using `@Retry` over `RuntimeException` and `TimeoutException`:

```
@Retry(retryOn = {RuntimeException.class, TimeoutException.class},
maxRetries = 3)
```

Now, let's learn how to apply a fault tolerance pattern named **Circuit Breaker** to our services.

Circuit Breaker

Circuit Breaker is a core pattern for creating resilient services. It can be used to prevent repeatable exceptions by instantly denying new requests. The MicroProfile Fault Tolerance API uses the `@CircuitBreaker` annotation to control incoming requests. A software Circuit Breaker is similar to an electrical circuit breaker since it has the following states:

- **Closed state**: A closed-circuit represents a fully functional system that's available to its clients.
- **Half-open circuit**: When some failures are detected, the state can change to half-open. In this state, it checks whether the failed component is restored. If so, it closes the circuit. Otherwise, it moves to an open state.
- **Open state**: An open state means the service is temporarily disabled. After checks have been made, you can verify whether it's safe to switch to a half-open state.

Here is an example:

```
@CircuitBreaker(successThreshold = 5, requestVolumeThreshold = 4,
failureRatio=0.75,
        delay = 1000)
public List<Orders> findAll(Long customerId) {

    possibleFailure();
    return   (List<Orders>)
    entityManager.createNamedQuery("Orders.findAll")
            .setParameter("customerId", customerId)
            .getResultList();
}
private void possibleFailure() {
    if (new Random().nextFloat() < 0.5f) {
    throw new RuntimeException("Resource failure.");
    }
}
```

In the preceding example, the @CircuitBreaker policy applies to the findAll method of the OrderRepository class. Because of that, if, within the last four invocations, 75% failed, then the circuit transits to an open state. The circuit will stay open for 1,000 ms. When a circuit is open, a CircuitBreakerOpenException will be thrown instead of actually invoking the method.

Please note that, like the retry method, the @CircuitBreaker also allows us to define failure criteria through the failon annotation parameter. This can be seen in the following example:

```
@CircuitBreaker(failOn={RuntimeException.class}, successThreshold = 5,
requestVolumeThreshold = 4, failureRatio=0.75, delay = 1000)
```

In the preceding example, if a RuntimeException is thrown in the method, then the execution is counted by the CircuitBreaker as a failure; otherwise, it is counted as a success.

Now that we know about the background of the core Fault Tolerance API, let's learn how to further enhance our application's robustness with bulkhead and asynchronous patterns.

Using asynchronous and bulkhead policies

Asynchronous programming is not a new pattern for Enterprise developers. However, when used in combination with the BulkHead policy, you can achieve a powerful fault tolerance pattern for your microservices. In a nutshell, if you annotate a method with @Asynchronous, it will be executed asynchronously on a separate thread.

In the following example, we are performing some logic in the createOrder method, which spins off some debugging in a separate thread by means of the writeSomeLogging method, which returns a CompletableFuture instance:

```
public void createOrder(Orders order, Customer c) {
    order.setCustomer(c);
    entityManager.persist(order);
    writeSomeLogging(order.getItem());

}
@Asynchronous
private Future writeSomeLogging(String item) {
        LOGGER.info("New Customer order at: "+new java.util.Date());
        LOGGER.info("Item: {}", item);
        return CompletableFuture.completedFuture("ok");
}
```

When `@Bulkhead` is used with `@Asynchronous`, the thread pool isolation approach will be used. The thread pool approach allows us to configure the maximum concurrent requests together with a certain queue size, just like a semaphore. Here is the updated example, which includes the `@Bulkhead` policy:

```
// maximum 5 concurrent requests allowed, maximum 10 requests allowed in
the waiting queue
@Asynchronous
@Bulkhead(value = 5, waitingTaskQueue = 10)
private Future writeSomeLogging(String item) {
        LOGGER.info("New Customer order at: "+new java.util.Date());
        LOGGER.info("Item: {}", item);
        return CompletableFuture.completedFuture("ok");
}
```

That was a whirlwind tour of the fault tolerance policies that are available in the MicroProfile API. Let's move on to the next section, which is about capturing service metrics.

The Eclipse MicroProfile Metrics API

The MicroProfile Metrics specification provides us with a unified way of exporting your services' monitored data to management agents. This helps us perform proactive checks on some key statistics indicators, such as the number of times and the rate at which a service has been requested, the duration of each request, and so on.

Let's get coding. Here, we will focus on the `Chapter06/metrics` example. First off, in order to use the metrics extension, we have included the following dependency in the `pom.xml` file:

```
<dependency>
  <groupId>io.quarkus</groupId>
  <artifactId>io.quarkus:quarkus-smallrye-metrics</artifactId>
</dependency>
```

Now, we'll provide an overview of the metrics annotations that have been added on top of our REST service. Let's start with the `@Counted` annotation, which tracks how many times a request has been made:

```
@GET
@Counted(description = "Customer list count", absolute = true)
public List<Customer> getAll() {
    return customerRepository.findAll();
}
```

Within the `@Counted` annotation, we have provided a description and set the `absolute` flag to `true`, which means the class's package name will not be prepended to the metric name.

Let's compile and run the application:

```
$ mvn compile quarkus:dev
```

Now, let's reload the home page, which will trigger a list of customers. Next, we'll gather some metrics. There are two entry points for our metrics:

- `http://localhost:8080/metrics`: This endpoint will return all the metrics, including system metrics where the application is running.
- `http://localhost:8080/metrics/application`: This endpoint will just return metrics that are emitted by the applications that have been deployed.

We will choose the latter option here, as follows:

```
$ curl http:/localhost:8080/metrics/applications
```

Since we have loaded the home page twice, the expected output should be as follows:

```
# HELP application:get_all Customer list count
# TYPE application:get_all counter
application:get_all 2.0
```

The next annotation is the `@Timed` annotation, which keeps track of the duration of an event. Let's apply it to the `getAll` method as well:

```
@Timed(name = "timerCheck", description = "How much time it takes to load
the Customer list", unit = MetricUnits.MILLISECONDS)
public List<Customer> getAll() {
    return customerRepository.findAll();
}
```

You should be able to retrieve a detailed report about the invocation rates of the preceding method (which includes rate/sec, rate/min rate/5 min, plus statistics quantile metrics). For the sake of brevity, here is an excerpt from it:

```
# TYPE
application:com_packt_quarkus_chapter6_customer_endpoint_timer_check_rate_p
er_second
application:com_packt_quarkus_chapter6_customer_endpoint_timer_check_rate_p
er_second 0.04980015712212517
# TYPE
application:com_packt_quarkus_chapter6_customer_endpoint_timer_check_one_mi
n_rate_per_second
```

ation:com_packt_quarkus_chapter6_customer_endpoint_timer_check_one_mi

```
application:com_packt_quarkus_chapter6_customer_endpoint_timer_check_one_mi
n_rate_per_second 0.09447331054820299
# TYPE
application:com_packt_quarkus_chapter6_customer_endpoint_timer_check_five_m
in_rate_per_second
application:com_packt_quarkus_chapter6_customer_endpoint_timer_check_five_m
in_rate_per_second 0.17214159528501158

. . . .
application:com_packt_quarkus_chapter6_customer_endpoint_timer_check_second
s{quantile="0.999"} 0.004191615
```

On the other hand, if you need just a basic metric that records a single unit of data, you can use the @Gauge annotation:

```
@Gauge(name = "peakOfOrders", unit = MetricUnits.NONE, description =
"Highest number of orders")
public Number highestNumberOfOrders() {
    return orderRepository.countAll();
}
```

The Gauge metric will display the following metric after two requests have landed on the preceding method:

```
# HELP application:com_packt_quarkus_chapter6_order_endpoint_peak_of_orders
Highest number of orders
# TYPE application:com_packt_quarkus_chapter6_order_endpoint_peak_of_orders
gauge
application:com_packt_quarkus_chapter6_order_endpoint_peak_of_orders 2.0
```

After this fast-paced introduction to MicroProfile metrics, let's learn how to document our endpoint resources with OpenAPI and Swagger.

Configuring OpenAPI and the Swagger UI

The OpenAPI specification aims to provide a set of Java interfaces and programming models that can natively produce OpenAPI v3 documents from JAX-RS services. The default OpenAPI implementation in Quarkus provides an out-of-the-box standard documentation for all the exposed services that can be generated through the /openapi endpoint.

Nevertheless, you can augment JAX-RS services even further using specific annotations to provide more insights about the endpoint, its parameters, and the response. Moving on to the code, we will focus on the Chapter06/openapi-swagger example. As you can check from its configuration, we have added the following extension to the project:

```
<dependency>
    <groupId>io.quarkus</groupId>
    <artifactId>quarkus-smallrye-openapi</artifactId>
</dependency>
```

Since we have several REST endpoints available in our project, we can check the generated OpenAPI document at http://localhost:8080/openapi. Here is the (truncated) output for our customer service application:

```
$ curl http://localhost:8080/openapi
---
openapi: 3.0.1
info:
  title: Generated API
  version: "1.0"
paths:
  /customers:
    get:
      responses:
        200:
          description: OK
          content:
            application/json:
              schema:
                type: array
                items:
                  type: object
                  properties:
                    id:
                      format: int64
                      type: integer
                    name:
                      type: string
                    orders:
                      type: array
                      items:
                        type: object
                        properties:
                          id:
                            format: int64
                            type: integer
                          item:
```

```
            type: string
         price:
            format: int64
            type: integer
surname:
   type: string
```

As you can see, with minimal effort we have produced a JSON document that describes the functionalities of our service without requiring direct access to the underlying source code or any other documentation.

Apart from this, the OpenAPI can be used as a foundation for powerful UIs such as **Swagger**, which is a great tool for visualizing and interacting with your APIs. Its UI is automatically generated from your OpenAPI specification.

In order to get rolling with Swagger, you just need to point to `http://localhost:8080/swagger-ui/`. By doing this, you will end up on the Swagger home page:

From there, you can easily test any available operation by expanding it and clicking on the **Try it out** button:

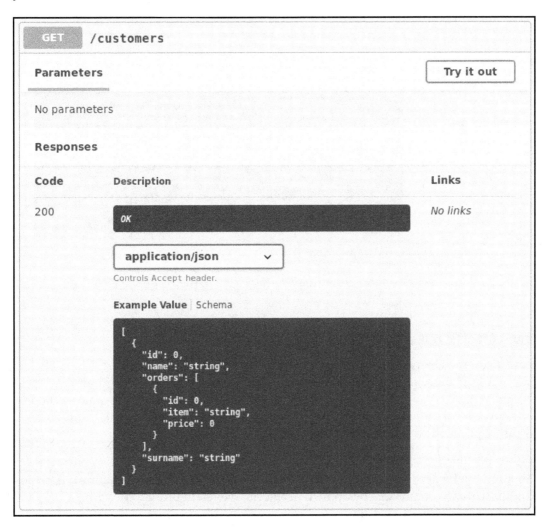

A default Response body will be generated. Adjust it to your needs and click on **Execute**. As a result, you will see the returned value (if any) from our operation in the **Response body** text area:

Optionally, you can click on the **Download** button to save the response locally.

Customizing the output of OpenAPI

According to the OpenAPI specification (`https://swagger.io/specification/`), it is possible to customize the full schema of objects that are returned by the `/openapi` Servlet. This can be done by adding specific annotations to your endpoints classes and methods. Although none of these annotations are mandatory, we will mention some common ones that can improve the readability of your OpenAPI schema.

For example, the `@org.eclipse.microprofile.openapi.annotations.tags.Tag` annotation can be used as a qualifier to describe a group of specific operations related to the endpoint. This annotation can be applied at the class level. In order to describe a single resource method, you can use the `org.eclipse.microprofile.openapi.annotations.Operation` tag, which can be applied at the method level. Then, a description of the operation parameters can be included with the `org.eclipse.microprofile.openapi.annotations.parameters.Parameter` tag. Finally, the `org.eclipse.microprofile.openapi.annotations.responses.APIResponse` tag describes a single response from an API operation. You can attach multiple `APIResponse` annotations to a single method to control the response for each response code.

The following example shows the customization being applied to the `CustomerEndpoint` class in practice:

```
@Tag(name = "OpenAPI Example", description = "Quarkus CRUD Example")
public class CustomerEndpoint {

    @Inject CustomerRepository customerRepository;

    @Operation(operationId = "all", description = "Getting All
      customers")
    @APIResponse(responseCode = "200", description = "Successful
      response.")
    @GET
    public List<Customer> getAll() {
        return customerRepository.findAll();
    }

    @POST
    public Response create( @Parameter(description = "The new
      customer.", required = true) Customer customer) {

        customerRepository.createCustomer(customer);
        return Response.status(201).build();
    }

    @PUT
    public Response update(@Parameter(description = "The customer to
      update.", required = true) Customer customer) {
        customerRepository.updateCustomer(customer);
        return Response.status(204).build();
    }
    @DELETE
    public Response delete(@Parameter(description = "The customer to
      delete.", required = true) @QueryParam("id") Long customerId) {
        customerRepository.deleteCustomer(customerId);
        return Response.status(204).build();
    }

}
```

For the sake of brevity, we have just tagged the `CustomerEndpoint` service with OpenAPI annotations. We leave it to you to update the `OrderEndpoint` service so that you can verify your new skills.

The Eclipse MicroProfile OpenTracing API

Distributed tracing plays a key role in the era of microservices as it lets you trace the flow of a request across different services. In order to accomplish microservice tracing, we can instrument our services to log messages to a distributed tracing server that can collect, store, and display this information in various formats.

The `OpenTracing` specification does not address which distributed system is in charge of collecting the tracing data, but a widely adopted end-to-end open source solution is **Jaeger** (`https://www.jaegertracing.io/`),which fully implements the `OpenTracing` standard.

Let's see OpenTracing in action by switching to the `Chapter06/opentracing` example. First off, in order to use the opentracing extension, the following dependency must be added to your project:

```
<dependency>
  <groupId>io.quarkus</groupId>
  <artifactId>io.quarkus:quarkus-smallrye-opentracing</artifactId>
</dependency>
```

 As a matter of fact, when adding this extension, an implementation of an `io.opentracing.Tracer` object will be made available to your application. This means that all your HTTP requests will be automatically traced.

In terms of configuration, we need to provide some details about the Jaeger endpoint. This can be done either with the `application.properties` file or using environment variables. The following shows how we have configured the `application.properties` file to emit a tracing notification to a Jaeger endpoint running on localhost and listening to port `14268`:

```
quarkus.jaeger.service-name=quarkus-service
quarkus.jaeger.sampler-type=const
quarkus.jaeger.sampler-param=1
quarkus.jaeger.endpoint=http://localhost:14268/api/traces
```

Within the preceding configuration, we have also defined the service name (`quarkus-service`) and the sampler type. In the sampler type definition, " always makes the same decision for all traces. It either samples all the traces (`sampler-param=1`) or none of them (`sampler-param=2`).

Now, we can start the Jaeger service. The simplest way to do this is by running it as a Docker container. The following command will start the `jaegertracing/all-in-one` container image, forwarding the UDP/TCP port of the Docker container to localhost:

```
docker run -e COLLECTOR_ZIPKIN_HTTP_PORT=9411 -p 5775:5775/udp -p
6831:6831/udp -p 6832:6832/udp -p 5778:5778 -p 16686:16686 -p 14268:14268 -
p 9411:9411 jaegertracing/all-in-one:latest
```

Now, we can start using our customer service application and execute some operations with it. Then, we can log into the Jaeger console, which is available at `http://localhost:16686`:

As shown in the preceding screenshot, in the left panel of the Jaeger UI you can see a combo box named **Service**, which contains a list of the services that are available for tracing. You should see in it the default **jaeger query service**, which allows us to trace the query service. Provided that you have configured your Quarkus application to emit notifications, you should be able to see **quarkus-service** enlisted. Select it and then check the next combo box, which is **Operation**. This combo box contains all the operations that have been traced for that particular service. Here is a partial view of the UI that contains the combo box:

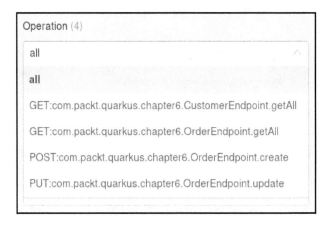

If you select **all**, on the screen you should be able to see all the traces for all the HTTP requests to quarkus-service, as shown in the following screenshot:

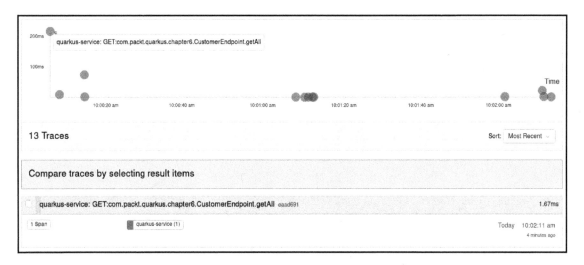

From there, you can choose to gather more details about a single trace by clicking on it. You will see a comprehensive timeline with details such as the execution time, remote caller, and errors reported:

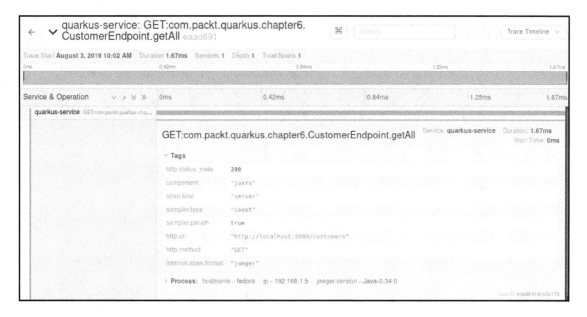

If you want to download and elaborate on the trace file, you can also choose to trace your operation as JSON by selecting **Trace JSON** in the top-right corner.

There are quite a lot of possibilities for tracing your application with Jaeger. We advise referring to `https://www.jaegertracing.io/` if you want to become a ninja at tracing your microservices!

The Eclipse MicroProfile REST Client API

The last MicroProfile extension we will discuss in this chapter is the REST client extension. The goal of this API is to provide you with a type safe way to invoke REST services in a microservice architecture.

Don't confuse the MicroProfile REST client API with the JAX-RS Client API! They implement different standards: the JAX-RS Client API is implemented according to JSR 370 (`https://www.jcp.org/en/jsr/detail?id=370`), while the MicroProfile REST Client API follows the standard specified here: `http://microprofile.io/project/eclipse/microprofile-rest-client`.

In order to learn about the REST client API, we will be using it as a template for the `Chapter06/rest-client` application. This project is nothing but a cut-down version of our customer service, which just contains interfaces instead of service implementations. In terms of configuration, we have added the following dependency to the `pom.xml` file of our `rest-client` project:

```
<dependency>
  <groupId>io.quarkus</groupId>
  <artifactId>quarkus-rest-client</artifactId>
</dependency>
```

Next, we have replaced the concrete service implementations with two interfaces: one named `CustomerEndpointItf` and another named `OrdersEndpointItf`. Here is `CustomerEndpointITf`:

```
@RegisterRestClient
@Path("customers")
@Produces("application/json")
@Consumes("application/json")
public interface CustomerEndpointItf {
    @GET
    List<Customer> getAll();

    @POST
    Response create(Customer customer);

    @PUT
    Response update(Customer customer);

    @DELETE
    Response delete(Long customerId);
}
```

Here is `OrdersEndpointItf`:

```java
@RegisterRestClient
@Path("orders")
@Produces("application/json")
@Consumes("application/json")
public interface OrderEndpointItf {
    @GET
    List<Orders> getAll(@QueryParam("customerId") Long customerId);

    @POST
    @Path("/{customer}")
    Response create(Orders order, @PathParam("customer") Long
     customerId);

    @PUT
    Response update(Orders order);

    @DELETE
    @Path("/{order}")
    Response delete(@PathParam("order") Long orderId);
}
```

Note the `@org.eclipse.microprofile.rest.client.inject.RegisterRestClient`
annotation, which makes the REST client injectable through the CDI using the
`@org.eclipse.microprofile.rest.client.inject.RestClient` annotation. Let's
learn how to do this in practice in the `CustomerEndpoint`:

```java
public class CustomerEndpoint {

    @Inject
    @RestClient
    CustomerEndpointItf customer;

    @GET
    public List<Customer> getAll() {
        return customer.getAll();
    }
    @POST
    public Response create(Customer c) {
        return customer.create(c);
    }
    @PUT
    public Response update(Customer c) {
        return customer.update(c);
    }
    @DELETE
```

```
public Response delete(Long customerId) {
    return customer.delete(customerId);
}

}
```

As you can see, we have replaced the REST client implementation by delegating the execution to the interface we have registered as a REST client. At this point, you may be wondering how the REST client knows about the remote endpoint. That's a good question, and the answer is contained in the `application.properties` file:

```
com.packt.quarkus.chapter6.restclient.CustomerEndpointItf/mp-rest/url=http:
//localhost:8080
com.packt.quarkus.chapter6.restclient.CustomerEndpointItf/mp-
rest/scope=java.inject.Singleton
com.packt.quarkus.chapter6.restclient.OrderEndpointItf/mp-rest/url=http://l
ocalhost:8080
com.packt.quarkus.chapter6.restclient.OrderEndpointItf/mp-
rest/scope=java.inject.Singleton
```

As you can see from the first line, all the requests to the REST client interface will result in a call to the remote endpoint base URL, which is qualified using the following expression:

```
<Fully Qualified REST Client Interface>/mp-rest/url=<Remote REST base URL>
```

Also, the default scope of the REST client interface has been configured as a **singleton**, which instructs Quarkus to instantiate the singleton once, passing its reference to other objects during the injection. Other supported scope values are @Dependent, @ApplicationScoped, and @RequestScoped, the latter being the default one. Check the CDI specifications for more details about the different scopes (http://www.cdi-spec.org/).

In order to run the test, we need an application that returns a list of Customers through the http://localhost:8080/customers endpoint and a list of Orders through the http://localhost:8080/orders endpoint. For this purpose, we can launch any version of our customer service application that implements the preceding endpoints, as follows:

cd Chapter05/hibernate

$ mvn quarkus:dev

Let's go back to our example:

```
cd Chapter06/rest-client
```

Now, we can run the REST Client test with the following command:

```
$ mvn compile test
```

You should see the following output in the console:

```
[INFO] Tests run: 1, Failures: 0, Errors: 0, Skipped: 0, Time elapsed:
3.988 s - in com.packt.quarkus.chapter6.restclient.CustomerEndpointTest
 2019-08-04 19:29:43,592 INFO  [io.quarkus] (main) Quarkus stopped in
0.003s
[INFO] Results:
[INFO] Tests run: 1, Failures: 0, Errors: 0, Skipped: 0
```

This means that you managed to run full CRUD operations against the remote customer endpoint. As proof of this, you should be able to see the SQL statements that were executed on the service console:

```
select
    orders0_.id as id1_1_0_,
    orders0_.customer_id as customer4_1_0_,
    orders0_.item as item2_1_0_,
    orders0_.price as price3_1_0_,
    customer1_.id as id1_0_1_,
    customer1_.name as name2_0_1_,
    customer1_.surname as surname3_0_1_
from
    Orders orders0_
left outer join
    Customer customer1_
        on orders0_.customer_id=customer1_.id
where
    orders0_.id=?
```

Please note that the preceding log requires that you have turned on SQL tracing, as discussed in Chapter 5, *Managing Data Persistence with Quarkus.*

Summary

In this chapter, we took a comprehensive overview of the MicroProfile specification and how to integrate it with Quarkus applications.

We started with an overview of the MicroProfile API and how it fits into the overall picture of cloud-based microservices. Then, we covered the major MicroProfile specifications.

First, we looked at the Health API and how it can report the liveness and readiness of your services. Then, we covered the Fault Tolerance API, which can be used to design resilient services. Next, we discussed the application's telemetry data and how it can be collected using the Metrics API. Another key aspect we covered was documenting of services and tracing the flow of requests, which can be carried out using the OpenAPI and tracing specifications. Finally, we learned how to create REST clients to simplify our interaction with remote services.

By now, you should have a clear picture of how to design a complete Quarkus Enterprise application, although we still haven't mastered a key aspect: Quarkus application security. That's what we are going to learn about in the next chapter.

Securing Applications

Security is a key requirement of every enterprise system. In this chapter, we will learn how to effectively secure Quarkus services using a variety of approaches. The first approach we will put into practice embeds the security layer within our service. This can still be considered a valid solution for rapid application development and testing. On the other hand, when moving our service into production, we need to avoid this extreme centralization. Therefore, the next strategy we will learn about is how the Quarkus service can connect to a distributed security system such as Keycloak. The last topic in this chapter is about encrypting the HTTP channel through some easy configuration steps.

In this chapter, we will cover the following topics:

- Securing our customer service
- Securing Quarkus services with Elytron
- Securing Quarkus services with Keycloak
- Securing Quarkus services with MicroProfile JWT
- Using HTTPS with Quarkus

Technical requirements

You can find the source code for the project in this chapter on GitHub at `https://github.com/PacktPublishing/Hands-On-Cloud-Native-Applications-with-Java-and-Quarkus/tree/master/Chapter07`.

Securing our customer service

The Quarkus security infrastructure derives from the standard **Java Enterprise Edition (Java EE)** specification, which is based on a simple role-based security model. By using that, you can specify your security constraints through annotations and configuration files.

In terms of Java annotations, the following ones can be used to specify security constraints that can be applied either on a single method or on a class:

- `@javax.annotation.security.RolesAllowed`: This is the most common annotation as it specifies one or more roles that have been authorized to invoke a certain method or class.
- `@javax.annotation.security.RunAs`: This annotation assigns a role dynamically during the invocation of a method or class. It can be a handy option if we need to temporarily allow the execution of some methods.
- `@javax.annotation.security.PermitAll`: This annotation allows us to release security constraints from methods. It can be useful in some scenarios where you haven't identified which role will be entitled to invoke a method.
- `@javax.annotation.security.DenyAll`: This annotation is the exact opposite of `@PermitAll` as it denies access to a method or class that bears this annotation.

To keep things simple, we will define a simple security policy for our customer service application. This will include two roles:

- **User role**: This role will be entitled to perform *read-only* operations, such as querying the `Customer` list.
- **Admin role**: This role will be entitled to perform all the available operations, including create, update, and delete.

The following is the code for our `CustomerEndpoint` class, which has been decorated with the `@RolesAllowed` security annotation:

```
public class CustomerEndpoint {

    @Inject CustomerRepository customerRepository;

    @GET
    @RolesAllowed("user")
    public List<Customer> getAll() {
        return customerRepository.findAll();
    }

    @POST
```

```
@RolesAllowed("admin")
public Response create(Customer customer) {

    customerRepository.createCustomer(customer);
    return Response.status(201).build();

}


@PUT
@RolesAllowed("admin")
public Response update(Customer customer) {
    customerRepository.updateCustomer(customer);
    return Response.status(204).build();
}
@DELETE
@RolesAllowed("admin")
public Response delete(@QueryParam("id") Long customerId) {
    customerRepository.deleteCustomer(customerId);
    return Response.status(204).build();
}

}
```

For the sake of brevity, we won't include the OrderEndpoint class here, which has been updated in the same way in order to secure read methods with the **user** role and the write methods with the **admin** role.

Having defined our security policy, we can now choose which security provider will be applied to our service. This will require us to add the right settings in application.properties and include the dependencies in our project's pom.xml file.

We will start with the Elytron security provider, which doesn't require us to install any external applications or tools to secure our service.

Securing Quarkus services with Elytron

Elytron is a security framework that has been created to unify the security aspects of WildFly and JBoss' **Enterprise Application Platform** (**EAP**). It comes as a consequence that this framework has been initially designed for monolithic applications in order to provide coverage on every aspect of security. What is the advantage of using Elytron in a container-ready native platform such as Quarkus?

Although it may look like an oversimplified solution to securing your assets, it can prove to be advantageous when developing or testing applications that include security roles. Out of the box, Quarkus provides an implementation of a **file-based security realm** in order to provide **role-based access control** (**RBAC**) to our basic endpoints with minimal configuration requirements.

In terms of libraries, at the time of writing this book, there are three available Elytron extensions we can use to secure our applications:

- `quarkus-elytron-security-properties-file`: Provides support for basic authentication via property files.
- `quarkus-elytron-security-jdbc`: Provides support for database authentication via JDBC.
- `quarkus-elytron-security-oauth2`: Provides support for OAuth2 authentication. This extension may be deprecated in future versions of Quarkus and replaced by a reactive Vert.x version.

Since our customer application already uses a database as a backend, we will show you how to use database authentication. Please check out the source code in the `Chapter07/elytron-demo` folder before you move on.

As shown in the `pom.xml` file, we have added the following extension to our project:

```
<dependency>
  <groupId>io.quarkus</groupId>
  <artifactId>quarkus-elytron-security-jdbc</artifactId>
</dependency>
```

To configure authentication, we need to specify which table contains the list of users and roles. We also need to add a couple of users with different roles. For this purpose, we have included the following SQL statements in the `import.sql` script, which are located in the `src/main/resources` folder:

```
CREATE TABLE quarkus_user (
    id INT,
    username VARCHAR(255),
    password VARCHAR(255),
    role VARCHAR(255)
);
INSERT INTO quarkus_user (id, username, password, role) VALUES (1, 'admin',
'password123', 'admin');
INSERT INTO quarkus_user (id, username, password, role) VALUES (2,
'frank','password123', 'user');
```

Now, within the `application.properties` file, we need to activate JDBC authentication by providing some basic configuration parameters for it. Here is the list of properties we have added:

```
quarkus.security.jdbc.enabled=true
quarkus.security.jdbc.principal-query.sql=SELECT u.password, u.role FROM
quarkus_user u WHERE u.username=?
quarkus.security.jdbc.principal-query.clear-password-mapper.enabled=true
quarkus.security.jdbc.principal-query.clear-password-mapper.password-
index=1
quarkus.security.jdbc.principal-query.attribute-mappings.0.index=2
quarkus.security.jdbc.principal-query.attribute-mappings.0.to=groups
```

Let's quickly discuss these properties:

- The `quarkus.security.jdbc.enabled` property, when set to true, enables JDBC authentication.
- The `quarkus.security.jdbc.principal-query.sql` property is used to specify the SQL statements that will check for a valid username/password combination.
- The `quarkus.security.jdbc.principal-query.clear-password-mapper.enabled` property, when set to true, configures a mapper that maps a column that's returned from a SQL query to a clear password key type.
- The `quarkus.security.jdbc.principal-query.clear-password-mapper.password-index` property sets the column index from the clear text authentication query.
- Finally, `quarkus.security.jdbc.principal-query.attribute-mappings.0.index` and `quarkus.security.jdbc.principal-query.attribute-mappings.0.to` are used to bind the second field in the authentication query (`index=2`) with the principal's role (groups).

That's all you need to secure your service using the Elytron security domain. With all the pieces in the right place, we will be using a test class that verifies authentication against the REST endpoints.

Creating a test class that performs basic authentication

Our test class needs to be adjusted so that it can fit the new secured scenario. In practice, we need to send the header files with the user's credentials, along with the HTTP request, with them to authorize the service's execution. Thanks to the Fluent RestAssured API, it is fairly easy to plug the auth() method into our HTTP request, as shown in the following code:

```
@Test
public void testCustomerService() {
    // Test GET for Customer size
    given()
            .auth()
            .preemptive()
            .basic("frank", "password123")
            .when().get("/customers")
            .then()
            .statusCode(200)
            .body("$.size()", is(2));


    JsonObject objOrder = Json.createObjectBuilder()
            .add("item", "bike")
            .add("price", new Long(100))
            .build();


    // Test POST Order for Customer #1
    given()
            .auth()
            .preemptive()
            .basic("admin", "password123")
            .contentType("application/json")
            .body(objOrder.toString())
            .when()
            .post("/orders/1")
            .then()
            .statusCode(201);

    // Create new JSON for Order #1
    objOrder = Json.createObjectBuilder()
            .add("id", new Long(1))
            .add("item", "mountain bike")
            .add("price", new Long(100))
            .build();
```

```
        // Test UPDATE Order #1
        given()
                .auth()
                .preemptive()
                .basic("admin", "password123")
                .contentType("application/json")
                .body(objOrder.toString())
                .when()
                .put("/orders")
                .then()
                .statusCode(204);

        // Test GET for Order #1
        given()
                .auth()
                .preemptive()
                .basic("admin", "password123")
                .when().get("/orders?customerId=1")
                .then()
                .statusCode(200)
                .body(containsString("mountain bike"));

        // Test DELETE Order #1
        given()
                .auth()
                .preemptive()
                .basic("admin", "password123")
                .when().delete("/orders/1")
                .then()
                .statusCode(204);


    }
```

Please note that we have to use a preemptive basic authentication. This means that the authentication details are sent in the request header immediately, regardless of whether the server has already challenged the authentication. Without that, the current Vert.x implementation in Quarkus would return an unauthorized response.

Assuming that the PostgreSQL database has been started, our test class is ready to be executed:

```
mvn compile test
```

You should see that all of the CRUD operations have completed successfully:

```
[INFO] Tests run: 1, Failures: 0, Errors: 0, Skipped: 0, Time elapsed:
5.799 s - in com.packt.quarkus.chapter7.CustomerEndpointTest
 2019-08-16 15:30:12,281 INFO  [io.quarkus] (main) Quarkus stopped in
0.012s
[INFO]
[INFO] Results:
[INFO]
[INFO] Tests run: 1, Failures: 0, Errors: 0, Skipped: 0
```

In the next section, we will cover how to use Keycloak to leverage OpenID (`https://openid.net/`) security standards in our application.

Securing Quarkus services with Keycloak

Keycloak (`https://www.keycloak.org/`) is an open source access management solution that builds on top of the WildFly application server. You can adopt it in your architecture to leverage a wide variety of features, such as the following:

- **Client adapters**
- **Single Sign-On** (SSO)
- **Identity management and social login**
- **Standard protocols (OpenID Connect or SAML)**
- **A rich admin console**
- **A user account management console**

Thanks to these features and the ability to connect to existing identity standards, Keycloak has become a de facto standard for many large organizations. A supported version of it, known as **Red Hat Single Sign-On** (**RH-SSO**: `https://access.redhat.com/products/red-hat-single-sign-on`), is also available for enterprise customers.

Once installed, Keycloak acts as the main security endpoint for the applications in your network. Therefore, your applications don't have to add login forms to authenticate users and store their credentials. Instead, applications are configured to point to Keycloak, which supports protocol standards such as OpenID or SAML to secure your endpoints.

In short, client applications will be redirected from their domain to Keycloak's identity server, where they exhibit their credentials. This way, your services are completely isolated from your security policies and from your user's credentials. Instead, services are granted a digitally signed identity token or assertion. These tokens hold identity information (such as name or email address) but can also hold information about roles that are authorized to perform business operations. In the next section, we will learn how to configure Keycloak so that we can issue tokens that can be used to access our example customer service.

Adding a Keycloak extension to our service

Within the `Chapter07/keycloak-demo` folder, you will find another version of our customer service application that uses Keycloak to secure the REST endpoints. To use Keycloak authorization and the OpenID extension, we have included the following set of dependencies in the `pom.xml` file:

```
<dependency>
    <groupId>io.quarkus</groupId>
    <artifactId>quarkus-keycloak-authorization</artifactId>
</dependency>
<dependency>
    <groupId>io.quarkus</groupId>
    <artifactId>quarkus-oidc</artifactId>
</dependency>
```

Now that all the required libraries are in place, let's learn how to install Keycloak Identity Server and load a security realm in it.

Setting up Keycloak

In this section, we will be using Docker to quickly take the reins of Keycloak. First, we need to pull the Keycloak image and start a container instance. The following command will start the Keycloak Server in the background and choose `8180` as the HTTP port and expose the host and port locally:

```
docker run --rm \
    --name keycloak \
    -e KEYCLOAK_USER=admin \
    -e KEYCLOAK_PASSWORD=admin \
    -p 8180:8180 \
    -it quay.io/keycloak/keycloak:7.0.1 \
    -b 0.0.0.0 \
```

```
-Djboss.http.port=8180 \
-Dkeycloak.profile.feature.upload_scripts=enabled
```

In the console, you should see that the server has managed to start successfully:

```
10:33:15,519 INFO  [org.jboss.as] (Controller Boot Thread) WFLYSRV0060:
Http management interface listening on http://127.0.0.1:9990/management
 10:33:15,519 INFO  [org.jboss.as] (Controller Boot Thread) WFLYSRV0051:
Admin console listening on http://127.0.0.1:9990
 10:33:15,519 INFO  [org.jboss.as] (Controller Boot Thread) WFLYSRV0025:
Keycloak 6.0.1 (WildFly Core 8.0.0.Final) started in 15991ms - Started 672
of 937 services (652 services are lazy, passive or on-demand)
```

Now that Keycloak is up and running, let's load a realm, which contains a valid security configuration that we will apply to our service.

Defining the security realm

A key aspect of Keycloak configuration is the security realm, which contains all the configuration (user, roles, client policies, and many others) that are pertinent to one security context. When you start Keycloak for the first time, it will contain just one realm: the **master** realm. This is the top level in the hierarchy of realms. You shouldn't use this realm to configure users and services in your organization. Instead, consider using the master realm for administrators who are in charge of defining the other realms in your organization.

Our GitHub repository for this chapter contains an application realm named **Quarkus realm** that will be useful for our purposes. We will show you how to import it and then we will walk through its configuration so that you will be able to create new realms based on this template. Let's proceed with the following steps:

1. Start by connecting to the Keycloak console, which is available at `http://localhost:8180`. An authentication challenge will be displayed. Log in with `admin/admin`:

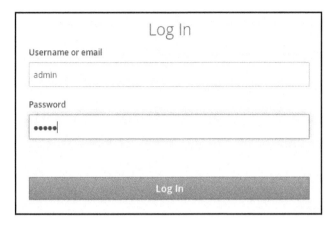

2. Now, from the top-left panel, choose to add a new realm, as shown in the following screenshot:

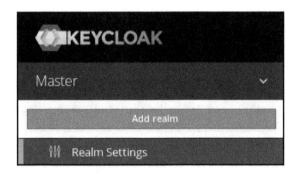

3. Choose to **Import** a realm and point to the JSON file (quarkus-realm.json) that contains an export of Quarkus' realm:

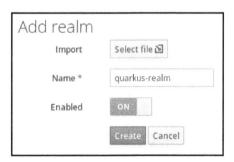

4. Click on **Create** to continue. Now, let's look at a short overview of the realm's options.

Within the realm settings window, you will be able to define some core settings, such as the domain name, and your login settings, predefine your tokens' lifespan and timeouts, and more:

For the purpose of our learning path, we will not vary these settings. In the realm panel, you will be able to verify that we have included the same roles (**admin** and **user**) so that they match our existing security constraints:

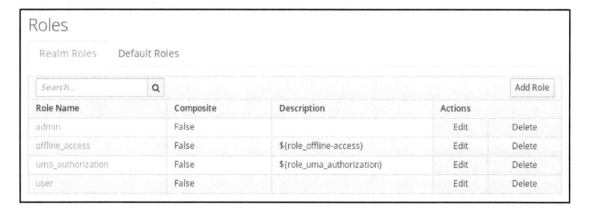

Here, we have recreated the same list of users that we tested in our file-based Elytron domain:

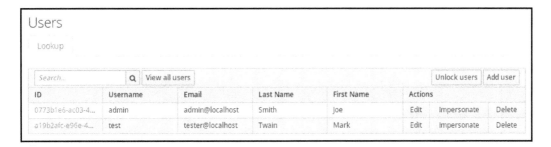

From within the **Role Mappings** tab, you can check that the **test** user is a member of the **user** role:

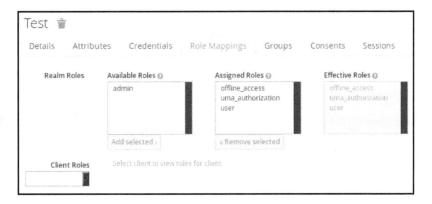

On the other hand, the **admin** user will be assigned to both the **admin** and the **user** role:

Now that we've looked at the users and roles, let's discuss a key aspect of the realm's client configuration, which is displayed in the following UI:

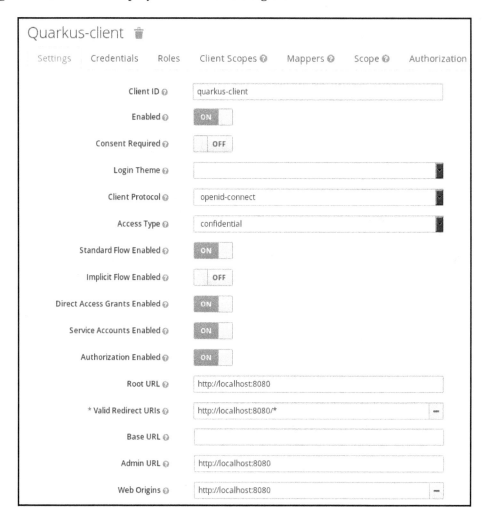

Let's look at some of the key aspects of the client configuration. First and foremost, we have to define the client protocol. There are two types of client authentication protocols:

- **OpenID Connect** (**OIDC**) is an authentication system where the client requests an access token that's used to call other services on behalf of the authenticated user.
- **SAML** authentication requires Keycloak to provide an SSO for the users of your organization.

For our needs, OIDC token-based authentication is what we need to grant access to our services. We also need to select whether we will be using the standard flow or the implicit flow for authentication.

The default option (**Standard Flow Enabled**) involves an initial browser redirection to/from the OIDC provider (Keycloak) for user authentication and consent. Then, a second back-channel request is needed to retrieve the ID token. This flow offers optimal security since tokens aren't revealed to the browser and the client can be safely authenticated.

Let's depict this flow in the form of a sequence diagram:

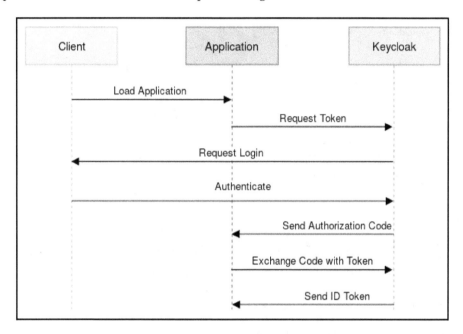

To provide a better performance, Keycloak also supports **implicit flows**, which occur when the access token is sent immediately after successful authentication. Although this option may scale better (since there is no additional request to exchange the code for tokens), you will be in charge of monitoring when the token expires so that you can issue a fresh one.

Since we've chosen to use the standard flow, we will specify an appropriate **Valid Redirect URI**, which needs to be set to the default HTTP port of our application running on Quarkus.

For the **Access Type**, we have configured it to be **confidential**, which requires client applications to provide a secret in order to obtain an ID token. When you set the **Access Type** to **confidential**, you will be able to choose the **Client Authenticator** from the **Credentials** tab, which defines the type of credential you will use for your client and its secret. The secret that's defined for this client ID is **mysecret**, as shown in the following screenshot:

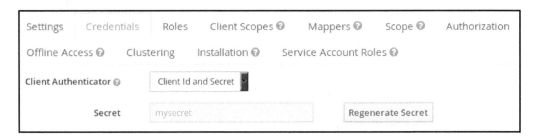

If you want to change the default secret, just click on the **Regenerate Secret** button and update your client applications accordingly.

Now that we have configured Keycloak, we will use this realm to execute a test using a bearer token authentication. However, before that, we will configure our Quarkus service accordingly.

Configuring Quarkus for Keycloak

Believe it or not, once we have configured the identity server, we don't have much work to do in our Quarkus application. We only need to provide the Keycloak URL and client settings to the `application.properties` configuration file of our application:

```
keycloak.url=http://localhost:8180

quarkus.oidc.enabled=true
quarkus.oidc.auth-server-url=${keycloak.url}/auth/realms/quarkus-realm
quarkus.oidc.client-id=quarkus-client
quarkus.oidc.credentials.secret=mysecret# Enable Policy Enforcement
quarkus.keycloak.policy-enforcer.enable=true

quarkus.http.cors=true
```

In the preceding configuration, we have provided the mandatory settings to connect to the Keycloak Identity Server. We have also added a property named `keycloak.url` to define Keycloak's IP address and port. In the following table, we have added some details about each parameter:

Parameter	Description
`quarkus.oidc.enabled`	When set to true, the OIDC extension will be enabled.
`quarkus.oidc.auth-server-url`	The root URL where Keycloak authenticates client requests.
`quarkus.oidc.client-id`	The client ID.
`quarkus.oidc.credentials.secret`	The client secret.
`quarkus.keycloak.policy-enforcer.enable`	By enabling the policy enforcer, requests are not allowed in, although there is no policy associated with that resource.

Other than this, if you are planning to run Keycloak on a different machine from your application, it is recommended to enable HTTP CORS so that you can access Keycloak across domain boundaries (check out `Chapter 5`, *Managing Data Persistence with Quarkus*, for more details about this).

Now, let's dive into the test class that will be used to perform CRUD operations that have been authorized through Keycloak's Identity Server.

Coding the test class

Our test class is composed of two blocks. In the first block, we retrieve a token for the `test` user and the `admin` user. Then, we use both tokens to test the application. More specifically, the `test` token, which belongs to the user role, will be used for GET requests. On the other hand, the `admin` token will be used to authorize POST, PUT, and DELETE requests.

Here is the first block of the test class:

```
@ConfigProperty(name = "keycloak.url")
String keycloakURL;

    @Test
    public void testHelloEndpoint() {

        RestAssured.baseURI = keycloakURL;
        Response response = given().urlEncodingEnabled(true)
                .auth().preemptive().basic("quarkus-client",
                  "mysecret")
                .param("grant_type", "password")
                .param("client_id", "quarkus-client")
                .param("username", "test")
                .param("password", "test")
                .header("Accept", ContentType.JSON.getAcceptHeader())
                .post("/auth/realms/quarkus-realm/protocol/openid-
                  connect/token")
                .then().statusCode(200).extract()
                .response();

        JsonReader jsonReader = Json.createReader(new
          StringReader(response.getBody().asString()));
        JsonObject object = jsonReader.readObject();
        String userToken = object.getString("access_token");

        response = given().urlEncodingEnabled(true)
                .auth().preemptive().basic("quarkus-client",
                  "mysecret")
                .param("grant_type", "password")
                .param("client_id", "quarkus-client")
                .param("username", "admin")
                .param("password", "test")
                .header("Accept", ContentType.JSON.getAcceptHeader())
                .post("/auth/realms/quarkus-realm/protocol/openid-
                  connect/token")
                .then().statusCode(200).extract()
                .response();

        jsonReader = Json.createReader(new
          StringReader(response.getBody().asString()));
        object = jsonReader.readObject();
        String adminToken = object.getString("access_token");

        // Test CRUD Methods here

    }
```

This code issues a POST request against the auth URL of our Keycloak realm. The request contains the username and password, along with the client's ID (quarkus_client) and its secret (mysecret) as parameters. The RESTAssured API verifies that a status code of 200 is returned and returns the response object. Then, we extracted the token contained in the JSON response, which is under the access_token key.

If you want to debug the low-level details of your token claim, you can use a tool such as curl to inspect the response returned by Keycloak. For example, if you are going to request a token for the test user, then here is a plain curl command that will do the job:

```
curl -X POST
http://localhost:8180/auth/realms/quarkus-realm/protocol/openid-connect/tok
en \
    --user quarkus-client:mysecret \
    -H 'content-type: application/x-www-form-urlencoded' \
    -d 'username=test&password=test&grant_type=password'
```

In the second block of code, we access our service by including the user's token in each REST call. We do this using the oauth2 method:

```
RestAssured.baseURI = "http://localhost:8081";
given().auth().preemptive()
        .oauth2(userToken)
        .when().get("/customers")
        .then()
        .statusCode(200)
        .body("$.size()", is(2));


JsonObject objOrder = Json.createObjectBuilder()
        .add("item", "bike")
        .add("price", new Long(100))
        .build();

// Test POST Order for Customer #1

given().auth()
        .oauth2(adminToken)
        .contentType("application/json")
        .body(objOrder.toString())
        .when()
        .post("/orders/1")
        .then()
        .statusCode(201);

// Create new JSON for Order #1
objOrder = Json.createObjectBuilder()
```

```
            .add("id", new Long(1))
            .add("item", "mountain bike")
            .add("price", new Long(100))
            .build();

// Test UPDATE Order #1
given().auth()
        .oauth2(adminToken)
        .contentType("application/json")
        .body(objOrder.toString())
        .when()
        .put("/orders")
        .then()
        .statusCode(204);

// Test GET for Order #1
given().auth()
        .oauth2(adminToken)
        .when().get("/orders?customerId=1")
        .then()
        .statusCode(200)
        .body(containsString("mountain bike"));

// Test DELETE Order #1
given().auth()
        .oauth2(adminToken)
        .when().delete("/orders/1")
        .then()
        .statusCode(204);
```

The test can be executed will the following command:

```
$ mvn compile test
```

You should expect it to complete successfully, as follows:

```
[INFO] Tests run: 1, Failures: 0, Errors: 0, Skipped: 0, Time elapsed: 6.84
s - in com.packt.quarkus.chapter7.CustomerEndpointTest
2019-08-24 12:28:28,056 INFO  [io.quarkus] (main) Quarkus stopped in 0.011s
[INFO]
[INFO] Results:
[INFO]
[INFO] Tests run: 1, Failures: 0, Errors: 0, Skipped: 0
```

Congratulations! You have just managed to set up an enterprise-grade security infrastructure for your service.

Gathering principal and role information at runtime

Before moving on to the next authentication schema, it's worth noting that you can determine the principal name and roles at runtime by injecting the SecurityIdentity interface that represents the currently logged-in user. In this short excerpt, we will learn how to retrieve and log the user that's connected, the name/surname they used to register, and the set of roles they are entitled to:

```
@Inject SecurityIdentity securityContext;
@Inject CustomerRepository customerRepository;

@GET
@RolesAllowed("user")
public List<Customer> getAll() {

    LOGGER.info("Connected with User
      "+securityContext.getPrincipal().getName());
    Iterator<String> roles = securityContext.getRoles().iterator();
    while (roles.hasNext()) {
       LOGGER.info("Role: "+roles.next());
    }
    return customerRepository.findAll();
}
```

In this case, when accessing the list of customers, the service will log the following information:

```
Connected with User test
Role: offline_access
Role: uma_authorization
Role: user
```

You can check all the available methods in the SecurityIdentity interface by having a look at its source code, which is available at https://github.com/quarkusio/quarkus-security/blob/master/src/main/java/io/quarkus/security/identity/SecurityIdentity.java.

Securing Quarkus services with MicroProfile JWT

In the previous example, we covered how to use Keycloak to authenticate and authorize requests using a bearer token. A bearer token alone, however, is a simplified security schema since it's based on exchanging a potentially arbitrary string.

Any client in possession of a valid bearer token can use it to get access to the associated resources without demonstrating his/her identity, which can only be verified with a cryptographic key. In order to fill this gap, we will learn how to use **JSON Web Tokens** (**JWTs**), an encoding standard for tokens, using a JSON data payload that can be signed and encrypted. A JWT includes the following sections:

- **Header**: This is a Base64-encoded string and consists of two parts: the type of the token, which is JWT, and the hashing algorithm being used, such as HMAC SHA256 or RSA. Here is a sample decoded header JWT:

```
HEADER: ALGORITHM & TOKEN TYPE

{
  "alg": "RS256",
  "typ": "JWT",
  "kid": "uio51ZiUOm7_QgRHI4X9jpEqeVCwLp_zFL91T1byNDw"
}
```

- **Payload**: This is also a Base64-encoded string that contains claims. Claims are statements about an entity (user or group) and additional metadata. Here is a sample payload that's been returned to our service:

PAYLOAD: DATA

```
{
  "jti": "4b3a73df-df09-43fe-a7ae-61f779b12e35",
  "exp": 1566654148,
  "nbf": 0,
  "iat": 1566653848,
  "iss": "http://localhost:8180/auth/realms/quarkus-
realm",
  "aud": "account",
  "sub": "a19b2afc-e96e-4939-82bf-aa4b589de136",
  "typ": "Bearer",
  "azp": "quarkus-client",
  "auth_time": 0,
  "session_state": "5984834c-7b6b-49a0-a84e-
ec711f9cf08a",
  "acr": "1",
  "allowed-origins": [
    "http://localhost:8080"
  ],
  "realm_access": {
    "roles": [
      "offline_access",
      "uma_authorization",
      "user"
    ]
  },
  "resource_access": {
    "account": {
      "roles": [
        "manage-account",
        "manage-account-links",
        "view-profile"
      ]
    }
  },
  "scope": "email profile",
  "email_verified": false,
  "name": "Mark Twain",
  "groups": [
    "offline_access",
    "uma_authorization",
    "user"
  ],
  "preferred_username": "test",
  "given_name": "Mark",
  "family_name": "Twain",
  "email": "tester@localhost"
}
```

- **Signature**: The signature is used to verify that the message wasn't altered along the way. In the case of tokens that have been signed with a private key, it can also assert that the sender of the JWT is who they say they are:

The JWT token can also be provided by Keycloak, so we don't have to change our realm configuration to use it with JWT. On the other hand, we had to include the **groups claim** so that the JWT token will map the token subject's group memberships to the application-level roles defined in the services.

This information has been included in our realm (in the **Mappers** section of our client configuration) through the **Token Claim Name** field:

Now, let's configure our service so that it can use this authentication schema.

Configuring our service to use JWT

Our proof of concept project can be located in the `Chapter07/jwt-demo` folder. We recommend that you import it into your IDE to compare it with the other projects in this chapter.

First off, we have replaced the Keycloak authorization and the OpenID extension with the `quarkus-smallrye-jwt` extension:

```
<dependency>
  <groupId>io.quarkus</groupId>
  <artifactId>quarkus-smallrye-jwt</artifactId>
</dependency>
```

Then, we included a different set of properties for our project. The following is the code for the `application.properties` configuration file, which targets the same Keycloak Server and provides details about the public key location and authentication mechanism:

```
keycloak.url=http://localhost:8180

# MP-JWT Config
mp.jwt.verify.publickey.location=${keycloak.url}/auth/realms/quarkus-
realm/protocol/openid-connect/certs
mp.jwt.verify.issuer=${keycloak.url}/auth/realms/quarkus-realm
quarkus.smallrye-jwt.realmName=quarkus-realm
```

The following table provides a brief description of each property:

Parameter	Description
`mp.jwt.verify.publickey.location`	The location where the provider's public key is stored. It can be a relative path or a URL.
`mp.jwt.verify.issuer`	Specifies the value of the **iss** (short for **issuer**) claim of the JWT that the server will accept as valid.
`quarkus.smallrye-jwt.realmName`	The security realm that's used for authentication.

Now, we are ready to execute our test class using the JWT authentication mechanism.

Running our test

Our `CustomerEndpointTest` class contains the same code we used to verify the Keycloak authentication. Behind the scenes, however, it will execute the following steps:

1. Request the access token.
2. Validate the access token fields.
3. Perform signature verification using the realm's RSA public key, which is available at the location defined in the `mp.jwt.verify.publickey.location` system property.

The test can be executed with the following command:

```
$ mvn compile test
```

You should see that it completes successfully, as follows:

```
 [INFO] Tests run: 1, Failures: 0, Errors: 0, Skipped: 0, Time elapsed:
 6.463 s - in com.packt.quarkus.chapter7.CustomerEndpointTest
 2019-08-24 15:37:29,879 INFO  [io.quarkus] (main) Quarkus stopped in 0.006s
 [INFO]
 [INFO] Results:
 [INFO]
 [INFO] Tests run: 1, Failures: 0, Errors: 0, Skipped: 0
```

As for pure Keycloak authentication, let's learn how to gather more information from the JWT context.

Injecting JWT claims and token information

To manage the information contained in the JWT programmatically, we can inject the relevant API into our services. The main class, `org.eclipse.microprofile.jwt.JsonWebToken`, can be injected plainly with the following command:

```
@Inject
JsonWebToken jwt;
```

This class provides methods that we can use to retrieve the token itself, its subject, and the claims contained in the token. More details can be found in the source code, which is available at https://github.com/eclipse/microprofile-jwt-auth/blob/master/api/src/main/java/org/eclipse/microprofile/jwt/JsonWebToken.java.

On the other hand, a shortcut for retrieving a specific claim can be done through the `@Claim` annotation, which includes its `standard` attribute and the name of the `Claim`. Use the following code to inject the groups and the username contained in the token's claim:

```
@Inject
@Claim(standard = Claims.groups)
Optional<JsonString> groups;

@Inject
@Claim(standard = Claims.preferred_username)
Optional<JsonString> currentUsername;
```

That was our last topic on Keycloak for this chapter. Now, let's dissect one more security topic, which is about using SSL for HTTP communication.

Using HTTPS with Quarkus

The last section of this chapter is dedicated to encrypting the HTTP communication in Quarkus. In order to do that, you need to provide a valid (either self-signed or signed by a CA) Keystore or PEM certificate in your configuration.

First, let's learn how to generate a self-signed PEM key and certificate pair. The simplest way to do this is by using the OpenSSL tool, as follows:

```
$ openssl req -newkey rsa:2048 -new -nodes -x509 -days 3650 -keyout
key.pem -out cert.pem
```

The preceding command will generate a certificate named `cert.pem` and a related key file named `key.pem` in the current directory. Next, configure the filesystem path to your certificate and the key file in your `application.properties`:

```
quarkus.http.ssl.certificate.file=/path/cert.pem
quarkus.http.ssl.certificate.key-file=/path/key.pem
```

On the other hand, you can also generate and use a Keystore that already contains a default entry with a certificate. You can generate it using the `keytool` utility and provide a password for it:

```
$ keytool -genkey -keyalg RSA -alias quarkus -keystore keystore.jks -
storepass password -validity 365 -keysize 2048

  Enter key password for <quarkus>
      (RETURN if same as keystore password):
```

In our case, the only file that will be created will be `keystore.jks`; we can include it in our configuration as follows:

```
quarkus.http.ssl.certificate.key-store-file=/path/keystore.jks
quarkus.http.ssl.certificate.key-store-password=password
```

Finally, we can specify the port that's used by the Undertow server to bind the HTTPS protocol:

```
quarkus.http.ssl-port=8443
```

As a proof of concept, you can build and run the application contained in `Chapter07/https` to verify that it can be accessed through the SSL port:

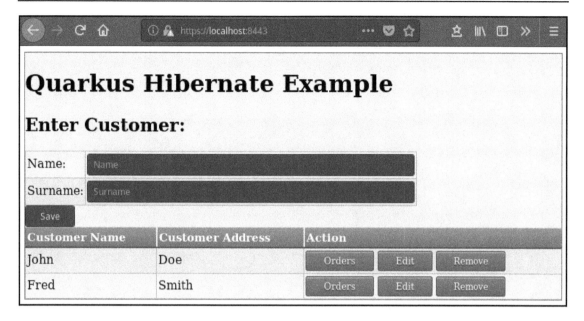

The warning you can see in the browser's bar simply means that the SSL certificate that's being used isn't being issued by a trusted authority.

In this section, we have covered the basic configuration steps that we need to follow in order to secure our application at the transport level. Now, we don't communicate with our customer service through a clear text channel; instead, we use a **Secure Sockets Layer** (**SSL**) to secure our connection.

Summary

We started this chapter by discussing the security policies that can be applied to Quarkus services. Out of the box, you can provide file-based security authentication and authorization by using the Elytron extension. Then, we took a closer look at Keycloak, which can be used to provide enterprise-grade security standards by supporting the OpenID standards. We covered a basic example using a bearer token and a more complex one using a digitally signed token, both in compliance with the JWT specification. Finally, we discovered how to generate and configure certificates to secure access to our Quarkus endpoints using HTTPS.

In the next chapter, we will cover some advanced tactics that can improve the untapped potential of Quarkus services!

3
Section 3: Advanced Development Tactics

In this section, we will cover advanced configuration concepts. Then, we will learn how to implement reactive and non-blocking APIs with Vert.x and how to build a streaming platform on top of that using Apache Kafka and ActiveMQ.

This section includes the following chapters:

- Chapter 8, *Advanced Application Development*
- Chapter 9, *Unifying Imperative and Reactive*
- Chapter 10, *Reactive Messaging with Quarkus*

Advanced Application Development

8

In this chapter, we will explore some advanced features of Quarkus that will help you design and code cutting-edge Quarkus applications. The topics we will learn about will cover different areas of Quarkus API, ranging from advanced configuration options to controlling the life cycle of a Quarkus application and firing time-based events using the Quarkus scheduler.

By the end of this chapter, you will be able to leverage the following advanced features:

- Using advanced MicroProfile configuration options
- Controlling the life cycle events of your services
- Scheduling periodic tasks in your services

Technical requirements

You can find the source code for the project in this chapter on GitHub at `https://github. com/PacktPublishing/Hands-On-Cloud-Native-Applications-with-Java-and-Quarkus/ tree/master/Chapter08`.

Using advanced configuration options

As we have already learned, Quarkus relies on the MicroProfile Config specification to inject configuration properties into our application. So far, we have used the default configuration file (named `application.properties`) to provide initial values for the application's initial settings.

```
@Inject
@ConfigProperty(name="tempFileName", defaultValue="file.tmp")
String fileName;
```

In the preceding code, we are injecting an application property into the `fileName` variable. Note that property names should be carefully planned since Quarkus ships with an extensive set of system properties that can be used to manage its environment. Luckily, you don't need to have your documentation at hand to check for all the available system properties. As a matter of fact, you can use Maven's `generate-config` command to list all the built-in system properties, based on the extensions that you have currently installed:

mvn quarkus:generate-config

This command will create a file named `application.properties.example` under the `src/main/resources` folder. If you open this file, you will see that it contains a commented list of all the available configuration options, which are located under the `quarkus` namespace. Here is a brief excerpt of it:

```
# The name of the application.
# If not set, defaults to the name of the project.
#
#quarkus.application.name=

# The version of the application.
# If not set, defaults to the version of the project
#
#quarkus.application.version=
```

As a side note, you can choose a different filename for `generate-command` by adding the `-Dfile=<filename>` option.

In the upcoming sections, we will learn about some advanced configuration drills using the examples located in the `Chapter08/advanced-config` folder of this book's GitHub repository as references. We recommend importing the project into your IDE before you move on.

Multiple configuration sources

The `application.properties` file is not the only option when it comes to setting application properties. As per MicroProfile's Config specification, you can also use the following:

- **Java system properties**: Java system properties can be read/written programmatically by means of the `System.getProperty()` and `System.setProperty()` APIs. As an alternative, you can set a property on the command line with the `-D` option, as follows:

      java -Dquarkus.http.port=8180 app.jar

- **Environment variables**: This requires setting an environment variable for the property, as follows:

      export QUARKUS_HTTP_PORT=8180

As you may have noticed, the matching environment variable name has been set to uppercase and the dot has been replaced with an underscore.

 Please note that, in the current version of Quarkus, it is required that the variable is also defined in `application.properties` so that it can be overridden by the environment variable.

Finally, it is also possible to collect our configuration from an external source by adding a new configuration source to our application. The next section will show us how to do this.

Configuring custom configuration sources

In all the examples we've created so far, we have assumed that the application configuration is picked up from the `src/main/resources/application.properties` file, which is the default for Quarkus applications. Nevertheless, since Quarkus fully supports the **MicroProfile Config** specification, it is entirely possible to load the configuration from another source, which could be an external filesystem, a database, or anything that can be loaded by a Java application!

In order to do that, you have to implement the `org.eclipse.microprofile.config.spi.ConfigSource` interface, which exposes a set of methods for loading properties (`getProperties`), retrieving the properties' names (`getPropertyNames`), and retrieving the corresponding value (`getValue`).

As proof of concept, take a look at the following implementation, which is available in the Chapter08/advanced-config project:

```java
public class FileConfigSource implements ConfigSource {
    private final String CONFIG_FILE = "/tmp/config.properties";
    private final String CONFIG_SOURCE_NAME = "ExternalConfigSource";
    private final int ORDINAL = 900;

    @Override
    public Map getProperties() {

        try(InputStream in = new FileInputStream( CONFIG_FILE )){

            Properties properties = new Properties();
            properties.load( in );

            Map map = new HashMap();
            properties.stringPropertyNames()
                    .stream()
                    .forEach(key-> map.put(key,
                     properties.getProperty(key)));

            return map;

        } catch (IOException e) {
            e.printStackTrace();
        }

        return null;
    }

    @Override
    public Set getPropertyNames() {

        try(InputStream in = new FileInputStream( CONFIG_FILE )){

            Properties properties = new Properties();
            properties.load( in );

            return properties.stringPropertyNames();

        } catch (IOException e) {
            e.printStackTrace();
        }

        return null;
    }
```

```
    @Override
    public int getOrdinal() {
        return ORDINAL;
    }

    @Override
    public String getValue(String s) {

        try(InputStream in = new FileInputStream( CONFIG_FILE )){
            Properties properties = new Properties();
            properties.load( in );
            return properties.getProperty(s);

        } catch (IOException e) {
            e.printStackTrace();
        }

        return null;
    }

    @Override
    public String getName() {
        return CONFIG_SOURCE_NAME;
    }
}
```

The code itself is pretty simple if you are familiar with the `java.io` API. The
`FileConfigSource` class attempts to load an external configuration from the
`/tmp/config.properties` path of your filesystem. It is worth mentioning that an
`ORDINAL` variable has been set to specify the order for this `ConfigSource` class in case
some properties are loaded from multiple sources.

The default value for a `ConfigSource` is set to `100`, and sources with the highest ordinal
value have priority in case the property is defined across multiple sources. Here is the
ranking of the available configuration sources:

Config source	Value
`application.properties`	100
Environment variables	300
System properties	400

Since we have set the `ORDINAL` variable to `900` in our example, it will prevail over the other configuration sources, if any.

Once the custom `ConfigSource` is available in the project, we need to register for this class. For this purpose, we have added a file named `org.eclipse.microprofile.config.spi.ConfigSource` under the `resources/META-INF/services` folder of the project. Here's a tree view of the project, under the `resources` folder:

```
|       └── resources
|             └── META-INF
|                     └── services
|                           ├── org.eclipse.microprofile.config.spi.ConfigSource
```

Within this file, we have specified the fully qualified name of `ConfigSource`. In our case, this is as follows:

```
com.packt.chapter8.FileConfigSource
```

Now, as soon as the application is started, the custom `ConfigSource` will be loaded and its properties will prevail over other potential duplicates of the same attributes.

Within the `AdvancedConfigTest` class of your project, you will find one assertion, which verifies that one property has been loaded from the external `FileConfigSource` class:

```
given()
        .when().get("/hello")
        .then()
        .statusCode(200)
        .body(is("custom greeting"));
```

More details about the `AdvancedConfigTest` class will be discussed later in this chapter.

Using converters in your configuration

To discuss configuration converters, let's take this simple configuration example:

```
year=2019
isUser=true
```

Here, it's perfectly fine to inject the preceding properties into our code:

```
@ConfigProperty(name = "year", defaultValue = "2020")
Integer year;

@ConfigProperty(name = "isUser", defaultValue = "false")
Boolean isUser;
```

Under the hood, the MicroProfile Config API provides a type-safe conversion for values that are not just plain strings.

 Also, note that we can provide a default value for a property, which will be used if the property hasn't been defined in our configuration.

This happens by providing converters in the configuration model. Out of the box, some converters are already provided by the MicroProfile Config API by default. Here's a list of the built-in converters:

- `boolean` and `java.lang.Boolean`. The following values are converted into Booleans (case-insensitive): `true`, `YES`, `Y`, `1`, and `ON`. Any other value will be `false`.
- `byte` and `java.lang.Byte`.
- `short` and `java.lang.Short`.
- `int` and `java.lang.Integer`.
- `long` and `java.lang.Long`.
- `float` and `java.lang.Float`. A dot . is used to separate the fractional digits.
- `double` and `java.lang.Double`. A dot . is used to separate the fractional digits.
- `char` and `java.lang.Character`.
- `java.lang.Class`. This is based on the result of `Class.forName`.

Array, list, and set are also supported. In order to inject one of these Collections into a class variable, you can use the comma (,) char as a delimiter and \ as the escape character. For example, take the following configuration:

```
students=Tom,Pat,Steve,Lucy
```

The following code will inject the preceding configuration into a `java.util.List` element:

```
@ConfigProperty(name = "students")
List<String> studentList;
```

In much the same way, you can use built-in converters to generate an `Array` from a list of values. Take a look at the following configuration example:

```
pets=dog,cat,bunny
```

The preceding configuration can be injected into an array of strings as follows:

```
@ConfigProperty(name = "pets")
String[] petsArray;
```

Even classes can be injected as part of the configuration:

```
myclass=TestClass
```

At runtime, the class will be searched by the class loader and created using the `Class.forName` construct. We can put it in our code as follows:

```
@ConfigProperty(name = "myclass")
TestClass clazz;
```

Finally, it's worth mentioning that you can inject the whole `Config` object and retrieve the single properties each time you need them:

```
@Inject
Config config;

@GET
@Produces(MediaType.TEXT_PLAIN)
public String hello() {
    Integer y = config.getValue("year", Integer.class);
    return "Year is " +y;
}
```

Now, let's explore some more advanced strategies for creating type converters.

Adding custom converters

If the list of built-in converters is not enough, you can still create custom converters by implementing the generic interface, that is, `org.eclipse.microprofile.config.spi.Converter`. The `Type` parameter of the interface is the target type the string is converted into:

```
public class MicroProfileCustomValueConverter implements
Converter<CustomConfigValue> {

    public MicroProfileCustomValueConverter() {
    }

    @Override
    public CustomConfigValue convert(String value) {
        return new CustomConfigValue(value);
    }
}
```

The following code is for the target `Type` parameter, which derives from a plain Java string that we have included in the configuration:

```
public class CustomConfigValue {
    private final String email;
    private final String user;

    public CustomConfigValue(String value) {

        StringTokenizer st = new StringTokenizer(value,";");
        this.user = st.nextToken();
        this.email = st.nextToken();
    }

    public String getEmail() {
        return email;
    }

    public String getUser() {
        return user;
    }
}
```

You have to register your converter in a file named `resources/META-INF/services/org.eclipse.microprofile.config.spi.Converter`. Include the fully qualified class name of the custom implementation. For example, in our case, we have added the following line:

```
com.packt.chapter8.MicroProfileCustomValueConverter
```

Now, let's learn how to use our custom converter in practice. To do that, we will add the following line to the `application.properties` file, which uses the pattern coded in the constructor of the `CustomConfigValue` class:

```
customconfig=john;johnsmith@gmail.com
```

Now, the custom converter can be injected into our code as a class attribute:

```
@ConfigProperty(name = "customconfig")
CustomConfigValue value;

@Path("/email")
@GET
@Produces(MediaType.TEXT_PLAIN)
public String getEmail() {
    return value.getEmail();
}
```

Although the preceding example does nothing fancy, it shows us how we can create a customized property based on class definitions.

Testing advanced configuration options

Within the `Chapter08/advanced-config/src/test` folder of this chapter, you will find a test class named `AdvancedConfigTest`, which will verify the key concepts that we've learned about so far.

To run all of these tests successfully, copy the `customconfig.properties` file into the `/tmp` folder of your drive, otherwise one of the assertions contained in the `AdvancedConfigTest` class will fail:

```
cp Chapter08/customconfig.properties /tmp
```

Then, simply run the `install` goal, which will trigger the test's execution:

```
mvn install
```

You should see that all the tests contained in `AdvancedConfigTest` pass.

Configuration profiles

We have just learned how to create complex configurations using built-in converters and, for the most demanding, custom converters. What about if we need to switch between different configurations, for example, when moving from a development environment to a production one? Here, you can duplicate your configuration. However, the proliferation of configuration files is not always welcome in IT projects. Let's learn how to deal with this concern using **configuration profiles**.

In a nutshell, configuration profiles allow us to specify namespaces for our profiles in our configuration so that we can bind each property to a specific profile in the same file.

Out of the box, Quarkus ships with the following configuration profiles:

- `dev`: This is triggered when running in development mode (that is, `quarkus:dev`).
- `test`: This is triggered when running tests.
- `prod`: This is picked up when we're not running in development or test mode.

 Besides the preceding profiles, you can define your own custom profiles, which will be activated according to the rules we specified in the *Activating profiles* section.

You can use the following syntax to bind a configuration parameter to a specific profile:

```
%{profile}.config.key=value
```

To see a practical example of this, we will go through the source code in the `Chapter08/profiles` folder of this book's GitHub repository. We recommend importing the project into your IDE before you move on.

Let's start by checking its `application.properties` configuration file, which defines multiple profiles:

```
%dev.quarkus.datasource.url=jdbc:postgresql://localhost:5432/postgresDev
%test.quarkus.datasource.url=jdbc:postgresql://localhost:6432/postgresTest
%prod.quarkus.datasource.url=jdbc:postgresql://localhost:7432/postgresProd

quarkus.datasource.driver=org.postgresql.Driver
quarkus.datasource.username-quarkus
quarkus.datasource.password=quarkus

quarkus.datasource.initial-size=1
```

```
quarkus.datasource.min-size=2
quarkus.datasource.max-size=8

%prod.quarkus.datasource.initial-size=10
%prod.quarkus.datasource.min-size=10
%prod.quarkus.datasource.max-size=20
```

In the preceding configuration, we have specified three different JDBC URLs for our data source connection. Each one is bound to a different profile. We have also set a specific connection pool setting for the production profile in order to grant a larger number of database connections. In the next section, we will learn how to activate every single profile.

Activating profiles

Let's learn how to activate a specific profile by taking the `prod` profile in the preceding configuration as an example. First of all, we need to start a PostgreSQL instance named `postgresProd` and bind it to port `7432`:

```
docker run --ulimit memlock=-1:-1 -it --rm=true --memory-swappiness=0 --
name quarkus_Prod -e POSTGRES_USER=quarkus -e POSTGRES_PASSWORD=quarkus -e
POSTGRES_DB=postgresProd -e PGPORT=7432 -p 7432:7432 postgres:10.5
```

Then, we need to provide profile information during the `package` phase, as follows:

```
mvn clean package -Dquarkus.profile=prod -DskipTests=true
```

When running the application, it will pick up the profile you specified in the `package` phase:

```
java -jar target/profiles-demo-1.0-SNAPSHOT-runner.jar
```

As an alternative, it is also possible to specify the profile using the `QUARKUS_PROFILE` environment variable, like so:

```
export QUARKUS_PROFILE=dev
java -jar target/profiles-demo-1.0-SNAPSHOT-runner.jar
```

Finally, it's worth mentioning that the same strategy can be used to define non standard profiles. For example, let's say we want to add a **staging** profile for applications that need to be checked before production:

```
%staging.quarkus.datasource.url=jdbc:postgresql://localhost:8432/postgresStage
```

Here, we can apply the same strategy we've used for other profiles, that is, we can either specify the profile at application startup using the Java system property (`quarkus-profile`) or add the necessary information to the `QUARKUS_PROFILE` environment variable.

Automatic profile selection

To simplify development and testing, the `dev` and `test` profiles can be automatically triggered by the Maven plugin. So, for example, if you are executing Quarkus in development mode, the `dev` profile will be used eventually:

```
mvn quarkus:dev
```

In much the same way, the `test` profile will be activated when tests are executed, for example, during the `install` life cycle phase:

```
mvn quarkus:install
```

The `test` profile will be activated when you execute the Maven `test` goal. Additionally, it's worth knowing that you can set a different profile for your tests through `maven-surfire-plugin`, within its system properties:

```
<groupId>org.apache.maven.plugins</groupId>
<artifactId>maven-surefire-plugin</artifactId>
<version>${surefire-plugin.version}</version>
<configuration>
    <systemPropertyVariables>
        <quarkus.test.profile>custom-test</quarkus.test.profile>
        <buildDirectory>${project.build.directory}</buildDirectory>
    </systemPropertyVariables>
</configuration>
```

In this section, we walked through application profiles. In the next section, we'll learn how to control the life cycle of our Quarkus applications.

Controlling the application life cycle

Controlling the application life cycle is a common requirement for your services to be able to bootstrap some external resources or verify the status of your components. One simple strategy, borrowed from the Java Enterprise API, is to include the **Undertow** extension (or any upper layer, such as rest services) so that you can leverage `ServletContextListener`, which is notified when a web application is created or destroyed. Here is a minimal implementation of it:

```
public final class ContextListener implements ServletContextListener {

    private ServletContext context = null;

    public void contextInitialized(ServletContextEvent event) {
        context = event.getServletContext();
        System.out.println("Web application started!");

    }
    public void contextDestroyed(ServletContextEvent event) {
        context = event.getServletContext();
        System.out.println("Web application stopped!");

    }
}
```

Although it is perfectly fine to reuse this strategy in a Quarkus web application, it is recommended to use this approach for any kind of Quarkus service. This can be done by observing the `io.quarkus.runtime.StartupEvent` and `io.quarkus.runtime.ShutdownEvent` events. Additionally, in CDI applications, you can observe an event with the `@Initialized(ApplicationScoped.class)` qualifier, which is fired when the application context is initialized. This can be particularly useful for bootstrapping resources such as databases, which are required before the configuration is read by Quarkus.

To see a practical example of this, check the source code that's available in the `Chapter08/lifecycle` folder of this book's GitHub repository. As usual, it's advised to import the project into your IDE before you move on. The purpose of this example is to show you how to replace the PostgreSQL database, in our customer service, with the H2 database (`https://www.h2database.com/`).

Starting with the configuration, the life cycle project doesn't contain the PostgreSQL JDBC dependency anymore. To replace this, the following one has been included:

```
<dependency>
  <groupId>io.quarkus</groupId>
  <artifactId>quarkus-jdbc-h2</artifactId>
</dependency>
```

To test our customer service, we have included two H2 database configuration profiles: one that's bound to the `dev` profile and one that's bound to the `test` profile:

```
%dev.quarkus.datasource.url=jdbc:h2:tcp://localhost:19092/mem:test
%test.quarkus.datasource.url=jdbc:h2:tcp://localhost/mem:test
quarkus.datasource.driver=org.h2.Driver
```

To bind the H2 database before the application context is started, we can use the following `DBLifeCycleBean` class:

```
@ApplicationScoped
public class DBLifeCycleBean {

    protected final Logger log =
     LoggerFactory.getLogger(this.getClass());

    // H2 Database
    private Server tcpServer;

    public void observeContextInit(@Observes
     @Initialized(ApplicationScoped.class) Object event) {
        try {
            tcpServer =  Server.createTcpServer("-tcpPort",
             "19092", "-tcpAllowOthers").start();
            log.info("H2 database started in TCP server
            mode on Port 19092");
        } catch (SQLException e) {

            throw new RuntimeException(e);

        }
    }
    void onStart(@Observes StartupEvent ev) {
        log.info("Application is starting");
    }

    void onStop(@Observes ShutdownEvent ev) {
        if (tcpServer != null) {
            tcpServer.stop();
            log.info("H2 database was shut down");
```

```
                    tcpServer = null;
            }
        }
    }
```

This class is able to intercept the following events:

- **Context startup**: This is captured through the `observeContextInit` method. The database is bootstrapped in this method.
- **Application startup**: This is captured through the `onStart` method. We are simply performing some logs when this event is fired.
- **Application shutdown**: This is captured through the `onStop` method. We are shutting down the database in this method.

Now, you can start Quarkus in the `dev` profile as usual with the following command:

```
mvn quarkus:dev
```

When the application is started, we will be notified that the H2 database has been started:

```
INFO  [com.pac.qua.cha.DBLifeCycleBean] (main) H2 database started in TCP
server mode on Port 19092
```

Then, we will receive one more notification on application startup, where we can include some extra tasks to be completed:

```
[com.pac.qua.cha.DBLifeCycleBean] (main) Application is starting
```

Finally, when we stop the application, the resource will be dismissed, as shown in the following console logs:

```
[com.pac.qua.cha.DBLifeCycleBean] (main) H2 database was shut down
```

Before shutting down the database, you can enjoy running your customer service example with a tiny in-memory database layer.

Activating a database test resource

As a bonus tip, we will show you how to activate the H2 database during the test life cycle. This can be done by adding a class, annotated as `@QuarkusTestResource`, to your test classes while passing the `H2DatabaseTestResource` class as an attribute.

Here is an example:

```
@QuarkusTestResource(H2DatabaseTestResource.class)
public class TestResources {
}
```

H2DatabaseTestResource basically performs the same actions
that DBLifeCycleBean does, before our tests are fired. Note that the following
dependency has been added into the project to run the preceding test class:

```
<dependency>
    <groupId>io.quarkus</groupId>
    <artifactId>quarkus-test-h2</artifactId>
    <scope>test</scope>
</dependency>
```

Now, you can safely run tests against the test profile with the following command:

mvn install

Note that, before our tests are executed, the following log will confirm that the H2 database
has been started on one of our available IP addresses:

```
[INFO] H2 database started in TCP server mode; server status: TCP server
running at tcp://10.5.126.52:9092 (only local connections)
```

Bootstrapping external resources is indeed a common use case for life cycle managers.
Another frequent use case consists of scheduling events at the application startup phase. In
the next section, we will discuss how to fire events using Quarkus' scheduler.

Firing events with the Quarkus scheduler

Quarkus includes an extension called **scheduler**, which can be used to schedule tasks for
single or repeated execution. We can use the cron format to specify the number of times the
scheduler fires the event.

The source code for the following example is located in the Chapter08/scheduler folder
of this book's GitHub repository. If you check the pom.xml file, you will notice that the
following extension has been added to it:

```
<dependency>
        <groupId>io.quarkus</groupId>
        <artifactId>quarkus-scheduler</artifactId>
</dependency>
```

Our sample project generates a random token (for the sake of simplicity, a random string is used) every 30 seconds. The class that's in charge of generating random tokens is the following `TokenGenerator` class:

```
@ApplicationScoped
public class TokenGenerator {

    private String token;

    public String getToken() {
        return token;
    }

    @Scheduled(every="30s")
    void generateToken() {
        token= UUID.randomUUID().toString();
        log.info("New Token generated");
    }

}
```

Now, we can have our token injected into the built-in REST endpoint, as follows:

```
@Path("/token")
public class Endpoint {

    @Inject
    TokenGenerator token;

    @GET
    @Produces(MediaType.TEXT_PLAIN)
    public String getToken() {

        return token.getToken();
    }
}
```

Start the application as usual with the following command:

```
mvn quarkus:dev
```

You will notice that, every 30 seconds, the following message is printed in the console logs:

```
[INFO] New Token generated
```

Then, by requesting the /token URL, the randomly generated string will be returned:

```
curl http://localhost:8080/token
  3304a8de-9fd7-43e7-9d25-6e8896ca67dd
```

Using the cron scheduler format

Besides using time expressions (**s=seconds**, **m=minutes**, **h=hours**, **d=days**), you can opt for the more compact expression of the cron scheduler. Therefore, if you wanted to fire the event every second, then you could use the following cron expression:

```
@Scheduled(cron="* * * * ?")
void generateToken() {
    token= UUID.randomUUID().toString();
    log.info("New token generated");
}
```

Check the cron main page for more information about the cron format: http://man7.org/linux/man-pages/man5/crontab.5.html.

Firing one-time events

If you need to execute one-time events, then you can inject the io.quarkus.scheduler.Scheduler class into your code directly and use the startTimer method, which will fire the execution of an action in a separate thread. This can be seen in the following example:

```
@Inject
Scheduler scheduler;

public void oneTimeEvnt() {

    scheduler.startTimer(300, () -> oneTimeAction());
}

public void oneTimeAction() {
    // Do something
}
```

In this brief excerpt, we can see how a single event, which will be executed in the oneTimeAction() method, can fire a one-time action after 300 milliseconds.

Summary

In this chapter, we presented some advanced techniques that we can use to manage our configuration using converters and configuration profiles. We have also demonstrated how different configuration sources can be injected and prioritized over the standard configuration file. In the second part of this chapter, we had a look at how to capture the application life cycle's events and how to schedule the execution of future tasks.

To make our applications even more scalable, in the next chapter, we will discuss how to build reactive applications, which are event-driven and non-blocking. Hold on tight!

9
Unifying Imperative and Reactive with Vert.x

One of the greatest challenges for enterprise applications has traditionally been combining business operations, which are inherently synchronous, with dispatching the results of these operations, which can be also asynchronous and event-driven. In this chapter, we will learn how the Vert.x toolkit can address this challenge in Quarkus applications by combining standard imperative programming with asynchronous data streams that can be created, changed, or combined at runtime. By the end of this chapter, you should be proficient in writing reactive applications on the JVM using Vert.x.

In this chapter, we will cover the following topics:

- An introduction to Reactive Programming and the Vert.x toolkit
- Vert.x API models available in Quarkus
- Managing the Reactive SQL Client with Vert.x

Technical requirements

You can find the source code for the project in this chapter on GitHub at `https://github.com/PacktPublishing/Hands-On-Cloud-Native-Applications-with-Java-and-Quarkus/tree/master/Chapter09`.

Demystifying Reactive Programming and Vert.x

Imperative programming is the way most programmers write their code every day. Wait a minute – what does imperative programming mean? In a concise statement, we can say that imperative programming means that lines of code get executed in a sequence, statement by statement, as shown in the following example:

```
URL url = new URL("http://acme.com/");
BufferedReader in = new BufferedReader(new
InputStreamReader(url.openStream()));

String line;
while ((line = in.readLine()) != null) {
  System.out.println(line);
}
in.close();
```

As you can see, imperative programming can use loops or conditional statements to jump to different parts of code. Don't be fooled by this, though. As long as your debugger clearly points to a statement in your code (and thus it's obvious what line will be executed next), you are definitely using imperative programming.

While the imperative programming model is clearly simpler to understand, it can badly impact scalability as the number of connections tends to grow. As a matter of fact, the number of system threads will have to be increased accordingly, causing your OS to spend significant CPU cycles just for thread scheduling management. That's where Vert.x comes into play.

Let's start with a definition: what exactly is Vert.x? Vert.x is not an application server or a framework but merely a toolkit or, if you prefer, a set of plain JAR files that can be added as a dependency to your projects. Easy-peasy. You don't need a specific development environment or plugin to develop applications with Vert.x either.

At its core, Vert.x is a reactive toolkit that fulfills the requirements dictated by the **Reactive Manifesto** (https://www.reactivemanifesto.org/). These requirements can be summarized in the following points:

- **Responsive**: A reactive system needs to be capable of handling requests in a reasonable time.
- **Resilient**: A reactive system must be designed to handle failures and deal with them appropriately.

- **Elastic**: A reactive system must be able to scale up and down according to loads without compromising the responsiveness of the system.
- **Message-driven**: The reactive system's components interact with each other by exchanging asynchronous messages.

Based on the preceding points, it's clear that Vert.x promotes a new way of designing and building distributed systems while infusing asynchrony, scalability, and reactiveness into the core of your applications. Therefore, with regard to our former example, it can be rewritten in a reactive way, as follows:

```
vertx.createHttpClient().getNow(80, "acme.com", "", response -> {
    response.bodyHandler(System.out::println);
});
```

Unlike the former example, by using Vert.x, the running thread is released while the connection with the HTTP server is being established. Then, when the response has been received, a handler coded as a Lambda expression (https://docs.oracle.com/javase/tutorial/java/javaOO/lambdaexpressions.html) is called back to deal with the response.

In the preceding example, the `vertx` field can be used in your code each time you extend the Vert.x basic unit of deployment, which is called a **Verticle**. In essence, a Verticle processes incoming events over an event loop, creating the foundation for an asynchronous programming model. Verticles can be written in various languages, not only Java, so you can mix different environments as part of a larger reactive system.

The main tool for allowing different Verticles to communicate with each other is called the **Event Bus**, and communication happens through asynchronous message passing. The following diagram shows how the **Event Bus** fits into this schema:

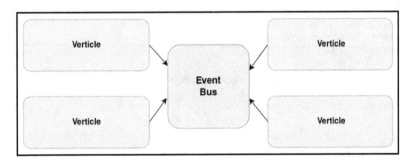

The Event Bus doesn't pose any restrictions on the kind of data format you use, although JSON is the preferred exchange format since it is a popular option for structuring data, allowing Verticles written in different languages to communicate. The Event Bus supports the following communication patterns:

- **Point-to-point** messaging, which means that messages are routed to just one of the handlers registered at that address.
- **Request-response** messaging, which is similar to point-to-point messaging, except that it includes an optional reply handler that can be specified while sending the message so that the recipient can decide whether to reply to the message. If they do so, the reply handler will be called.
- **Publish-subscribe**, which allows you to broadcast messages using a publish function. In this case, the event bus will route messages to all the handlers that are registered against that address.

Since there are multiple communication patterns, several API models have been designed for Vert.x and are all based around the concept of executing the flow in an asynchronous way via callbacks. The next section discusses a variety of Vert.x API models that are available in Quarkus.

Vert.x API models in Quarkus

Vert.x provides a large ecosystem of reactive APIs that are integrated into Quarkus. More specifically, Quarkus uses Vert.x as the reactive engine by providing a single dependency to your applications:

```
<dependency>
    <groupId>io.quarkus</groupId>
    <artifactId>quarkus-vertx</artifactId>
</dependency>
```

This allows you to access a managed Vert.x instance with simple code injection:

```
@Inject io.vertx.core.Vertx vertx;
```

The `Vertx` object is the control center of a Vert.x application. It's your pass to Vert.x land and allows you to create an asynchronous and non-blocking client and servers, get a reference to the Event Bus, and many other things.

When using Vert.x API in Quarkus, however, there's no `Vertx` object for you to access. As a matter of fact, Quarkus provides three different Vert.x APIs:

- `io.vertx.core.Vertx`: This is the entry point into the Vert.x core API and allows you to achieve asynchronous and non-blocking clients and servers using callbacks.
- `io.vertx.reactivex.core.Vertx`: This API allows us to use observable patterns in our Vert.x applications wherever we can use streams or asynchronous results. Additionally, it allows us to use a large set of data transformation operators on our streams.
- `io.vertx.axle.core.Vertx`: This API has been specifically designed to integrate with Quarkus' MicroProfile patterns, proving a solid foundation for sending and receiving asynchronous messages, thus enforcing loose coupling between services.

In order to learn about all three different variations of Vert.x, we have provided an equal number of examples in the `Chapter09` folder in this book's GitHub repository. Let's take a look at them in detail.

Managing the Vert.x core API

For the purpose of learning about the Vert.x core API, we will be using a modified version of our basic customer service application, which we discussed in `Chapter 4`, *Adding Web Interfaces to Quarkus Services*. You can find the source code for this example of the `Chapter09/core/customer-service` folder in this book's GitHub repository. We recommend that you import the project into your IDE.

Now, let's dive straight into the code. Since the Vert.x core API is based around the callback mechanism, in order to leverage asynchronous and non-blocking APIs, for our customer service example we have added two functions that will read and write a list of customers from the filesystem in JSON format. Where shall we write our customer list? The answer is into the `application.properties` file, which defines a property named `file.path`, which is where the customer list will be written:

```
file.path=/tmp/customer.json
```

Now, let's look at the code. The core class that's responsible for providing customer data is `CustomerRepository`. There we'll inject an instance of `io.vertx.core.Vertx` at this point. We will also inject the path where the data will be stored:

```
public class CustomerRepository {
    @Inject io.vertx.core.Vertx vertx;
    @ConfigProperty(name = "file.path" )
    String path;
```

Now comes the interesting bit, that is, writing a method that uses the `vertx` instance to flatten our list of customers on the filesystem:

```
public CompletionStage<String> writeFile( ) {

    JsonArrayBuilder jsonArray = javax.json.Json.createArrayBuilder();
    for (Customer customer:customerList) {
        jsonArray.add(javax.json.Json.createObjectBuilder().
                add("id", customer.getId())
              .add("name", customer.getName())
              .add("surname", customer.getSurname()).build());
    }

    JsonArray array = jsonArray.build();
    CompletableFuture<String> future = new CompletableFuture<>();

    vertx.fileSystem().writeFile(path, Buffer.buffer(array

    .toString()), handler -> {
        if (handler.succeeded()) {
            future.complete("Written JSON file in " +path);
        } else {
            System.err.println("Error while writing in file:
              " + handler.cause().getMessage());
        }
    });
    return future;
}
```

The first thing you may have noticed is the `CompletionStage` method's signature. If you have been programming async Java code, you may be familiar with the `java.util.concurrent.Future` API. It's used to do the following:

- Check whether the execution has completed via the `isDone()` method
- Cancel the execution using the `cancel()` method
- Fetch the result of the execution using the blocking `get()` method

The major limitation of this approach is that the caller cannot manually complete the task, nor can it chain multiple `Future` executions.

On the other hand, `CompletionStage` is based on the concept of stages, which are thought of as multiple intermediate computations and may or may not be asynchronous. In any case, we have to complete them before we reach the final result. These intermediate computations are known as **completion stages**.

By using the `CompletionStage` stage, you can easily address the `java.util.concurrent.Future` API's limitations by doing the following:

- Manually completing `CompletableStage` using `complete(T value)`
- Chaining multiple `CompletableStage` in a block

Let's get back to our example. Once we have created `JsonArray` out of our customer list, we can access our `FileSystem` using the Vert.x core API. We can also register a handler that is in charge of completing our `CompletionStage` as soon as the file has been successfully written.

Let's take a look at the `readFile` method, which is in charge of reading the file that contains the customer list:

```java
public CompletionStage<String> readFile() {
    CompletableFuture<String> future = new CompletableFuture<>();
    long start = System.nanoTime();

    // Delay reply by 100ms
    vertx.setTimer(100, l -> {
        // Compute elapsed time in milliseconds
        long duration = MILLISECONDS.convert(System.nanoTime() -
          start, NANOSECONDS);

        vertx.fileSystem().readFile(path, ar -> {
            if (ar.succeeded()) {
                String response = ar.result().toString("UTF-8");
                future.complete(response);
            } else {
                future.complete("Cannot read the file: " +
                  ar.cause().getMessage());
            }
        });

    });
    return future;
}
```

The `readFile` method is intentionally a bit more complex. As a matter of fact, we have chained two different stages into it. The first one executes a one-time timer that will fire the next execution in 100 ms. Timers are a core construct of Vert.x and should be used wherever you want to delay the execution of some code or execute it repeatedly:

```
vertx.setPeriodic(1000, 1 -> {
    // This code will be called every second
    System.out.println("timer fired!");
});
```

In any case, timers are how you can delay the execution in Vert.x terms in place of other mechanisms, such as `Thread.sleep`, which would block the event loop and therefore should **never**, ever be used in the Vert.x context.

 If you forget our gentle warning, Vert.x will remind you each time you attempt to use a blocking code in the Vert.x context with a log message similar to *Thread vertx-eventloop-thread-1 has been blocked for 22258 ms.*

The remaining part of the `readFile` method does exactly the opposite of the `writeFile` method; that is, it reads the JSON file and completes the stage as soon as the file has been read.

In order to expose this feature to the client application, we have added two wrapper methods to our `CustomerEndpoint` class in order to expose the functions via the REST API:

```
@GET
@Path("writefile")
@Produces("text/plain")
public CompletionStage<String> writeFile() {
    return customerRepository.writeFile();
}

@GET
@Path("readfile")
public CompletionStage<String> readFile() {
    return customerRepository.readFile();
}
```

It's worth noting that the `writeFile` method produces text information since it's supposed to return a simple text message to the caller. On the other hand, the `readFile` method relies on the class' default `application/json` format to display the JSON text file.

Now, let's move on to the client-side. We can easily capture the `CompletionStage` event using two more AngularJS handlers, which will capture the result as soon as it's available:

```
$scope.writefile = function () {

$http({
    method: 'GET',
    url: SERVER_URL+'/writefile'
  }).then(_successStage, _error);
};

scope.readfile = function () {

  $http({
    method: 'GET',
    url: SERVER_URL+'/readfile'
  }).then(_successStage, _error);
};

function _successStage(response) {
    _clearForm()
    $scope.jsonfile = JSON.stringify(response.data);
}
```

Both functions will be triggered with the addition of two simple buttons to our home page:

```
<a ng-click="writefile()" class="myButton">Write File</a>
<a ng-click="readfile()"  class="myButton">Read File</a>
```

Besides doing this, we have also added a `div` section to our HTML schema, which is where information will be displayed:

```
<div ng-app="displayfile"  >
        <span ng-bind="jsonfile"></span>
</div>
```

Without further ado, let's build and run the application with the following command:

```
mvn install quarkus:dev
```

The following is our new UI, which includes the **Read File** and **Write File** buttons. We have just saved a set of `Customer` objects, as shown in the following screenshot:

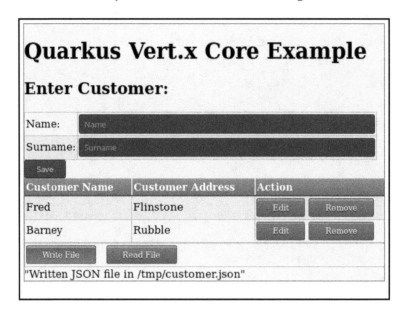

Conversely, if we hit the **Read File** button, its content will be displayed in the lower `div` of the page in JSON format:

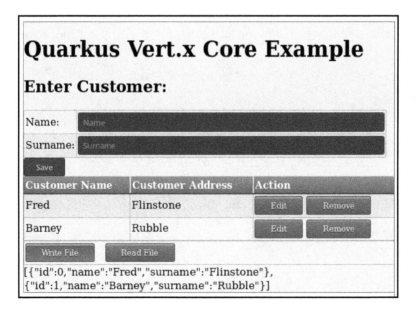

We have completed the first round with Vert.x core. Now, let's move on and look at using Vert.x with **ReactiveX (RxJava)**.

Managing Vert.x API for RxJava

RxJava (`https://github.com/ReactiveX/RxJava`) is a Java library that lets you create asynchronous and event-based applications using `Observable` sequences for the Java VM. In order to understand the core features of this framework, we need to define the core actors of ReactiveX, which are as follows:

- **Observables**: These represent the source of data to be emitted. An observable starts providing data once a subscriber starts to listen. An observable may emit a variable number of items and will eventually terminate with success or with an error.

- **Subscribers:** These listen to events that are emitted by observables. There can be one or more subscribers for one observable.

The following diagram shows the relationship between these two components:

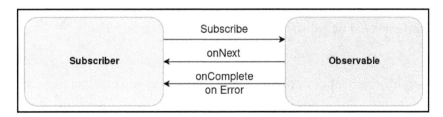

Based on the number of items emitted and the control of the flow of items, we can distinguish between different types of observables:

Observable type	Description
`Flowable<T>`	Emits *0* or *n* items and terminates with a success or an error event. Supports backpressure, which allows us to control the rate of source emission.
`Observable<T>`	Emits *0* or *n* items and terminates with a success or an error event.
`Single<T>`	Emits either one value or an error notification.
`Maybe<T>`	Emits a single item, no items, or an error event. The reactive version of an optional call.
`Completable`	Wraps the deferred computation without any value but only as an indication of completion or an exception.

Let's provide a minimalist example of this. The following is a `Hello world` example of an `Observable` that emits a single item:

```
Observable.just("Hello world!").subscribe(System.out::println);
```

When the subscriber receives the item, it simply prints it on the out stream. The following code is slightly different as it uses a `Flowable` observable to control the flow of items in the event you are pushing out data at a high rate, which could overflood your subscribers:

```
Flowable.just("Hello world!").subscribe(System.out::println);
```

One important concept of RxJava programming is **operators**; an operator is a function that defines an `Observable` and how and when it should emit the data stream. We have already met one, that is, the `just` operator, which allows you to convert an object or a set of objects into an `Observable`. In our first example, the object was the `Hello world` string.

There are many more operators, all of which can be found in RxJava's documentation (`http://reactivex.io/documentation/operators.html`). For example, you can suppress duplicates in a stream of data using the `distinct` operator:

```
Observable.just(2, 3, 4, 4, 2, 1)
        .distinct()
        .subscribe(System.out::println);
```

In this case, the expected output from the subscriber will be as follows:

```
2,3,4,1
```

You can also chain another operator to filter out items that don't meet a pattern, as follows:

```
Observable.just(1, 2, 3, 4, 5, 6)
        .distinct()
        .filter(x -> x % 2 == 0)
        .subscribe(System.out::println);
```

As you may have guessed, the output will be further restricted to the following:

```
2,4
```

Although we have barely scratched the surface of RxJava's power, we have a minimal background to how we plug these concepts into our example application.

Using RxJava with Quarkus

In order to learn about RxJava, we will go through the example contained in the `Chapter09/rx2java/customer-service` folder in this book's GitHub repository.

The first thing you should be aware of is that, in order to use RxJava with Quarkus, you have to add an instance of `Vertx`, which can be found under the `io.vertx.reativex.core` namespace:

```
@Inject io.vertx.reactivex.core.Vertx vertx;
```

That being said, one of the main advantages of including ReactiveX in our project is that it will greatly enhance the capability of **transforming** data that flows between the observable and the subscriber.

For example, let's take a look at the following use case:

- We want to produce a file with a list of customers to be imported in a spreadsheet. Therefore, we will create a plain CSV file out of our customer list.
- Then, we want to convert the CSV file into any other format is coded in the customer's `toString` method.

Let's learn how to operate the right changes on the `CustomerRepository` class. As we mentioned previously, the first change is to replace the `io.vertx.core.Vertx` instance with the corresponding `io.vertx.reativex.core.Vertx`. Then, we will apply some changes to the `writeFile` and `readFile` methods. Let's begin with the `writeFile` method first:

```
public CompletionStage<String> writeFile() {
    CompletableFuture<String> future = new CompletableFuture<>();
    StringBuffer sb = new StringBuffer("id,name,surname");
    sb.append(System.lineSeparator());

    Observable.fromIterable(customerList)
            .map(c -> c.getId() + "," + c.getName() + "," +
            c.getSurname() + System.lineSeparator())
            .subscribe(
                    data ->   sb.append(data),
                    error -> System.err.println(error),
                    () ->  vertx.fileSystem().writeFile(path,
                     Buffer.buffer(sb.toString()), handler -> {
                        if (handler.succeeded()) {
                            future.complete("File written in "+path);
                        } else {
                            System.err.println("Error while
```

```
                                           writing in file: " + handler.cause()
                                           .getMessage());

                                  }
                        }));

            return future;
    }
```

If you have found our introduction to observables intuitive, the preceding code won't look overly complex, in spite of the proliferation of Lambda expressions. Here, we have added a long list of operators to produce the desired result.

First of all, we have produced a set of observables by iterating over the customer list using the Observable.fromIterable operator. Since we need to produce a CSV file, we need to map single customer fields with the CSV format, which uses a comma (,) to separate the values. We have used the map operator for this purpose. Then, we are done with transformation and the result will be a list of observables that are in the format we have chosen.

For an observer (or subscriber) to see items that are being emitted by Observable, along with errors or completed notifications from Observable, it must subscribe to that Observable using the subscribe operator. In a nutshell, the subscribe operator is the glue that connects a subscriber to an Observable.

Our subscriber will receive notifications when new items are added so that they can be appended to StringBuffer, which has already been initialized with the CSV header. The subscriber will also receive notifications in case of errors and eventually, when the stream of items gets completed, via the () handler. In this case, the CSV file will be written to the filesystem using the writeFile function, which is also available in the io.vertx.reativex.core.Vertx filesystem context.

Then, the readFile method will need to reverse the CSV file we have already written into the representation of the Customer object, as provided by its toString method. The code is as follows:

```java
public CompletionStage<String> readFile() {

    CompletableFuture<String> future = new CompletableFuture<>();
    StringBuffer sb = new StringBuffer();

    vertx.fileSystem().rxReadFile(path)
            .flatMapObservable(buffer ->
              Observable.fromArray(buffer.toString().split(System.
              lineSeparator())))
```

```
        .skip(1)
        .map(s -> s.split(","))
        .map(data-> new Customer(Integer.
         parseInt(data[0]),data[1],data[2]))
        .subscribe(
                data ->  sb.append(data.toString()),
                error -> System.err.println(error),
                () -> future.complete(sb.toString()));

    return future;

}
```

Here, we have to familiarize ourselves with some more operators. Since we want to read and process the file line by line, we are using the `flatMapObservable` operator to produce our array of multiple `Observable` instances. In practice, this operator allows us to produce a set of `Observable` instances that are the result of a function being emitted by a single item the line in our CSV file.

We have conveniently split the file into an array using the `split` method of the string's class. Then, we used the `skip` operator to skip the first item, which is the CSV header. After, we applied two `map` transformations to the data:

- The first one creates an array of string objects, out of the CSV line, using the comma (,) as a separator
- Next, we created an instance of the `Customer` object using the data arriving from the string array

Now that we have collected our target data, which is a `Customer` object, we are ready to stream this data, which will eventually be collected by the subscriber. The subscriber, in turn, receives each item and adds the `toString()` output from it to the `StringBuffer`. You can include any format in your `toString()` method, but to keep it simple, we have let our IDE (IntelliJ IDEA) self-generate it:

```
public String toString() {
    return "Customer{" +
            "id=" + id +
            ", name='" + name + '\'' +
            ", surname='" + surname + '\'' +
            '}';
}
```

The last thing we'll do is set the media type of `readFile` so that it's consistent with the format of our `toString` data. Since we are producing simple text, it will look as follows:

```
@GET
@Path("readfile")
@Produces("text/plain")
public CompletionStage<String> readFile() {
    return customerRepository.readFile();
}
```

Now, you can just run the application and check the new outcome. The following is what your UI should look like once you've added some customers and clicked on the **Write File** button:

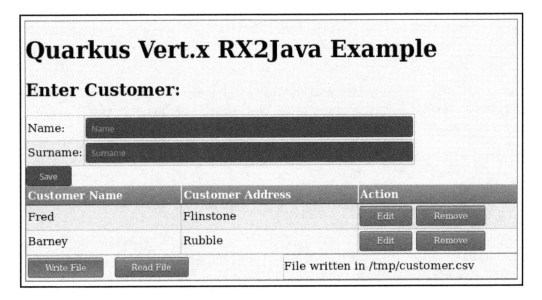

Then, by hitting the **Read File** button, the lower HTML `div` will contain the `toString` data for each customer:

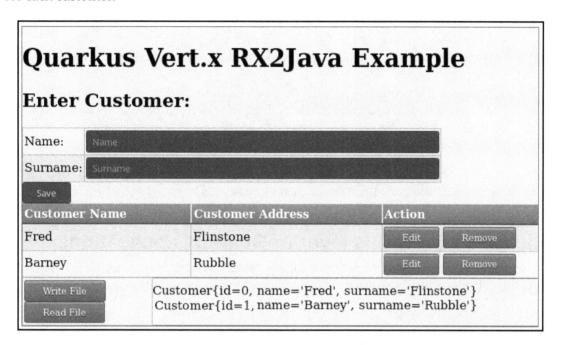

As you can see, in spite of the minimalist UI log, there is plenty of work being done under the hood to manage the transformation of data in different kinds of format.

That was our second implementation of Vert.x and Quarkus. We still have to deal with the third beast, which is `io.vertx.axle.core.Vertx`.

Decoupling events with Vert.x axle libraries

Typically, we want to separate our service entry points (adapters) from the business logic, which is part of the application. A common pattern is to keep the service in a distinct bean, which is injected into our service REST entry point. When approaching Reactive Programming, however, we can decouple even more of our components by bringing the Vert.x Event Bus into the picture.

In this kind of architecture, components communicate with each other by sending messages to virtual addresses. To manage the distribution of messages, the following components are available:

- **EventBus**: This is a lightweight distributed messaging system that allows communication between the different parts of your application in a loosely coupled way.
- **Message**: This contains data that is received from the Event Bus in a handler. Messages have a body and a header, both of which can be null. By adding a reply handler in the message, it is possible to apply a request-response pattern to the communication.

Let's learn how we can instrument a simple messaging pattern by using the example application that's available in the `Chapter09/axle/customer-service` folder.

Adding an EventBus layer to Quarkus applications

To include a distributed peer-to-peer messaging pattern in our application, we will need to inject the `EventBus` instance into a CDI bean, which will act as a receiver:

```
@Inject EventBus bus;
```

In our case, we will add the `EventBus` to the `CustomerEndpoint` class.

 Please note that there is only one single instance of the Event Bus per Vert.x instance.

Now, in the same class, let's create a new endpoint method, which will be in charge of dispatching messages:

```
@GET
@Path("/call")
@Produces("text/plain")
public CompletionStage<String> call(@QueryParam("id") Integer customerId) {
    return bus.<String>send("callcustomer",
    customerRepository.findCustomerById(customerId))
            .thenApply(Message::body)
            .exceptionally(Throwable::getMessage);
```

We are conveying messages on the bus through the `"callcustomer"` address. The body of the message contains the `Customer` object, which is retrieved by the `findCustomerById` method. In the event of an error, a throwable with the error's `getMessage` content will be thrown.

Now, we need a consumer for messages, so we will add another class named `CustomerService`, which contains a method annotated as `@ConsumeEvent`:

```
@ApplicationScoped
public class CustomerService {

        @ConsumeEvent("callcustomer")
        public String reply(Customer c) {
            return "Hello! I am " + c.getName() + " "
              +c.getSurname() + ". How are you doing?";
        }
}
```

Within the `@ConsumeEvent` annotation, we are specifying the address where messages are consumed. At the end of the day, we are merely returning a response containing a message from the customer.

To complete the loop, we need to make the following changes:

- We need to add one more button to the `index.html` page:

  ```
  <a ng-click="call( customer )" class="myButton">Call</a>
  ```

- We need to add one more AngularJS controller to handle the response, which will display (in an alert window) the message:

  ```
  $scope.call = function (customer) {

    $http({
      method: 'GET',
      url: SERVER_URL+'/call/?id='+customer.id
    }).then(_callCustomer, _error);
  };

  function _callCustomer(response) {
    window.alert(response.data);
  }
  ```

Now that we have added everything, let's run our application.

Rolling up the application

When all the changes are in place, you should be able to see that the **Call** button has been added to each customer's row, as shown in the following screenshot:

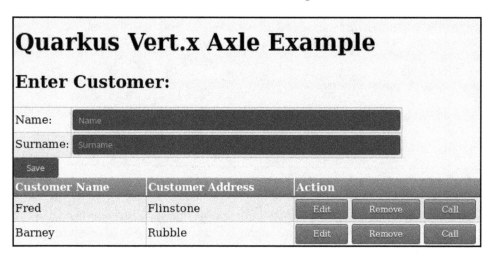

When you click on the **Call** button, a message will be sent through the Event Bus. As soon as it's consumed, you should see the following response:

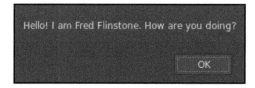

Besides peer-to-peer messaging, you can also use the Vert.x axle API to stream **Server-Side Events (SSEs)**.

Streaming SSE with Vert.x

Traditionally, web applications are capable of sending a request to servers to receive a response; that is the standard paradigm. With server-send events, however, it's possible for the server application to send new data to a web page at any time by pushing events (messages) to the web page. These incoming messages are treated as events combined with data inside the web page.

Now, let's demonstrate how to use the Vert.x axle API to stream SSEs in Quarkus. The following class, which has been included in our project, is in charge of sending an SSE to the home page every two seconds:

```
@Path("/streaming")
public class StreamingEndpoint {

    @Inject io.vertx.axle.core.Vertx vertx;

    @Inject CustomerRepository customerRepository;
    @GET
    @Produces(MediaType.SERVER_SENT_EVENTS)
    public Publisher<String> stream() {

        return
                ReactiveStreams.fromPublisher
                (vertx.periodicStream(2000).
                 toPublisher())
                        .map(l -> String.format
                    ("Number of Customers %s .
                    Last one added: %s %n",customerRepository.
                    findAll().size(),
                            customerRepository.findAll().size()
                             > 0 ?
                            (customerRepository.findAll().
                            get(customerRepository.findAll().
                            size() -1)).toString()   : "N/A"))
                    .buildRs();



    }
}
```

First off, notice that we are using an instance of `io.vertx.axle.core.Vertx` to handle the streaming of events. Then, our REST method, which is bound to the `"/streaming"` URI, is annotated with a different media type, that is, `SERVER_SENT_EVENTS`. The method returns a publisher type, which is required in order to publish Reactive Streams.

By using the `ReactiveStreams.fromPublisher` method, we push stream events based on the frequency specified by `vert.xperiodicStream`. In our case, messages will be dispatched every two seconds. Before sending the actual event, the content will be transformed by the `map` operator, which will create a message with some `Customer` statistics, such as the number of customers and the last one added. By using the ternary operator, we managed to compress this login into just one statement, at the expense of slightly more complex readability.

That's all you need on the server-side. On the client-side, we made some other adaptations:

- We added one more button to trigger the SSE:

```
<a ng-click="stats()" class="myButton">Stats</a></div>
```

- We added a callback method, in JavaScript, to handle the event that was received:

```
$scope.stats = function () {

    var eventSource = new EventSource("/streaming");
    eventSource.onmessage = function (event) {
    var container = document.getElementById("divcontainer");
    var paragraph = document.createElement("p");
    paragraph.innerHTML = event.data;
    container.appendChild(paragraph);
};
```

- We added a `div` where messages will be displayed:

```
<div id="divcontainer" style="width: 800px; height: 200px;
overflow-y: scroll;">
```

When we run the updated application, the expected outcome is a UI that includes the **Stats** button at the bottom of it:

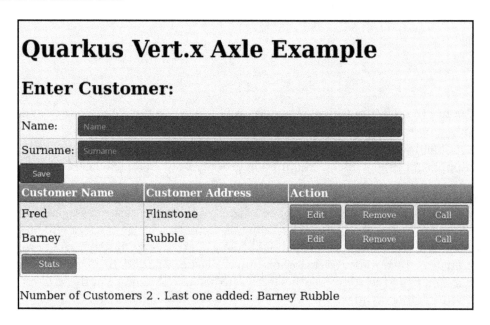

The lower `div` will be updated every two seconds, based on the data contained in the customer list.

Canceling events

It's worth mentioning that SSE subscriptions can be canceled by keeping a reference to the `Subscription` object so that you can cancel your subscription at any time:

```
publisher
    .subscribe(new Subscriber<String>() {
      volatile Subscription subscription;

      @Override
      public void onSubscribe(Subscription subscription) {
        this.subscription = subscription;
      }

      @Override
      public void onNext(String s) {
        // when no more event is needed
        subscription.cancel();
      }

      @Override
      public void onError(Throwable throwable) {
        // handle error
      }

      @Override
      public void onComplete() {
        // handle complete
      }
  });
```

In the preceding code snippet, when the event is emitted, the observer's `onNext` method is called with the item and the `onComplete` method is invoked immediately after. On the other hand, when the callback is a failure, the observer's `onError` method is called. Within any callback method, we can cancel the subscription using the `cancel` method on the subscription object.

This was our last piece of work with Reactive Events, but not the last with Vert.x. We still have one more thing to cover: Quarkus' Reactive SQL Clients. This is an API that focuses on scalable JDBC connections with minimal overhead.

Managing the Reactive SQL Client

The Reactive SQL Client is an API that allows you to use reactive and non-blocking features of Vert.x to access a relational database. This brings some changes in terms of how you access your data. Let's put the costs and benefits on the table:

- On one side, you will need to use SQL statements to enable your RDBMS to access data, instead of the abstract HQL. Also, automatic mapping between Java classes and DB is not available anymore since Hibernate is out of the game here.
- On the other hand, you will be able to use a fully event-driven, non-blocking, lightweight alternative to stream the result of your SQL statements.

Based on your requirements, you may stick with Hibernate's API or switch to Reactive's SQL Client. Let's say you're brave and want to switch to Reactive SQL. To do that, you will need to configure your application so that it can use the PostgreSQL Reactive Client API.

Configuring your application to use the PostgreSQL reactive client

In order to delve into the reactive Client API, please refer to the example contained in the `Chapter09/pgpool` folder in this book's GitHub repository. Since this example won't use the PostgreSQL JDBC driver, the following dependency has been added as a replacement:

```
<dependency>
  <groupId>io.quarkus</groupId>
  <artifactId>quarkus-reactive-pg-client</artifactId>
</dependency>
```

The other configuration we added was the JDBC URL, which needs to be in the following format:

```
vertx-reactive:postgresql://<Host>:<Port>/<DBName>
```

Therefore, in our example, we will add this setting in `application.properties`:

```
quarkus.datasource.url=vertx-reactive:postgresql://localhost:5432/quarkusdb
quarkus.datasource.username=quarkus
quarkus.datasource.password=quarkus
```

Now, let's look at the changes in our application. To keep things as simple as possible, we have broken down our example so that it just uses the `CustomerEndpoint` and the `Customer` POJO class.

Let's begin with the `CustomerEndpoint`, which requires access to `io.vertx.axle.pgclient.PgPool` and `io.vertx.core.Vertx`:

```
public class CustomerEndpoint {

    @Inject PgPool client;
    @Inject Vertx vertx;
```

Within the same class, we have added an `init` method to create some data at startup:

```
@PostConstruct
private void initdb() {

    client.query("DROP TABLE IF EXISTS CUSTOMER")
            .thenCompose(r -> client.query("CREATE SEQUENCE IF
              NOT EXISTS  customerId_seq"))
            .thenCompose(r -> client.query("CREATE TABLE CUSTOMER
              (id SERIAL PRIMARY KEY, name TEXT NOT NULL,surname
              TEXT NOT NULL)"))
            .thenCompose(r -> client.query("INSERT INTO CUSTOMER
              (id, name, surname) VALUES ( nextval('customerId
              _seq'), 'John','Doe')"))
            .thenCompose(r -> client.query("INSERT INTO CUSTOMER
              (id, name, surname) VALUES ( nextval('customerId
                _seq'), 'Fred','Smith')"))
            .toCompletableFuture()
            .join();
}
```

Pgpool's `query` method returns a `CompletionStage` object with a `RowSet` of data, as a result of the query. Please note how we can chain multiple statements to produce a `CompletableFuture`, which spins off the execution in another thread. Within this simple method, you can experience how powerful reactive SQL clients can be when it comes to creating event-driven, non-blocking SQL executions. You will eventually get the combined result of all the statements by executing the `join` method of `CompletableFuture` at the end.

The other methods of `CustomerEndpoint` delegate the execution of CRUD statements to the `Customer` class using the same composition pattern:

```
@GET
public CompletionStage<Response> getAll() {
    return Customer.findAll(client).thenApply(Response::ok)
            .thenApply(ResponseBuilder::build);
}


@POST
public CompletionStage<Response> create(Customer customer) {
    return customer.create(client).thenApply(Response::ok)
            .thenApply(ResponseBuilder::build);
 }

@PUT
public CompletionStage<Response> update(Customer customer) {
    return customer.update(client)
            .thenApply(updated -> updated ? Status.OK :
             Status.NOT_FOUND)
            .thenApply(status -> Response.status(status).build());
}

@DELETE
public CompletionStage<Response> delete(@QueryParam("id") Long customerId)
{
    return Customer.delete(client, customerId)
            .thenApply(deleted -> deleted ? Status.NO_CONTENT :
             Status.NOT_FOUND)
            .thenApply(status -> Response.status(status).build());
}
```

Within the `Customer` class, we have coded all the methods that are required to perform CRUD operations. The first one, `create`, performs an `INSERT` in the `CUSTOMER` table by using `PreparedStatement`, which applies a tuple containing the name and surname as an argument:

```
public CompletionStage<Long> create(PgPool client) {
    return client.preparedQuery("INSERT INTO CUSTOMER (id, name,
      surname) VALUES ( nextval('customerId_seq'), $1,$2)
      RETURNING (id)", Tuple.of(name,surname))
            .thenApply(pgRowSet -> pgRowSet.iterator()
            .next().getLong("id"));
}
```

In much the same way, the `update` method executes an `UPDATE` through a `PreparedStatement`, and applies the customer's tuple of data as a parameter:

```
public CompletionStage<Boolean> update(PgPool client) {
    return client.preparedQuery("UPDATE CUSTOMER SET name = $1,
    surname = $2 WHERE id = $3", Tuple.of(name, surname, id))
            .thenApply(pgRowSet -> pgRowSet.rowCount() == 1);
}
```

To remove a customer, the `delete` method executes `PreparedStatement`, which uses the customer `id` as a parameter:

```
public static CompletionStage<Boolean> delete(PgPool client, Long id) {
    return client.preparedQuery("DELETE FROM CUSTOMER WHERE
    id = $1", Tuple.of(id))
            .thenApply(pgRowSet -> pgRowSet.rowCount() == 1);
}
```

Finally, the `findAll` method is used to query a list of customers from the database and returns them as a Java list:

```
public static CompletionStage<List<Customer>> findAll(PgPool client) {
    return client.query("SELECT id, name, surname FROM CUSTOMER
    ORDER BY name ASC").thenApply(pgRowSet -> {
        List<Customer> list = new ArrayList<>(pgRowSet.size());
        for (Row row : pgRowSet) {
            list.add(from(row));
        }
        return list;
    });
}
```

We have finished coding our application. Let's get it running!

Running the example

Before running the example, make sure you have bootstrapped the PostgreSQL database; otherwise, the initial statements will fail when the application is deployed:

```
$ docker run --ulimit memlock=-1:-1 -it --rm=true --memory-swappiness=0 --
name quarkus_test -e POSTGRES_USER=quarkus -e POSTGRES_PASSWORD=quarkus -e
POSTGRES_DB=quarkusdb -p 5432:5432 postgres:10.5
```

Then, run the application as usual with the following command:

```
mvn  install quarkus:dev
```

The UI hides the fact that we have switched from plain objects to a real database, though you can work out that this has happened from the page title, which is now **Quarkus Vert.X PgPool Example**:

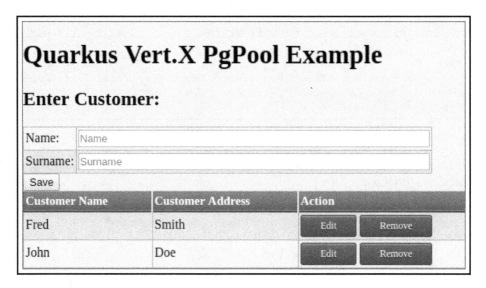

However, if you log in to the database container, you verify sure that the `Customer` table has been created with its items. Let's find the container ID for this purpose:

```
$ docker ps
  CONTAINER ID           IMAGE                  COMMAND                       CREATED
  STATUS                 PORTS                  NAMES
  6b1b13b0547f           postgres:10.5          "docker-entrypoint..."    2 minutes
  ago        Up 2 minutes           0.0.0.0:5432->5432/tcp    quarkus_test
```

Now, let's go into the bash shell of the PostgreSQL container by using the `docker exec` command:

```
$ docker exec -it 6b1b13b0547f /bin/bash

root@6b1b13b0547f:/# psql -U postgres
psql (10.5 (Debian 10.5-2.pgdg90+1))
Type "help" for help.
```

You can check the list of relationships using the `\dt` shortcut:

```
postgres=# \dt;
List of relations
 Schema |   Name   | Type  |  Owner
--------+----------+-------+----------
 public | customer | table | postgres
(1 row)
```

We can also query the `Customer` table's rows, as follows:

```
postgres=# select * from customer;
 id | name | surname
----+------+---------
  5 | John | Doe
  6 | Fred | Smith
(2 rows)
```

Great! We have completed our first reactive SQL application with Quarkus. This also marks the end of our journey into the land of Vert.x.

Summary

From this whirlwind tour of Reactive Programming, you should be proficient in writing reactive applications on the JVM. Your programming skills now include how to use the Vert.x core API to write asynchronous and non-blocking services. You have also learned how to combine the `Observable` pattern with streams or asynchronous results using the Vert.x Reactive API. Then, we quickly explored the last Vert.x paradigm, Vert.x Axle, which allows different beans to interact using asynchronous messages and enforces loose coupling. Finally, we applied a reactive API to access a relational database using the PostgreSQL client extension for Vert.x.

Although you've gotten to grips with the Reactive Programming API, note that much of its power can only be unleashed when building real-time data pipelines and streaming data. We will cover these in the next chapter.

10
Reactive Messaging with Quarkus

In this chapter, we will learn about the nuts and bolts of **SmallRye Reactive Messaging**, which can be used in Quarkus to implement the Eclipse MicroProfile Reactive Messaging specification. By the end of this chapter, you will have a solid development model for your data streaming applications and know how to connect to streaming platforms such as **Apache Kafka** and **ActiveMQ**.

In this chapter, we will cover the following topics:

- Getting started with Reactive Messaging
- Streaming messages with Apache Kafka
- Streaming messages with **Advanced Message Queuing Protocol** (**AMQP**)

Technical requirements

You can find the source code for the project in this chapter on GitHub at `https://github.com/PacktPublishing/Hands-On-Cloud-Native-Applications-with-Java-and-Quarkus/tree/master/Chapter10`.

Getting started with Reactive Messaging

Reactive Streams is an initiative that aims to provide a standard for exchanging data streams across an asynchronous boundary. At the same time, it guarantees that the receiving side is not forced to buffer arbitrary amounts of data.

There are several available implementations of Reactive Stream, and we have already learned how you can feature Reactive Programming in Vert.x. In this chapter, we will complement our knowledge using the SmallRye Reactive Messaging implementation to show you how we can integrate it with a streaming platform such as Apache Kafka or a messaging broker such as ActiveMQ with minimal configuration changes.

To familiarize ourselves with MicroProfile Reactive Messaging, we need proper knowledge of some key concepts. First of all, MicroProfile Reactive Messaging is a specification that uses CDI beans to drive the flow of messages toward some specific channels.

A message is a basic interface that contains a payload to be streamed. The `Message` interface is parameterized in order to describe the type of payload it contains. Additionally, a `Message` interface contains attributes and metadata that are specific to the broker that's used for message exchange (for example, Kafka or AMQ).

A channel, on the other hand, is a string indicating which source or destination of messages is used. There are two types of channels:

- Internal channels are local to the application and are used to implement a multi-step process for messages.
- Remote channels are connected to remote brokers (such as Apache Kafka or AMQ) through connectors.

Since MicroProfile Reactive Messaging is fully governed by the CDI model, two core annotations are used to indicate whether a method is a producer or a consumer of messages:

- `@Incoming`: This annotation is used on a method to indicate that it consumes messages from the specified channel. The name of the channel is added to the annotation as an attribute. Here is an example:

```
@Incoming("channel")
public void consume(Message<String> s) {
  // Consume message here:
}
```

The effect of placing this annotation on a method is that the method will be called each time a message is sent to that channel. From the user's perspective, it is totally transparent about whether the incoming message arrives from a collocated CDI bean or a remote broker. However, you may decide to make it clear that the method consumes a specific kind of message, such as `KafkaMessage` (which inherits from `Message`). Here is an example:

```
@Incoming("channel")
public void consume(KafkaMessage<String> s) {
    // Consume message here:
}
```

- `@Outgoing`: This annotation indicates that a method publishes messages to a channel. In much the same way, the name of the channel is stated in the annotation's attribute:

```
@Outgoing("channel")
 public Message<String> produce() {
    // Produce and return a Message implementation
 }
```

Within the method annotated with `@Outgoing`, we return a concrete implementation of the `Message` interface.

 Be aware that you can only annotate a single method with `@Outgoing` for one channel. If you attempt to use the same channel in more than one `@Outgoing` annotated method, an error will be emitted at deployment time.

You can also annotate a method with both `@Incoming` and `@Outgoing` so that it behaves like a **message processor**, which transforms the content of the message data:

```
@Incoming("from")
@Outgoing("to")
public String translate(String text) {
    return MyTranslator.translate(text);
}
```

From the preceding examples, we can see that messages flow from an `@Outgoing` stream producer to an `@Incoming` stream consumer and Reactive Messaging transparently connects the two endpoints. In order to decouple `Producer` and `Consumer` messages, you can add a component such as Apache Kafka by using the connectors provided by MicroProfile API. In the next section, we will introduce our first example of Reactive Messaging using Apache Kafka.

Streaming messages with Apache Kafka

Apache Kafka (`https://kafka.apache.org/`) is a distributed data streaming platform that can be used to publish, subscribe, store, and process streams of data from multiple sources in real time at amazing speeds.

Apache Kafka can be plugged into streaming data pipelines that distribute data between systems, and also into the systems and applications that consume that data. Since Apache Kafka reduces the need for point-to-point integrations for data sharing, it is a perfect fit for a range of use cases where high throughput and scalability are vital.

Additionally, once you combine Kafka with Kubernetes, you attain all the benefits of Kafka, as well as the advantages of Kubernetes, such as the following:

- **Scalability and high availability**: You can easily scale up and down resources with Kubernetes, which means you can automatically determine the pool of resources that Apache Kafka will share with other applications while guaranteeing the high availability of your Kafka cluster at the same time.
- **Portability**: By running Kafka with Kubernetes, your cluster of Kafka nodes can span across on-site and public, private, or hybrid clouds, even using different operating systems.

To manage the Kafka environment, you need a piece of software called **ZooKeeper**, which manages naming and configuring data in order to provide flexible and robust synchronization within distributed systems. ZooKeeper controls the status of the Kafka cluster nodes and also keeps track of Kafka topics, partitions, and all the Kafka services you need. We won't cover the details of ZooKeeper administration in this chapter, although it's worth mentioning its role as you will need to get to grips with it in order to land a Kafka Administrator job.

To demonstrate Apache Kafka and MicroProfile Streaming's powerful combination on Quarkus, we will design a simple application that simulates a stock trading ticker that's updated in real time by purchases and sales. Get ready and open for business!

Composing our stock trading application

Let's start with the architecture of our stock trading application. To set up an application that has a minimal level of complexity, we will create the following channels:

- An **outgoing** producer that's bound to the **"stock-quote"** channel, where messages containing stock orders will be written into a topic named **"stocks"**

- An **incoming** consumer that's bound to the **"stocks"** channel, which read messages that are available in the **"stocks"** topic
- An **outgoing** producer that's bound to the **"in-memory-stream"** channel, which broadcasts the new stock quote to all the available subscribers internally
- An **incoming** consumer that's bound to the **"in-memory-stream"** channel, which reads the new stock quote and sends it as SSE to clients

The following diagram depicts the basic stream of messages that will be used in our example:

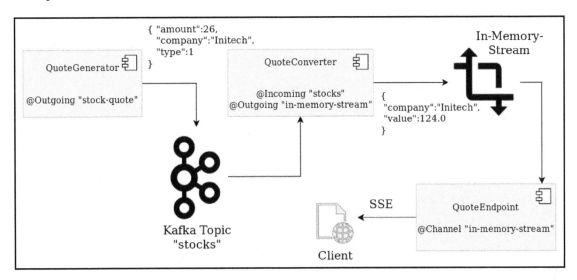

The example application can be found in the `Chapter10/kafka` folder of this book's GitHub repository. We recommend importing the project into your IDE before you move on.

As you can see from the `pom.xml` file of this project, we have included the following extension so that we can stream messages to the Apache Kafka server:

```
<dependency>
    <groupId>io.quarkus</groupId>
    <artifactId>quarkus-smallrye-reactive-messaging-kafka</artifactId>
</dependency>
```

Before we dive into the code, we need to fulfill some requirements to run Kafka in a container. As we mentioned previously, Kafka needs ZooKeeper to manage its cluster, so we need to start both services. A practical solution you can use in the development or test environment is to use **Docker Compose**, which is a tool that's used to manage and synchronize multiple container applications in a single configuration file written in YAML format.

The installation of Docker Compose is detailed on its documentation page (`https://docs.docker.com/compose/install/`), but for a Linux machine, you can install a stable release of it with the following shell command:

```
sudo curl -L
"https://github.com/docker/compose/releases/download/1.24.1/docker-compose-
$(uname -s)-$(uname -m)" -o /usr/local/bin/docker-compose
```

When you're done, apply for the right permission on the `docker-compose` tool:

```
chmod a+x /usr/local/bin/docker-compose
```

Now, you can verify the installed version, as follows:

```
docker-compose --version
```

You should see the following output:

```
docker-compose version 1.24.1, build 1110ad01
```

Now that we're done with our preliminary requirements, it's time to add some lines of code!

Coding bean classes

The first class we will add is `QuoteGenerated`, which is an `ApplicationScoped` CDI bean that produces random quotes for a company every two seconds. Here's the code for this:

```
@ApplicationScoped
public class QuoteGenerator {

    private Random random = new Random();

    @Outgoing("stock-quote")
    public Flowable<String> generate() {
        return Flowable.interval(2, TimeUnit.SECONDS)
          .map(tick -> generateOrder(random.nextInt(2),
           random.nextInt(5),   random.nextInt(100)));
```

```
    }

        private String generateOrder(int type, int company, int amount) {
            Jsonb jsonb = JsonbBuilder.create();
            Operation operation = new Operation(type, Company.values()
            [company], amount);
            return jsonb.toJson(operation);
        }
    }
```

This class produces messages that will be written to Kafka through the "stock-quote" channel. The message contains the stock order that is randomly generated through three parameters:

- The type of order (sale/purchase)
- The company name
- The number of shares purchased/sold

At the end of the day, the `generate` method will produce a message that contains a JSON string, similar to the following:

```
{"amount":32,"company":"Soylent","type":0}
```

So that we have a better understanding of the accessory components, here is the `Company` enumeration, which contains the following set of companies:

```
public enum Company {
        Acme, Globex, Umbrella, Soylent, Initech
}
```

We also need the core part of the `Operation` class, which is a Java POJO that holds the data of each stock order:

```
public class Operation {

    public static final int SELL = 0;
    public static final int BUY = 1;

    private int amount;
    private Company company;
    private int type;

    public Operation(int type, Company company, int amount) {
        this.amount = amount;
        this.company = company;
        this.type = type;
    }
```

```
    // Getters/Setters method omitted for brevity
}
```

Now, a brief Wall Street 101: each stock order will determine a change in the quotation of a company. Simply put, by selling stocks, the price of a company will decrease, while a buy order will make the stock more demanded, which means that the price will rise. The number of shares sold/purchased will eventually determine how much the price goes up and down.

The following QuoteConverter class will do the job of converting a stock order into a new quotation for the Company involved in the transaction:

```java
@ApplicationScoped
public class QuoteConverter {
    HashMap<String,Double> quotes;

    private Random random = new Random();
    @PostConstruct
    public void init() {
        quotes = new HashMap<>();
        for (Company company: Company.values())
        quotes.put(company.name(), new Double(random.nextInt
        (100) + 50));

    }

    @Incoming("stocks")
    @Outgoing("in-memory-stream")
    @Broadcast
    public String newQuote(String quoteJson) {
        Jsonb jsonb = JsonbBuilder.create();

        Operation operation = jsonb.fromJson(quoteJson,
         Operation.class);
        double currentQuote =
         quotes.get(operation.getCompany().name());
        double newQuote;
        double change = (operation.getAmount() / 25);

        if (operation.getType() == Operation.BUY) {
            newQuote = currentQuote + change;
        }
        else  {
            newQuote = currentQuote - change;
        }
        if (newQuote < 0) newQuote = 0;
```

```
        quotes.replace(operation.getCompany().name(), newQuote);
        Quote quote = new Quote(operation.getCompany().name(),
        newQuote);

        return jsonb.toJson(quote);

    }

}
```

The `init` method of this class simply bootstraps the initial quotation of every `Company` with some random values.

The `newQuote` method is at the heart of our transaction system. By reading the operation data contained in the JSON file, a new quote is generated using a basic algorithm: for any 25 stocks that are transacted, there will be one point's impact on the value of the stock. The returned JSON string wraps the `Quote` class, which is broadcasted to all the matching subscribers of the `"in-memory-stream"` channel by means of the `@Broadcast` annotation being on top of the method.

For the sake of completeness, we'll also include the `Quote` Java class, which will be sent as JSON to the client:

```
public class Quote {
    String company;
    Double value;

    public Quote(String company, Double value) {
        this.company = company;
        this.value = value;
    }

    // Getters Setters method omitted for brevity
}
```

Within our example, we have the following subscriber for the `"in-memory-stream"` channel, where `Quote` is published:

```
@Path("/quotes")
public class QuoteEndpoint {

    @Inject
    @Channel("in-memory-stream")
    Publisher<String> quote;

    @GET
    @Path("/stream")
```

```
@Produces(MediaType.SERVER_SENT_EVENTS)
@SseElementType("text/plain")
public Publisher<String> stream() {

    return quote;
}
}
```

QuoteEndpoint is our REST endpoint. Within this, we are using the @Channel qualifier to inject the "in-memory-stream" channel into the bean. That's exactly the point where the reactive world (governed by streams) unifies with the imperative world (the CDI bean, which executes code in sequence). Simply put, this is where our bean is able to retrieve channels that are managed by Reactive Messaging.

All the preceding components need a broker, which is where we publish the stock quotes and read them. Here is the application.properties file, which keeps all of these pieces together:

```
#Kafka destination
mp.messaging.outgoing.stock-quote.connector=smallrye-kafka
mp.messaging.outgoing.stock-quote.topic=stocks
mp.messaging.outgoing.stock-
quote.value.serializer=org.apache.kafka.common.serialization.StringSerializ
er

#Kafka source
mp.messaging.incoming.stocks.connector=smallrye-kafka
mp.messaging.incoming.stocks.topic=stocks
mp.messaging.incoming.stocks.value.deserializer=org.apache.kafka.common.ser
ialization.StringDeserializer
```

The first block is related to the Kafka destination, also known as a **sink** in streaming parlance, and is where we write the stock quote produced by QuoteGenerator. To replicate the data across the node of the classes, it is necessary to serialize its content. Byte streams are the standard language that the OS uses for I/O. In our case, since the data is in JSON format, we use StringSerializer.

In the second block, we configure the source topic and connector, where we read the stock quote as a JSON serialized stream.

Now, all we need to do is add a client application that is able to capture the SSE and display the text of it in a nicely formatted table of data. For the sake of brevity, we will just add the core JavaScript function that collects the SSE:

```
<script>
    var source = new EventSource("/quotes/stream");
    source.onmessage = function (event) {
    var data = JSON.parse(event.data);
    var company = data['company'];
    var value = data['value'];
        document.getElementById(company).innerHTML = value;
    };
</script>
```

The preceding code will be included in the `index.html` page, which can be found in the source code of this chapter. Let's see it in action! Before building the application, start the Kafka/ZooKeeper containers with the following command:

docker-compose up

The Docker Compose tool will search for the `docker-compose.yaml` file, which is in the root directory of this example. Here, we have configured the Kafka and ZooKeeper containers so that they start. A successful bootstrap will produce the following output at the bottom of your console:

```
kafka_1      | [2019-10-20 07:05:36,276] INFO Kafka version : 2.1.0
(org.apache.kafka.common.utils.AppInfoParser)
 kafka_1      | [2019-10-20 07:05:36,277] INFO Kafka commitId :
809be928f1ae004e (org.apache.kafka.common.utils.AppInfoParser)
 kafka_1      | [2019-10-20 07:05:36,279] INFO [KafkaServer id=0] started
(kafka.server.KafkaServer)
```

You can verify that the Kafka and ZooKeeper containers are up and running by executing the `docker ps` command:

docker ps --format '{{.Names}}'

The preceding command will display the following active processes:

```
kafka_kafka_1
kafka_zookeeper_1
```

Now, bootstrap the application as usual with the following command:

```
mvn install quarkus:dev
```

The welcome page of the application (available at `http://localhost:8080`) will show the stock quotes ticker in action, as shown in the following screenshot:

Quarkus Demo - Kafka messaging

Stock Quotes

Company	Stock Quote
Acme	85
Globex	116
Umbrella	67
Soylent	62
Initech	59

Each company in the list will start with an N/A quote until a random operation is executed on it. In the end, you will see that the preceding page is updated every two seconds, which is what we configured in the `QuoteGenerator` class. Pretty cool, isn't it?

When you're done with this example, stop all the running containers with the following command:

```
docker stop $(docker ps -a -q)
```

Once the `docker-compose` process terminates, the preceding command will display a list of all the container layers that have been stopped:

```
6a538738088f
f2d97de3520a
```

Then, verify that the Kafka and ZooKeeper containers have been stopped by executing the `docker ps` command once more:

```
docker ps --format '{{.Names}}'
```

The preceding command shouldn't produce any output, which means that no pending Docker process is running.

We've just got started with the Docker Compose tool. Now, let's move on and deploy the full application stack on OpenShift.

Streaming messages to Kafka in the cloud

To complete our next challenge, we strongly recommend using the latest OpenShift 4.X version. As a matter of fact, in order to orchestrate multiple services such as Kafka and ZooKeeper, it is much simpler to use OpenShift release 4 as it is built on top of the concept of **Operators**. A Kubernetes Operator is a piece of software running in a Pod on the cluster, which introduces new object types through **Custom Resource Definitions** (**CRDs**). A CRD is nothing but an extension mechanism in Kubernetes that lets you define interfaces for a user; for example, you can define a CRD for a Kafka server, which provides a simpler way for us to configure and run it in our cluster.

In addition, Operators already have a common directory (`https://operatorhub.io/`), where you can find an existing Operator or add your own.

You can evaluate OpenShift 4 by going to `https://www.openshift.com/trial/`. There, you can find several alternatives for evaluating OpenShift, either in the cloud or on your own machine. In this chapter, we are assuming that you have already completed the signup procedure and that you have OpenShift 4 up and running.

For the next project, please refer to the `Chapter10/kafka-openshift` directory, where you will find the stock trade application configured for OpenShift and the YAML files for setting up and configuring the Kafka cluster.

Installing Kafka on OpenShift

The simplest way to install and manage an Apache Kafka cluster on the OpenShift cluster is via the **Strimzi** project (`https://strimzi.io/`), which can be installed as an OpenShift Operator.

Start by creating a new OpenShift project named `kafka-demo`. You can either create it from the admin console or using the `oc` command-line utility, as follows:

```
oc new-project kafka-demo
```

The returned output will confirm that the project namespace has been created in your virtual address:

```
Now using project "kafka-demo" on server
"https://api.fmarchioni-openshift.rh.com:6443".
```

The server name will be different in your case, depending on the account name you chose when you signed in.

We recommend continuing from the OpenShift web-console. From the left-hand **Administrator** panel, select **OperatorHub**, as shown in the following screenshot:

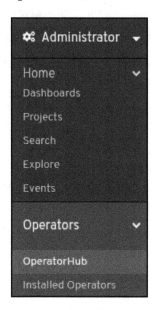

The **OperatorHub** Catalog will show up in the main OpenShift dashboard. Select the **Strimzi** Operator, as shown in the following screenshot:

Then, in the following UI, choose to **Install** the Operator:

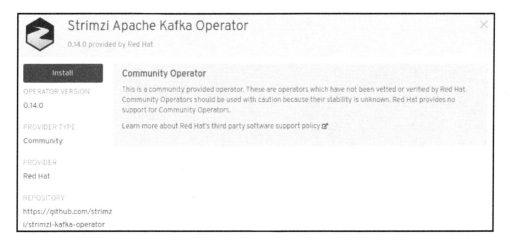

Next, you will be able to choose whether you want to install the Operator in all the available namespaces of your cluster or just in a specific project. Since we won't be using this Operator in other projects, just check the **A specific namespace on the cluster** option and pick up your project. Your selection should look as follows:

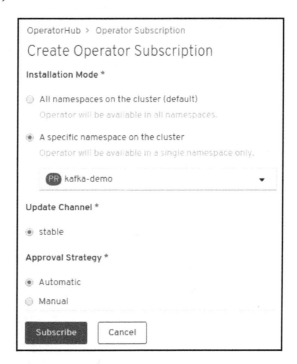

After a few seconds, in the main panel, you will be notified that the Operator has been installed, along with all its provided APIs:

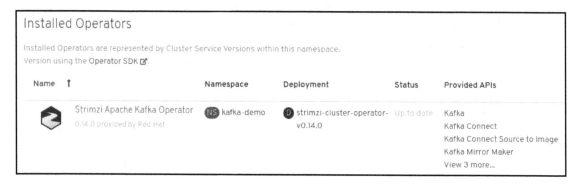

Now that you have the Strimzi Operator available, installing the Kafka cluster will be a piece of cake! Within the `Chapter10/kafka-openshift/strimzi` folder, you will find the following files:

- `kafka-cluster-descriptor.yaml`: This file contains a Kafka cluster definition based on the Strimzi Operator.
- `kafka-topic-queue-descriptor.yaml`: This file defines a resource (a Kafka topic) that we need to configure in our Kafka cluster.

You can install both of them with the `oc` command. Let's start from the cluster:

```
oc create -f strimzi/kafka-cluster-descriptor.yaml
```

The output of the preceding command is as follows:

```
kafka.kafka.strimzi.io/my-kafka created
```

Now, wait a few seconds until the Kafka cluster is up and running. You can check the status of your Pods in the current project with the following command:

```
oc get pods
```

Then, wait until all the Pods are running, as follows:

```
NAME                                              READY   STATUS
RESTARTS     AGE
my-kafka-entity-operator-58d546cf6c-dw85n         3/3     Running    0
5m50s
my-kafka-kafka-0                                  2/2     Running    1
6m27s
my-kafka-kafka-1                                  2/2     Running    1
```

```
6m27s
my-kafka-kafka-2                                        2/2      Running    0
6m27s
my-kafka-zookeeper-0                                    2/2      Running    0
7m5s
my-kafka-zookeeper-1                                    2/2      Running    0
7m5s
my-kafka-zookeeper-2                                    2/2      Running    0
7m5s
strimzi-cluster-operator-v0.14.0-59744f8569-d7j44       1/1      Running    0
7m47s
```

A successful cluster setup will be made up of the following components:

- Three Kafka cluster nodes in a running state
- Three ZooKeeper cluster nodes also in a running state

The name of the cluster (`my-kafka`) has been assigned within the `kafka-cluster-descriptor.yaml` file, as follows:

```
apiVersion: kafka.strimzi.io/v1beta1
  kind: Kafka
  metadata:
    name: my-kafka
```

Now, let's move on by adding a queue named `stock`, as defined in the `kafka-topic-queue-descriptor.yaml` folder. You can create it with the following command:

```
oc create -f strimzi/kafka-topic-queue-descriptor.yaml
```

You will see the following output:

```
kafkatopic.kafka.strimzi.io/stocks created
```

If you want some insights into the Kafka cluster, you can check whether the topic is available. To do that, log in to any of the available Kafka nodes with `oc rsh`:

```
oc rsh my-kafka-kafka-0
```

By doing this, you will have access to the Terminal of that container. From there, execute the following command:

```
sh-4.2$ ./bin/kafka-topics.sh --list --zookeeper localhost:2181
```

The minimal output you will see in the console is `stocks`, which is our topic name:

```
stocks
```

To connect to the Kafka cluster, we won't use an IP address or a Pod name (which will vary upon restarts). Instead, we will use the service name, which will let you reach the cluster through an alias. You can check the available service names with the following command:

```
oc get services -o=name
```

The output of the preceding command will be restricted to the `name` column. In our case, it will look as follows:

```
service/my-kafka-kafka-bootstrap
service/my-kafka-kafka-brokers
service/my-kafka-zookeeper-client
service/my-kafka-zookeeper-nodes
```

The service name we are interested in is `my-kafka-kafka-bootstrap`, which we will add to our Quarkus project soon.

Shaping up our project for native cloud execution

To run our project on OpenShift, we will apply some minimal changes to the configuration file so that we can reach the Kafka service name we have just determined. In the following code, we have highlighted the changes that we have to apply to the `application.properties` file:

```
mp.messaging.outgoing.stock-quote.connector=smallrye-kafka
mp.messaging.outgoing.stock-quote.topic=stocks
mp.messaging.outgoing.stock-quote.value.serializer=org.apache.kafka.common.serialization.StringSerializer
mp.messaging.outgoing.stock-quote.bootstrap.servers=my-kafka-kafka-bootstrap:9092

mp.messaging.incoming.stocks.connector=smallrye-kafka
mp.messaging.incoming.stocks.topic=stocks
mp.messaging.incoming.stocks.value.deserializer=org.apache.kafka.common.serialization.StringDeserializer
mp.messaging.incoming.stocks.bootstrap.servers=my-kafka-kafka-bootstrap:9092
```

As you can see, in the preceding configuration, we have used the
`bootstrap.servers` property to specify the list of Kafka servers (`host:port`).

 Multiple servers can be added in the configuration by using a comma to separate each entry.

Within the source code of this example, you will also find that all POJO classes that have
been serialized in the messaging stream are annotated with
`@io.quarkus.runtime.annotations.RegisterForReflection`, as follows:

```
@RegisterForReflection
public class Quote    { . . . }
```

As a matter of fact, when building a native executable, GraalVM does some assumptions to
remove all the classes, methods, and fields that are not used directly in your code. The
elements that are used via reflection are not part of the call tree, so they are candidates
when it comes to eliminating them from the native executable. Since JSON libraries heavily
rely on reflection to perform their job, we must explicitly tell GraalVM not to exclude them
by using the `@RegisterForReflection` annotation.

That's the small change we have applied in order to publish it to the cloud. Now, build and
deploy the native application with the following commands:

```
#Build the native application
mvn clean package -Pnative -Dnative-image.docker-build=true

#Create a new build for it
oc new-build --binary --name=quarkus-kafka -l app=quarkus-kafka

#Patch the Docker.native file
oc patch bc/quarkus-kafka -p
"{\"spec\":{\"strategy\":{\"dockerStrategy\":{\"dockerfilePath\":\"src/main
/docker/Dockerfile.native\"}}}}"

#Deploy the application in the build
oc start-build quarkus-kafka --from-dir=. --follow

# To instantiate the image as new app
oc new-app --image-stream=quarkus-kafka:latest

# To create the route
oc expose service quarkus-kafka
```

Please note that you can find the preceding script, that is, `deploy-openshift.sh`, in the `Chapter10/kafka-openshift` folder.

Once the preceding script has been executed, verify that the `quarkus-kafka` Pod is up and running by using the following command:

```
oc get pods
```

The output will confirm this:

```
NAME                      READY   STATUS       RESTARTS   AGE
kafka-demo-1-deploy       0/1     Completed    0          30s
kafka-demo-1-p9qdr        1/1     Running      0          36s
```

You can check the route address as follows:

```
oc get routes
```

The route will be under the `HOST/PORT` column output:

```
NAME              HOST/PORT
PATH     SERVICES       PORT       TERMINATION   WILDCARD
quarkus-kafka     quarkus-kafka-kafka-demo.apps.fmarchio-qe.qe.rh-ocs.com
quarkus-kafka     8080-tcp                  None
```

If you want to reach your application with just a click, head to the **Administration** console and select **Networking** | **Routes**. Then, click on the **Route Location**, as shown in the following screenshot:

Name ↑	Namespace ↓	Location ↓	Service ↓	Status
RT quarkus-kafka	NS kafka-demo	http://quarkus-kafka-kafka-demo.apps.fmarchio-qe.qe.rh-ocs.com ☑	S quarkus-kafka	✔ Accepted

Once the configured timeout for emitting quotes elapses, you will see the stock trading application in action on OpenShift:

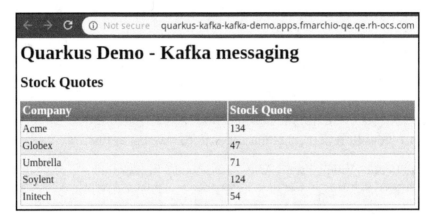

We've come to the end of our glorious journey of Apache Kafka Streaming! In the next section, we will learn how to approach another candidate solution for streaming messaging, which is based on the AMQP protocol instead.

Streaming messages with AMQP

If you have only just found Quarkus after years in the Java Enterprise community, you will already be familiar with message brokers, which are used to allow different Java applications to communicate using JMS as a standard protocol. Although JMS is a robust and mature solution for implementing a messaging system, one of the main limitations of it is that it's focused exclusively on Java. In the microservices world, it's fairly common to use different languages to compose the overall system architecture, so a platform-independent solution is required. In this context, AMQP offers a set of advantages that make it a perfect fit for implementing the Reactive Streams API when it comes to microservices in a distributed system.

In a nutshell, the following are some of the main features of the AMQP protocol:

- It provides a platform-independent wire-level messaging protocol that allows interoperability across multiple languages and platforms.
- It is a wire-level protocol, by which data is sent across the network as a stream of bytes.

- It can achieve high performance while working at low-level byte streams.
- It supports long-lived messaging and classic message queues.
- It supports distribution patterns such as round-robin (where the load is equally distributed across servers) and store and forward (where messages are stored at the sender side in a persistence store and are then forwarded to the receiver side).
- It provides support for transactions (across message destination), as well as distributed transactions using common standards (XA, X/Open, MS DTC).
- It provides support for data encryption using SASL and TLS protocols.
- It allows us to control the message flow with metadata.
- It provides flow control of messages to control backpressure.

To let our applications interact with AMQP, we need a broker that supports this protocol. A commonly adopted solution in the Java Enterprise is **Apache Artemis ActiveMQ** (`https://activemq.apache.org/components/artemis/`), which is compatible with Java Enterprise **Message-Oriented Middleware** (**MOM**) as well. In the next section, we will learn how to start it and configure it in our stock quotes application.

Configuring the AMQP broker

In order to kick-start our application as quickly as possible, we will use a Docker Compose script. This will download a suitable version of the message broker and set some environment variables that are needed so that we can reach the broker.

Simply start the `docker-compose.yaml` file contained in the `amqp` folder with the following command:

```
docker-compose up
```

If the startup is successful, you should see the following output:

```
artemis_1  | 2019-10-26 17:20:47,584 INFO  [org.apache.activemq.artemis]
AMQ241001: HTTP Server started at http://0.0.0.0:8161
artemis_1  | 2019-10-26 17:20:47,584 INFO  [org.apache.activemq.artemis]
AMQ241002: Artemis Jolokia REST API available at
http://0.0.0.0:8161/console/jolokia
artemis_1  | 2019-10-26 17:20:47,584 INFO  [org.apache.activemq.artemis]
AMQ241004: Artemis Console available at http://0.0.0.0:8161/console
```

You can verify that the Kafka and ZooKeeper containers are up and running by executing the `docker ps` command:

```
docker ps --format '{{.Names}}'
```

The preceding command will display the following active processes:

```
amqp_artemis_1
```

Now, let's configure our application so that it can use ActiveMQ. You will find the updated application in the `Chapter10/amqp` folder of this book's GitHub repository. First of all, we need to replace Kafka's Reactive Messaging dependency with the AMQP Reactive Messaging dependency:

```
<dependency>
        <groupId>io.quarkus</groupId>
        <artifactId>quarkus-smallrye-reactive-messaging-amqp</artifactId>
</dependency>
```

In terms of application configuration, some changes need to be made to our `application.properties` file. First of all, we need to include the username and password that we have set in `docker-compose.yaml` (quarkus/quarkus):

```
amqp-username=quarkus
amqp-password=quarkus
```

Then, we need to configure the AMQP connector so that we can write to the `stock-quote` queue, by specifying that the queue is durable (for example, persists to disk and survives a broker restart):

```
mp.messaging.outgoing.stock-quote.connector=smallrye-amqp
mp.messaging.outgoing.stock-quote.address=stocks
mp.messaging.outgoing.stock-quote.durable=true
```

Conversely, we need to configure the AMQP connector so that it can read from the `stocks` queue:

```
mp.messaging.incoming.stocks.connector=smallrye-amqp
mp.messaging.incoming.stocks.durable=true
```

Now, we can bootstrap the application as usual with the following command:

```
mvn install quarkus:dev
```

The welcome page of the application (available at `http://localhost:8080`) will show the stock quotes ticker in action, which now uses ActiveMQ as its broker. As you can see, a minimal adjustment has been made to the UI (just the title), but it accurately masks the changes that were made under the hood:

Quarkus Demo - AMQP messaging

Stock Quotes

Company	Stock Quote
Acme	52
Globex	134
Umbrella	132
Soylent	51
Initech	119

You can find out more about this process by logging in to the AMQ management console, which is available at `http://localhost:8161/console`. Once you've logged in with your configured credentials (`quarkus/quarkus`), you can check that the destination queue has been created in the list of available addresses:

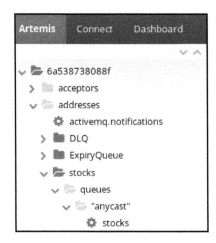

By selecting the `stocks` destination, you can check any further details in the main panel of the management console, as shown in the following screenshot:

When you're done, stop all the running containers with the following command:

```
docker stop $(docker ps -a -q)
```

The preceding command will display a list of all the container layers that have been stopped, like so:

```
6a538738088f
f2d97de3520a
```

Then, verify that the ActiveMQ containers have been stopped by executing the `docker ps` command once more:

```
docker ps --format '{{.Names}}'
```

The preceding command shouldn't produce any output. Now, let's test the same application stack in the cloud.

Streaming messages to AMQ in the cloud

The last thing we will do is deploy the Quarkus application to the cloud while using AMQ as a messaging broker. For this purpose, we will plug the ActiveMQ Docker image that we tested previously into OpenShift (more details about this image can be found on GitHub at `https://github.com/vromero/activemq-artemis-docker`).

First of all, create a new project named `amq-demo`:

```
oc new-project amq-demo
```

The output will confirm that the project namespace has been created in your virtual address:

```
Now using project "amq-demo" on server
"https://api.fmarchioni-openshift.rh.com:6443"
```

Next, deploy the AMQ server to your project with the following command, which will set the username and password so that you can access the broker:

```
oc new-app --name=artemis vromero/activemq-artemis:2.9.0-alpine -e
ARTEMIS_USERNAME=quarkus -e ARTEMIS_PASSWORD=quarkus -e
RESTORE_CONFIGURATION=true
```

Take note of the RESTORE_CONFIGURATION=true environment variable. This is needed since OpenShift automounts empty volumes in all the declared volumes. Since this behavior impacts the /etc folder of this image, which is where the configuration is stored, we need to set the RESTORE_CONFIGURATION environment variable to true.

After executing the new-app command, the following output will be displayed:

```
--> Found container image 2fe0af6 (10 days old) from Docker Hub for
"vromero/activemq-artemis:2.9.0-alpine"

* An image stream tag will be created as "artemis:2.9.0-alpine" that will
track this image
* This image will be deployed in deployment config "artemis"
* Ports 1883/tcp, 5445/tcp, 5672/tcp, 61613/tcp, 61616/tcp, 8161/tcp,
9404/tcp will be load balanced by service "artemis"
* Other containers can access this service through the hostname "artemis"
* This image declares volumes and will default to use non-persistent, host-
local storage.
You can add persistent volumes later by running 'oc set volume dc/artemis -
-add ...'
--> Creating resources ...
    imagestream.image.openshift.io "artemis" created
    deploymentconfig.apps.openshift.io "artemis" created
    service "artemis" created
--> Succes
```

You can check the status of the Pods with the oc command:

```
oc get pods
```

The following output confirms that the `artemis` Pod is in a running state:

```
NAME                 READY   STATUS      RESTARTS   AGE
artemis-1-deploy     0/1     Completed   0          80s
artemis-1-p9qdr      1/1     Running     0          76s
```

Finally, let's check the service name, which will be `artemis`:

```
oc get services -o name
```

Check that the output that's returned matches the output shown here:

```
service/artemis
```

Now, let's go for the final kill: we will deploy the application located in the `Chapter10/amqp-openshift` directory. Within this folder, you will find the stock trade application, which has been configured to stream messages on AMQ.

Here is the updated `application.properties` file, which contains the AMQ username and password, along with the host and the port where the service runs:

```
amqp-username=quarkus
amqp-password=quarkus

# Configure the AMQP connector to write to the `stocks`  address
mp.messaging.outgoing.stock-quote.connector=smallrye-amqp
mp.messaging.outgoing.stock-quote.address=stocks
mp.messaging.outgoing.stock-quote.durable=true
mp.messaging.outgoing.stock-quote.host=artemis
mp.messaging.outgoing.stock-quote.port=5672

# Configure the AMQP connector to read from the `stocks` queue
mp.messaging.incoming.stocks.connector=smallrye-amqp
mp.messaging.incoming.stocks.durable=true
mp.messaging.incoming.stocks.host=artemis
mp.messaging.incoming.stocks.port=5672
```

Next, we will deploy the application contained in the same folder (`Chapter10/amqp-openshift`) into OpenShift. For convenience, you can simply run the `deploy-openshift.sh` script, which can be found in the same directory. Here is the content of the script, which should be pretty familiar to you:

```
#Build native image of the project
mvn clean package -Pnative -Dnative-image.docker-build=true

# Create a new binary build
oc new-build --binary --name=quarkus-amq -l app=quarkus-amq
```

```
# Patch the native file
oc patch bc/quarkus-amq -p
"{\"spec\":{\"strategy\":{\"dockerStrategy\":{\"dockerfilePath\":\"src/main
/docker/Dockerfile.native\"}}}}"

# Add project to the build
oc start-build quarkus-amq --from-dir=. --follow

# To instantiate the image
oc new-app --image-stream=quarkus-amq:latest

# To create the route
oc expose service quarkus-amq
```

Then, check that the `quarkus-amq` Pod is in a running state:

```
oc get pods
```

The output that you'll receive confirms this:

```
NAME                      READY   STATUS      RESTARTS   AGE
artemis-1-deploy          0/1     Completed   0          9m9s
artemis-1-p9qdr           1/1     Running     0          9m5s
quarkus-amq-1-deploy      0/1     Completed   0          14s
quarkus-amq-1-zbvrl       1/1     Running     0          10s
```

Now, you can verify that the application works by clicking on the route address. Just go to the **Networking** | **Routes** path in the console:

The output will be pretty much the same, except for the route name, which celebrates your last achievement in this book:

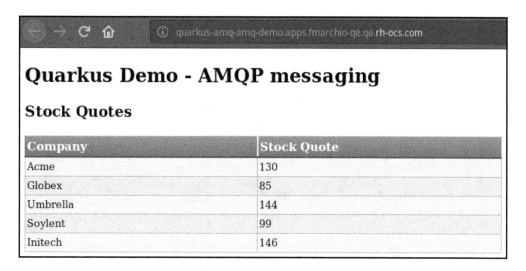

That's all, folks!

Summary

In this chapter, we learned how to use CDI beans to produce, consume, and process messages using the Reactive Messaging specification. We also learned how to bootstrap and configure Apache Kafka and Active MQ's broker so that it acts as a distributed streaming platform for our CDI Beans. To put our new skills in place, we created an example stock trade application, which was initially run in development mode and then deployed as a native image on top of OpenShift.

Now, we have reached the end of this book, where we learned about the story of the gradual renewal of the Java Enterprise application, from monolith to native microservices running in the cloud. It was an exciting journey that certainly set a milestone, but this isn't the end of our hard work – it's just the end of this story.

Other Books You May Enjoy

If you enjoyed this book, you may be interested in these other books by Packt:

Hands-On Microservices with Spring Boot and Spring Cloud
Magnus Larsson

ISBN: 978-1-78961-347-6

- Build reactive microservices using Spring Boot
- Develop resilient and scalable microservices using Spring Cloud
- Use OAuth 2.0/OIDC and Spring Security to protect public APIs
- Implement Docker to bridge the gap between development, testing, and production
- Deploy and manage microservices using Kubernetes
- Apply Istio for improved security, observability, and traffic management

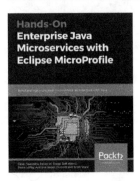

Hands-On Enterprise Java Microservices with Eclipse MicroProfile
Jeff Mesnil, Cesar Saavedra, Et al

ISBN: 978-1-83864-310-2

- Understand why microservices are important in the digital economy
- Analyze how MicroProfile addresses the need for enterprise Java microservices
- Test and secure your applications with Eclipse MicroProfile
- Get to grips with various MicroProfile capabilities such as OpenAPI and Typesafe REST Client
- Explore reactive programming with MicroProfile Stream and Messaging candidate APIs
- Discover and implement coding best practices using MicroProfile

Index

R

www.ingramcontent.com/pod-product-compliance
Lightning Source LLC
LaVergne TN
LVHW081517050326
832903LV00025B/1522